An Ethics of Interrogation

An Ethics of Interrogation

MICHAEL SKERKER

University of Chicago Press
Chicago and London

Michael Skerker is assistant professor in the Leadership, Ethics, and Law
Department at the U.S. Naval Academy.

The University of Chicago Press, Chicago 60637
The University of Chicago Press, Ltd., London
© 2010 by The University of Chicago
All rights reserved. Published 2010
Printed in the United States of America

19 18 17 16 15 14 13 12 11 10   1 2 3 4 5

ISBN-13: 978-0-226-76161-9 (cloth)
ISBN-10: 0-226-76161-4 (cloth)

Library of Congress Cataloging-in-Publication Data

Skerker, Michael.
  An ethics of interrogation / Michael Skerker.
      p. cm.
  Includes index.
  ISBN-13: 978-0-226-76161-9 (cloth: alk. paper)
  ISBN-10: 0-226-76161-4 (cloth: alk. paper)
1. Police questioning—Moral and ethical aspects. 2. Interviewing in law
enforcement—Moral and ethical aspects. 3. Legal ethics.   I. Title.
  HV8073.3.S57 2010
  174′.9363254—dc22

                                                         2009030508

♾ The paper used in this publication meets the minimum requirements of the
American National Standard for Information Sciences—Permanence of Paper
for Printed Library Materials, ANSI Z39.48-1992.

To my family, friends, and teachers

CONTENTS

ACKNOWLEDGMENTS

I would like to thank my professors at the University of Chicago Divinity School, especially Chris Gamwell. I would like to thank colleagues who read parts of the manuscript, including John Carlson, Erik Owens, Norman Bay, and Jan Goldman. I would also like to thank Father Jim Halstead for his support. Numerous student research assistants have helped me conduct research or offered critiques of early drafts, including Andy Manos, Rosalie Simmons, Robin Weiss, Laura Noe, Raphael Satter, and Tyler Williams—my thanks to them. Finally, thanks to my editor David Pervin as well as anonymous readers at the University of Chicago Press. Earlier versions of some chapters, much revised for this book, appeared as "Interrogation Ethics in the Context of Intelligence Collection," in *Ethics of Spying: A Reader for Intelligence Professionals*, ed. Jan Goldman (Scarecrow Press, 2006), "Intelligence Ethics and Interrogation," *Defense Intelligence Journal*, vol. 16, no. 1, pp. 61–76 (2007), and a paper presented at the Ethics and Intelligence Conference, Springfield, VA, January 2006.

Introduction

The public conversation about interrogation in America has been guided by pictures and letters. The Abu Ghraib photographs leaked in the spring of 2003 were horrifying both for what they revealed and what they concealed. Given the nature of what the photographs documented, one had to wonder what happened off camera and at other installations. Perhaps some were comforted by the Bush administration's assurances that the abuse of detainees at Abu Ghraib was isolated, the result of a few "bad apples," even if a steady stream of rumors and leaks suggested a vast enterprise of secret detention and harsh interrogation of terror suspects. We read of "ghost detainees" shuttled between secret prisons or delivered to dubious locales for clandestine interrogation. Novel ways of prosecuting terrorists were proposed, some believed, in order to allow testimony garnered through torture. Activists feared what treatment accompanied the incommunicado detention of terror suspects in the black hole of Guantanamo.

Revelations continue: As this book goes to press, four newly declassified memos from the Department of Justice to the CIA's Office of Legal Counsel confirm many of the darkest rumors. With exacting precision, the authors parse the international accords against torture to conclude that keeping an al-Qaeda agent awake for eleven days straight or suffocating him with a wet cloth does not meet the legal definition of torture since the techniques do not cause "pain" in the sense of blunt force or burns. The former vice president and CIA director publicly argue that such techniques were vital to gaining actionable intelligence from terrorists. CIA and FBI agents involved in the interrogations weigh in with their accounts of what happened, and a commission reporting to the new president will soon issue a report assessing the efficacy of harsh interrogations.

"Interrogation" has become part of the American vernacular, with a frequency of mention probably outstripping most people's understanding of the practice. Yet the presumption behind the practice surely deserves scrutiny: that there are times when a state is entitled to know the thoughts of one of its inhabitants (or even a foreign national), such that it can demand and compel their revelation. The idea that one person can have a claim to another person's secrets flies in the face of common morality and logic, and the practice of eliciting a person's secrets against his will seems a holdover from the Middle Ages, like alchemy or sorcery. While there have been some collections published recently addressing torture (which is involved in but one type of interrogation), there are no extant works addressing the range of moral issues related to interrogation per se. Disparate scholarly articles about the right to privacy, the Fifth Amendment, police-procured false confessions, military commissions, and detainee rights address some of the relevant moral and legal issues, but this literature often feels incomplete. If police or military interrogation tactics are condemned, alternatives are rarely proposed; if harsh interrogation tactics are promoted for use on terrorists, questions about the effects of such practices on interrogators and the government authorizing them are begged, along with the question of what to do with detainees following their torture. Appeals for greater latitude for law enforcement and national security actors typically abstract from the real limitations of state agents' knowledge and wrongly assume all suspects are guilty. Jurisprudential claims about the privilege against compelled self-incrimination or the right to silence are given scant philosophical justification, and philosophers, game to address the right to privacy, are largely silent on the subject of the privilege against compelled self-incrimination. This book means to address all the issues relevant to interrogation with an argument about the use of state power at home and abroad that is expansive enough to field broad conceptual questions and generate specific policy recommendations. It adopts an interdisciplinary approach for an interdisciplinary subject, encompassing moral and political philosophy, jurisprudence, and just war theory.

One of the two questions at the heart of this book was mentioned above. Under what circumstances is a state entitled to know a person's thoughts? If the first question can be satisfactorily answered, it prompts a second question regarding moral practice. How can information be procured from a person against his will in a morally upright manner? Full answers to these questions cannot be given in the language of professional ethics alone—in the sort of admonitions one might find in the appendix to an interrogators' handbook—since answers to these questions presuppose answers to broader questions in moral theory, political theory, and international relations. What sort of deference does one owe to another's privacy, and why? Why is keeping secrets morally important? What good might it do to say harboring *criminal* secrets is illicit if such activity is normally undetectable by others? Given some standard for acting when motivated by suspicion alone, may police compel criminals to incriminate themselves, or is this inherently perverse, like forcing someone to commit suicide? If domestic criminal suspects are due a given set of rights, what do authorities owe foreign nationals? Do terrorists get the same POW rights as captured conventional combatants? In short, interrogation ethics is more than an answer to the question "to waterboard or not to waterboard?"

This book has a particular applied focus but also contributes to current academic debates about self-defense, political obligation, political consent, the Fifth Amendment, military commissions, and the rights of "unlawful enemy combatants." It should therefore be of interest to academics and professionals in the fields of law, philosophy, criminal justice, and national security. Since readers outside of academia may not share professional philosophers' interest in some of the details of moral and political theory, I will indicate later which sections devoted to these matters may be skipped in favor of more concrete discussions of criminal justice and national security matters.

Part 1 of this book discusses interrogation in the context of domestic law enforcement, and part 2, interrogation in the context of military and intelligence operations. This division is indicated by the different issues in play when a state interacts with its own inhabitants as opposed to foreign nationals. The two parts are distinct but interconnected. While questions regarding conventional foreign combatants can readily be addressed with concepts from the just war tradition, the general theory of just coercion and the justification for the coercive behavior of state agents developed in part 1 are necessary to resolve questions in part 2 regarding the rights of nonstate actors like guerillas and terrorists who are not automatically covered by the prerogatives of state agents. The general theory of just coercion is also used to assess the permissibility of interrogatory torture in chapter 8 since just war theory's justifications for violence against active combatants is not relevant to detained and disarmed interrogatees.

Chapter 1 develops a general theory of just coercion (i.e., permitting one to compel someone to do something), expanding extant theories of self-defense to cover responses to rights violations other than assault. This chapter creates the groundwork for the justification of interrogators' efforts to learn of criminals' plots both in domestic law enforcement and irregular warfare contexts. Chapter 2 develops grounds for just political action in defense of inhabitants' lives and rights, linking a liberal state's police powers with the conditions for inhabitants' freedom. I argue that politically legitimate coercive actions (i.e., those compelling inhabitants to act or refrain from acting) are those that inhabitants cannot rationally reject, given that these actions are necessary for the protection of their lives and rights. This standard of political legitimacy entails that police actions materially infringing on inhabitants' freedom (e.g., questioning, arrest, interrogation, etc.) do not *violate* inhabitants' rights provided these actions are proportionate to a reasonable suspicion that the people affected are involved in criminal activity or have knowledge of criminal activity.

Chapter 3 explains the relationship between moral autonomy and rights to privacy and silence. It argues that criminal plotting is impermissible in the sense that acquiring contraband is impermissible and explains how an abuse of the rights to privacy and silence voids the right to keep certain secrets from others. The chapter also discusses how abuses of these rights are not as easily remedied by outsiders as are other types of misbehavior, because plotting is usually not as publicly obvious as is something like assault. In fact, the subjective and contextual nature of suspicion, coupled with the ordinary deference a liberal state affords its inhabitants, ground a series of rights for criminal suspects, including the right to silence during police interrogation.

Chapter 4 suggests that the constitutionally protected—but much maligned—privilege against compelled self-incrimination can be understood as integrating the state's necessarily rights-infringing investigative actions with the baseline deference it must show inhabitants before it has proven they are criminals. Critiques of the privilege can be met if it is conceived as based on a robust right to silence instead of as the basis for a more or less nominal right to silence in police custody, as is usually the case. Recognizing a suspect's right to silence in police interrogation expresses the deference a liberal state properly pays to an inhabitant it suspects of criminality: since the state does not have cause to *know* he is guilty, it cannot treat him as one who has voided his right to silence through criminal plotting or criminal activity. The chapter also develops a substantive standard for assessing police investigative behavior preferable to the relatively vague legal standard of "due process."

Chapter 5 describes contemporary American police interrogation techniques and finds certain deceptive techniques to be reasonably reliable, efficacious, and indispensable. These techniques are then assessed by the standard of police ethics developed over the previous chapters. I consider the possible negative side effects of police deception, including false confessions, police corruption, and soured police-community relations to see if they should lead us to reject otherwise permissible interrogation techniques.

Part 2 addresses interrogation in an international context where military or intelligence officers might interrogate conventional prisoners of war or irregular fighters who do not meet the conventional criteria for POW status, including some guerillas and terrorists. Chapter 6 introduces the Western just war tradition, the moral foundation for the arguments to follow. Different possible moral justifications for POWs' legal immunity and nonpunitive detention are assessed in order to determine if combatants' roles as state agents, "warrior's honor," or the self-interest of the detaining power is the salient justification to use in extending or denying POW status to various irregulars. The chapter categorizes different types of irregulars based on their relationship to a state, nascent state, or recently occupied state and concludes that since "unprivileged irregulars"—militants who fail to achieve POW status—have essentially criminal profiles to the detaining power, they may be tried in criminal court or in a court martial for war crimes.

Chapter 7 describes contemporary American military interrogation techniques and assesses them in reference to the rights of POWs as well as the rights of both suspected and positively identified unprivileged irregulars. I argue that there is no cause for creating a third interrogation style meant for unprivileged irregulars, apart from law enforcement-style interrogation (with standard due process protections) and POW-style interrogation (lacking these protections but also assuming legal immunity), because there are no efficacious techniques in principle permissible only for unprivileged irregulars that are not also practically counterproductive for the detaining power. I consider three different possibilities for postinterrogation treatment of unprivileged irregulars and conclude that the lack of due process protections in POW-style interrogation makes information extracted there unsuitable for use as evidence in either civilian or military trials. Tailoring the mode of unprivileged irregulars' detention to the interrogation needs of the detaining power entails foregoing prosecution and holding irregulars as de facto POWs (despite their failure to formally meet the criteria for POW status) until the end of hostilities.

Chapter 8 addresses arguments made about interrogatory torture, or coercive interrogation, as it is sometimes called. After giving a brief history of interrogatory torture in the West, the chapter discusses torture's dubious efficacy and systemic corrupting effects on both the personnel employing it and the government authorizing it. Torture is impermissible according to the model of just coercion defended in this book; I argue abandoning these moral limits has grotesque implications even proponents of coercive interrogation would likely abjure.

Method

The early chapters of this book assume conceptions of human beings and human rights that gained currency in the Enlightenment and have been passed down in concrete form by common law. I will not call these often-invoked rights into question or attempt to ground them in an all-encompassing philosophical system. Rather, my approach is hypothetical: *if* we are going to conceive of people as autonomous and equally provisioned with certain rights, then we must accept certain entailments regarding these rights by force of logic. With respect to certain contested rights, like the privilege against compelled self-incrimination and the right to silence, I will argue that my construal of such rights complements other, uncontroversial rights; meets standard critiques; provides a basis for answering practical questions about policing; and does so better than the alternatives available in the literature.

This book's contingent starting point with a particular conception of autonomy and an associated regime of rights means I will be operating in a deontological idiom when assessing questions of morality and taking deontology's salience to these questions as a given. In addition to recognizing certain entailments of autonomy on the moral level, I will assume that we should accept other entailments with respect to the political protection of moral autonomy if we wish to avoid certain political effects now typically condemned in the West. I take an aversion to these illiberal political effects as a second given.[1] Similarly, the second part of the book will take the well-established Western just war tradition as a given foundation for assessing combatant rights in an international context.

Finally, I know that no basic concept used here—rights, reason, autonomy, person, etc.—is uncontroversial, unproblematized, not already declared dead by some, and resurrected by others. By working with fairly classic moral terminology, and refraining from grounding my applied work on ideas unique to a more specialized modern wing of moral or political theory, my hope is to get a conversation about interrogation ethics *started*— and with an many interlocutors as possible.

PART ONE

Interrogation in Domestic Law Enforcement

ONE

Autonomy, Rights, and Coercion

The detectives lied to Eugene Livingston:

> Okay, as Sgt. Becker said Eugene, we have talked to a lot of people in this
> case. We've talked to you a couple of times, and every time we've talked to
> you, I think we were pretty, pretty honest with you. We were telling you what
> we were hearing, and we asked you a couple times to tell us what you know
> about this case. Now Mr. Young, as Sgt. Becker said, has uh given us a com-
> plete statement. He told us exactly what happened, what his role in the rob-
> bery was, and what everybody's role in the robbery was. He implicated you
> also in the robbery. He's identified you as being a participant. Now every-
> body who tells us things, at times may see things different, or may not be
> completely truthful. That's why we wanta come to you now and get your part
> of exactly what happened, and your participation in the robbery. In other
> words, we got a folder, about four or five folders thick of what the people are
> saying about Eugene Livingston. We have nothing on what Eugene Livingston
> had to say about this incident, and the best thing we can do now Eugene is be
> completely truthful, because it's over with.[1]

In fact, Young had not implicated Livingston in the robbery. The detectives, from the Vallejo, California, police department, made that up out of
whole cloth. Yet the police were not necessarily acting unprofessionally;
the most commonly used American police interrogation manual sometimes
instructs interrogators to lie to suspects or engage in other deceptive ploys
to trick them into confessing.[2] These techniques have even been condoned
by the U.S. Supreme Court.

The above monologue may seem familiar to fans of police dramas. Yet
consider the monologue and its context anew: is it not strange that in a liberal

democracy—where the government ostensibly serves the people—police may break down a man's door, drag him to a station house, then hold him against his will, in order to tell him lies and insult him? For that matter, as was asked in the introduction, is not the notion of interrogation itself strange? The underlying presumption that one man can have a claim to another man's secrets flies in the face of common morality and logic, and the practice of eliciting a person's secrets against his will seems like an exercise from a cruder age.

We need a framework for understanding what police are allowed to do generally in order to assess what it is morally acceptable for police to do in interrogation—a framework of police ethics. For that, we need two types of intellectual building blocks: first, a general account of just coercion identifying when it is acceptable for a person to force another person to do something against his or her will and, second, political theory, some account of what states may do to their inhabitants, including sometimes forcing them to do things against their wishes.

Political theory will be addressed in chapter 2. This chapter will address just coercion on a basic level apart from policing contexts in order to isolate the foundational issues involved in police interrogation. The various elements of this account of just coercion will later be used to resolve particular questions regarding police and military ethics. This chapter will extend theories of self-defense from traditional contexts of assault to broader contexts involving other types of rights violations. I will first outline in fairly general terms the conception of rights to be used in this project and then articulate the grounds for just coercion. This account of just coercion will strike a balance between an approach concerned with the defender's rights alone and an approach concerned solely with an objective consideration of the defensive action's consequences. The account will also address the rights of the offender and determine the status of third parties witnessing rights violations.

Some caveats about the scope and method of chapters 1 and 2: the discussion of rights and political obligation in these chapters are developed to the level of complexity I think necessary to adequately address the moral and political issues related to interrogation. Extended defenses of the foundational positions will be omitted in favor of more extended treatment of applied matters in the rest of Part 1. I have also tried to strike a balance in prose style in these foundational chapters between the precision expected by specialists and the nontechnical language desired by nonspecialists. The first two chapters are the most technical and abstract, dealing with fundamental questions in moral and political philosophy. A book's chapters are meant to be read in order, but readers who are more interested in the concrete application of moral theory in policing and war fighting contexts than in broader philosophical questions of rights, autonomy, and state power may wish to skip ahead now to chapter 3.

The "rule deontological" framework I will be using in this book draws from the common stock of ideas endorsed by the medieval theologian St. Thomas Aquinas and the Enlightenment philosophers Thomas Hobbes, John Locke, Jean-Jacques Rousseau, and Immanuel Kant.[3] The framework belongs to a family of moral systems that judges actions based on their conformity to universally binding rules (rules that may be geared toward the protection of people's rights) rather than based on the actions' consequences. The exposition concerning coercion below owes most in its idiom to Kant, and focuses in places on specific arguments Kant made, but it might have couched in the vocabulary of one of the other thinkers or of various modern authors.[4] The conclusions I reach about police powers and interrogation could have likely been reached with different starting points, but I prefer Kant's idiom because of its precision and his general approach because it marries well with the diverse approaches to interrogation in the philosophical and legal literature.

Rights and Coercion

A central moral claim made by deontological thinkers is that human beings are autonomous, meaning there are core areas of thought and action individuals should govern for themselves, all other things being equal. The deeds or titles to self-governance with respect to these areas of thought and action are *rights*. These titles grant their owners the liberty to think or act as they choose in these areas without uninvited interference from others. On the *moral* understanding of autonomy to be employed in this chapter, *moral rights* are understood to be a natural part of human beings, rather than conventionally recognized or bestowed on them by some entity like a state. All human beings have these rights, regardless of their citizenship, gender, religion, class, or profession. *Moral rights* are fostered by persons' reciprocal recognition of these rights on the parts of others. *Political rights* (to be discussed in chapter 3) are rights conventionally recognized by a state in self-limitation of its own power as well as by its promise to limit the power of inhabitants with respect to one another. In many cases, political rights overlap with moral ones.

This chapter will address what is owed persons as persons, based on the concepts of moral autonomy and rights, abstracted from any particular empirical (i.e., concrete, real-world) setting. In most empirical settings, in the context of a state, moral rights are relevant to private citizens' interpersonal behavior. No moral right is absolute in a system where all have equal rights; instead, every person's moral rights are dependent on and limited to the reciprocal recognition of the same rights, and same scope of rights exercise, for others.[5] This requires further explanation. If one has a moral right in a particular area, then it is an area properly self-governed instead of governed by others. For example, if we say that the right to own private property entails the right to own a car, that right might protect the following choices: whether or not to buy a car; what type of car to buy; and when and where to drive it. Just the same, one may not drive one's car anywhere or in any manner one wishes. The only coherent and stable picture of a society of independently self-directing agents is one in which all issue similar self-directions, at least on major issues where agents' behavior might come into conflict. For example, the only safe way for independently controlled automobiles to simultaneously travel in the same lane in close proximity to one another is if they all travel in the same direction and at roughly the same speed. Each driver is free to choose whether or not to drive, what to drive, and where to go but must follow certain rules enabling all other car owners to enjoy the same scope of freedom. Such behavior allows for all to get to where they want to go: provided they observe the same traffic rules, Smith's success at reaching his destination does not prevent Jones from reaching hers. The will to perform morally permissible actions (like "driving in accordance with traffic rules") can be universalized, meaning driving to a destination is still possible even if everyone desires to do the same—the idea of driving to a destination has not been rendered absurd by everyone in principle wishing to drive.[6]

Morally upright people, who will be defined here as people who respect other's rights, must in turn be treated deferentially by others, afforded the space to make their own decisions, and ford their way through the world. They can be trusted with this freedom because they are only going to embark on actions consistent with respect for others' rights. This respectful behavior does nothing to reduce others' opportunities to achieve their legitimate aims. Again, Smith's successful car trip does not prevent Jones from reaching her destination as well.

By contrast, Smith's fellow highway travelers *would* have cause to object if he broke the rules that accommodate everyone's freedom and, for example, drove south in a northbound lane. Generally then, one's rights are bounded where universal accord would break down—for those actions where all could not logically consent to one's actions, because such actions would be incoherent (i.e., self-contradictory or self-defeating) if universally adopted. Illicit actions—rights violations—then are those that could only issue from unreal "private rights areas," which one enjoys to the exclusion of others. These "private rights" foster self-direction depending parasitically on the majority's morally upright behavior for its success. For example, those lunatics one sees on the highway who weave in between other cars at a high rate of speed would be unable to drive this way if everyone else drove in the same unpredictable manner. The reckless drivers depend on the majority driving at a constant rate and observing several car lengths' distance so they can slalom past. Another example: the success of slander depends on the majority of actors speaking truthfully about others; if people habitually lied about other's character, no one would believe the slanderous things said by a character assassin. The slanderer grants himself a liberty—gives himself a right—that he cannot coherently grant others. Moreover, his slander likely inhibits his victim's ability to be heard and received on the same footing as the slanderer.

Rights violations often entail the use of coercion, which for our purposes will be defined as behavior where the recipient of the action is treated as a *means* to the actor's goal—instead of as a free, independent person whose preferences deserve respect—usually by restricting or controlling the victim's ability to do what he wants. Coercive measures include physical force, threats, extortion, emotional manipulation, lying, and other forms of deception.

The rights violator's failure to behave morally *cedes his otherwise legitimate expectation* to be treated with deference by others. (The reason for this formal phrasing will be explained below.) Since the ground for moral rights is reciprocal respect—rendered "horizontally" by rights-holders to other rights-holders like the strands of a web, rather than based "vertically" on a foundation like the bricks of a pyramid—the revocation of reciprocal respect eliminates the support for the rights. As a right is a claim against all other actors' claims (to unrestricted action), limiting their scope, the partial or complete voiding of a right by a rights violator exposes him to the claims of all other actors. They are now unrestrained in their behavior toward the violator to the extent he has ceded the otherwise legitimate expectation that his right(s) in the relevant area(s) will be respected. The rights violator cannot expect others to respect a "right" he was claiming to have for himself alone and that came at others' expense. The rights violator was not self-limiting his own freedom in deference to his neighbor's rights, so both the basis for respecting the violator's rights and the incentive for self-restraint is lost. His neighbors can now do things to him that would otherwise be impermissible, such as exercising some form of coercion. It may in fact be practically necessary to treat him *prudentially*,[7] as a means, as someone whose choices do not matter to the actor, in order to restrain his rights-violating actions.[8] As Kant puts it, a right can be thought of as a "title to coerce" or, as H. L. A. Hart writes, "a special justification for interference with another's freedom."[9]

A rights violator is not wronged if his victim or a proxy deals coercively with him to the extent necessary to restore the previolation status quo. Pushing him back to his original level of freedom does him no *moral* injury because the "extra" freedom he seized while violating another's rights was not a freedom he was due (a freedom consistent with all others having the same freedom). For example, if my neighbor and I have equal-sized, adjacent gardens, and he starts planting his crops in my plot without permission, I do not wrong him by demanding—or forcing him, if he refuses—to return to his land (taking his broccoli with him).

While in many instances, an agent will exercise his rights without any challenge or resistance from others, the fact that the relevant actions fall under the title of a "right" means that the agent can legitimately expect the following. (1) Others will restrict their own freedom to make room for the agent's rights exercise. (2) The agent may *demand* that others do this (and need not *request*, because they would not be giving something of their own but something that is already his). (3) The agent does not exceed the scope of his rights when coercing recalcitrant neighbors to respect the areas of freedom that were his all along. Coercing a rights violator to the status quo ante restores the freedom of the offended party but is also consistent with the freedom of the coerced party. This follows because the coercion is expressive of the limitations to the freedom of all necessary for the universal enjoyment of equal rights—a regime to which the coerced party belongs and from which he presumably benefited.

Specifications and Caveats

I will now explore the limits and applications of the foregoing account of just coercion. This account of just coercion is not meant to be a complete moral theory. It is an analysis of moral actions, rather than of persons or societies. Since this account of just coercion is but one type of permissible action, it is does not necessarily identify the best thing a person can do, nor what one must do to be a good person. (Rather, it identifies actions to avoid lest one be a bad person, or at least a person who has behaved badly in one instance.)

Rights grant their owners the liberty to think or act as they choose in core areas of thought or action without uninvited interference from others. It does not matter if a person was exercising a certain right when it was violated, as a right is a sort of reserved space in which one is allowed to operate if and when he chooses. Assaulting a man who is in a drunken stupor is still assault even though he is not making full use of his bodily autonomy at the time. Similarly, we can say a person is *abusing a right* in the sense of acting in a way that in nonuniversalizable even if the action does not directly, immediately violate another's right. For example, I am abusing my right to private property if I test-fire my new pistol from my apartment balcony, because I am acting with a gross disregard for other's safety and property. I have not violated anyone's rights in a direct, material way if the bullets I fire do not strike anyone or damage anyone's property, but I have wronged others in the abstract sense of taking a liberty I could not coherently extend to others. (I might not be in any shape to fire my gun if my neighbors routinely fired guns from their balconies.) Depending on the context, abusing a right can lead to an immediate and direct violation of another's right—for example, lying simultaneously violates the (innocent) hearer's right to honest-dealing— while other abuses, like the above example, may be objectionable for threatening other's rights or leading to their future violation.[10] (I will argue in chapter 3 that criminal plotting is an abuse of a right threatening to others.) Threats can be relatively direct or relatively indirect. For example, shooting a gun off a balcony when there are no people in sight is more of an indirect threat than pointing a gun at someone at close range.

In the following thought experiments, I will refer to the two men mentioned in the Vallejo detective's monologue, Young and Livingston. Say the two men had a falling out one day and Young decides to assault Livingston and steal the gold chain he wears (a family heirloom). Livingston is entitled to fight back, to coercively reassert the status quo ante, yet he cannot exceed that original balance of legitimate freedom (and associated material holdings) lest he seize more freedom than he is due. Generally speaking, he cannot use more force than necessary to defend himself or take more property from Young than the chain he snatched. Kant argues that a defender's reaction must match an unjust aggressor's action *precisely* in degree in order to be just.[11] This view needs slight emendations. Practical exigencies could require minor excesses in re-implementing the just balance of freedoms. Since the restoration of the status quo ante is morally relevant, the practical steps necessary to restore that state are also morally relevant—and what is practically required to restore the status quo ante will vary with circumstances and actors. If Young is physically assaulting Livingston, Livingston is entitled to fight back. Depending on Young's intentions and frame of mind, restoring the status quo ante of neither Livingston nor Young being physically assailed might require more than a strict blow-for-blow; for example, Young might need to be knocked out or locked in a room.

Further, for practical reasons, "fighting back" against rights violations other than *assault* could not entail exact reciprocal reactions. Fighting back, say, against one's kidnapping in order to free oneself would not entail kidnapping the kidnapper. Rather, it would entail doing what was necessary to escape his physical control: fighting with him, destroying his property (doors, locks, etc.), stealing his car, tricking him, and so on. In a second practical sense, when rights violations concern things external to the aggrieved party such as property crimes, the restoration of the status quo ante may entail more than reciprocal actions since the defender's symmetrical response may happen to be inadequate to that end. For example, if Young cons Livingston out of $50, it would not be unjust for Livingston to trick Young to get the $50 back. Justice would not be done if Livingston's trickery only netted $20; since the injustice of Young's act included not only his manipulation or deception of Livingston but the appropriation of his money under false pretenses, a just response needs to be oriented toward the reappropriation of the $50. Livingston, who is perhaps a bad liar, would be within his rights to forcibly wrest $50 from Young's hand or take it from Young's wallet when Young is asleep.[12] That said, focusing on the goal of the coercive response can engender new problems if unmitigated by other concerns, so our conversation will now turn to the limits one must observe in coercive reaction.

The innocent party's defense must be roughly symmetrical with the way and the degree to which the offender has ceded the otherwise legitimate expectation others will defer to his rights lest the defender create a new unjust imbalance of freedoms. Gross overreactions could occur if the sole focus was on the restoration of the defender's autonomy (and associated material holdings), with no attention paid to the original balance of rights.[13] On this view, *any* action necessary to restore the full enjoyment of the defender's rights would be justifiable, with the severity of the response linked to contingent factors concerning the defender's strength and arsenal.[14] Such a view could conceivably defend an elderly orchard keeper's shooting of a thief making off with an armload of apples.[15] Granted, the value of a life does not compare to that of an armload of apples, but the orchard keeper's rights were being violated, and shooting the thief was the only way he could retain his property. Were the orchard keeper a younger man, he could have perhaps chased and tackled the thief; and perhaps the thief would have escaped if the orchard keeper was unarmed; but on this view, the thief made himself vulnerable to *whatever* minimum level of force was necessary for the *particular victim* to defend his rights. (We will see in chapter 8 that a similar argument is sometimes used to defend the torture of terrorists.)

Life is more important than fruit—the desire to include this kind of analysis counsels against a purely deontological approach to just coercion that only takes into account the defender's rights. Yet to go to the other extreme is also inadequate, as an approach to the situation that only views consequences fails to address what we might call the moral violence of a rights violation.[16] If Young snatches $20 from Livingston's hand, and the only way for Livingston to get the money back is to tackle Young, the cost of injuries that might ensue (broken nose, cracked tooth, etc.) could far exceed $20. An approach that simply balances the parties' interests from an objective point of view (because both are doing things that are normally illicit) might say that physically harming Young in this way is disproportionate to the loss of the $20, and so Livingston should instead let Young escape if tackling is the only means of stopping him.[17] Yet this disembodied calculus is not apt. It is not the *universe* that suffered the loss of the $20; it was Livingston. Further, there is more to lament over a theft than a monetary loss. Young had no *right* to that money; he seems to have arrogated to himself a position in which Livingston's interests and rights were no impediment to him, a position in which Livingston was not viewed as a human being inherently deserving of respect. Something wrong has occurred even if Livingston is a billionaire who uses twenties for attic insulation; there is a difference between losing $20 and having it stolen.

Consequentialist approaches can also be insensitive to the defender's subjective circumstances. Shooting an unarmed attacker is excessive, viewed consequentially and objectively, apart from the actors' subjective situations, but what if the defender with the gun is physically weaker and cannot defend himself with his fists? To those who counsel retreat when the only alternative is lethal force,[18] we may ask: must the defender suffer the beating if retreat is impossible? Even if retreat is possible, apart from the question of the defender's arsenal, it seems wrong that the innocent defender should have to yield, for it is his attacker who is entirely in the wrong.[19]

Just the same, as the example of the apple thief indicates, a view of coercion's limits that is tied strictly to the defender's rights and subjective situation will not do, so what is needed is a mixed approach, neither purely deontological nor purely consequentialist. Drawing from the above arguments, a desirable approach should be sensitive to both parties' rights, to the defender's subjective situation, to an objective balancing of the actors'

interests, and to the fact that what triggered the conflict was a rights violation, and not simply a *harm* like pain or pecuniary loss.

By violating the orchard keeper's property rights, the thief ceded the otherwise legitimate expectation that others would defer to his normal privilege against coercion to the extent necessary to restore the status quo ante,
but not for other purposes or to greater extents. This is because a right is
a title to coerce others to respect the zone of freedom that the right delin-
eates—but not more than this—and a violation of the right is what triggers
enforcement. Remediating the situation coercively might practically entail
curtailing the thief's freedoms in areas other than those of property use
(e.g., bodily autonomy, right to honest-dealing, etc.), and these practical
considerations are morally relevant.

The offender looses at least the defender from deferring to the offender's
freedom in that area where he does not have a right to freely operate. The
area of action where the offender lacks a right therefore corresponds to the
defender's violated right(s); the offender retains his rights that are beyond
the extra areas of freedom he seized at the defender's expense. The apple
thief cannot complain if the orchard keeper snatches back his stolen apples, but the thief can complain if the orchard keeper seizes the apples *and*
steals the thief's watch. (The second action might be a fitting punishment,
but punishment is a separate issue from just coercion in the context of self-
defense.) Since practical exigencies may require reactions dissimilar in kind,
and the defender's violated right serves as a limit beyond which the defender
cannot justly coerce the offender, the defender may coerce the offender with
respect to areas of action corresponding to rights of an equal or lesser value
than the right(s) violated, directly threatened, or abused if subjectively necessary to restore the status quo ante. In sum, therefore, the defender may do
what is necessary to restore the status quo ante through means affecting the
offender in areas corresponding to rights of equal or lesser value to the right
the offender violated, directly threatened, or abused.

Further comment on these three conditions is warranted. When a right is
directly threatened, it is reasonable to assume it will be violated imminently in
the event that the threatening party is not stopped; a paradigmatic example
would be a private citizen drawing and pointing a gun at another. The potential victim's right to live out her natural life is in imminent danger of
being violated even though it is not yet being violated. The threatened right
therefore is the relevant standard for judging the appropriate response. The
potential victim could use lethal force to stop the gun-wielding aggressor.
We would speak of a person *abusing a right* in cases where the threat is more
indirect or indeterminate. I am clearly abusing my right to private property

when test-firing my gun from my balcony, but the number and identify of people threatened by my behavior is indeterminate, so it is difficult to use a particular person's life or property rights as the gauge for just coercion. In this case, the right I am abusing is the most determinate and salient point of reference. It would be just for my neighbor to act coercively in a way affecting my property rights by demanding I stop shooting; by wrenching the gun out of my hand; or sabotaging it while I slept (if he was afraid of me). However, it seems that his *shooting* me would be excessive unless he was in the line of fire; saw someone else in the line of fire; or if the nonlethal approaches failed and I continued shooting, regardless of whether he saw someone in imminent danger (because it is likely that eventually my bullets would find a target). Even though my activities place my neighbors in potential mortal danger, there may be other ways to halt my activities without lethal force if this danger does not appear to my neighbor as imminent.

To return to the case of the apple thief, ranking rights is certainly not a controversy-free endeavor, but I will beg a discussion of such ranking here and trust most would agree that the right to life or to bodily integrity is more central to the preservation of autonomy than is, say, the right to private property. The apple thief did not cede the legitimate expectation that others respect his right to live out his natural life, because he did not (I will stipulate) threaten the old man's life. Since the right to property is less central than the right to life, the orchard keeper would be wrong to shoot the fleeing thief.[20] It *would* be acceptable for the orchard keeper to act coercively in areas corresponding to rights on par with, or of lesser value than, the right to property in order to restore the status quo ante. I would suggest that these include taking some of the thief's property of equal value; tackling the thief; threatening him; or tricking him into surrendering the apples. In many cases, what is permissible for a defender to do will also be efficacious at restoring the status quo ante, including associated material holdings; in some cases, as with the elderly orchard keeper, the permissible means of response may not be sufficient to fully restore the moral status quo ante, including associated material holdings.

This limit addresses the complication introduced by the defender's variable abilities and arsenal *and* acknowledges that the trigger for a coercive response is a rights violation rather than a pecuniary loss or other material harm. If the defender's just response is indexed only to the restoration of the balance of rights (which is sometimes expressed in material holdings), there is no limit to what he might do to regain the status quo ante. If he is limited in his response to actions leading only to the same material harm that he suffered, practical exigencies may prevent him from restoring either the moral status quo ante (e.g., having an effective defense, if for example, the attacker has a high pain threshold and is not subdued by the same number of blows he delivered) or the material holdings that may have been associated with the status quo ante. Further, not all rights violations incur a material harm. On the other hand, there *is* a limit to what the defender may do, despite his personal circumstances, if the limits to the defender's response are pegged to the relative value of the right originally trespassed. This arrangement may fail to allow him to regain the material holdings associated with the original level of rights enjoyment but at least does so because geared toward the fact that the violation triggering the coercive response was an event in moral space; the just reaction is guided by the rights violation rather than the material effect alone.

The Status of the Rights Violator

A rights violator is vulnerable to a range of coercive actions aimed at restoring the status quo ante, limited by the value of the right he violated, directly threatened, or abused.[21] (Unless the three different conditions are relevant, I will from hereon refer only to the value of the right violated.) We need to consider the offender's status now to further specify the appropriate limits to the defender's reaction; this discussion will lay the groundwork for responses to claims in chapters 5 and 8 that heinous criminals and terrorists, respectively, have no rights that interrogators must observe.

One might ask if the attention to equity in the above account of just coercion is so strict that most defenders will end up being in the wrong when responding to rights violations. Locke famously argues that a defender cannot be certain what a rights violator intends—one does not know if a thief wants one's life in addition to one's purse—and so parceling out exact coercive quid for coercive quo (e.g., merely exerting enough force to get back one's purse) is not necessarily adequate for one's protection. Therefore, Locke argues, one may kill a thief. Further, even if one knew the exact level of force necessary and appropriate to halt a culpable attacker, most people cannot exactly measure the force of their kick, say, in pounds per square inch, relative to the one they received. It would be easy to use more force than (was retrospectively seen as) necessary to fend off an attacker. Similarly, a defender who tackled a thief and violently recovered his stolen money might realize in hindsight that there was a way to nonviolently trick the thief out of the money.

Locke and Aquinas, among others, conceive of a miscreant as dropping from the sphere of human moral respect to a bestial level because of his crime. A defender may do anything he wishes to protect his rights because the offender's rights are completely voided; he has no more moral claim against the defender's violence than a hog does the butcher's. This dismissive characterization of the offender following his departure from the "law of reason" (Locke), in which he may be "disposed of according as he is useful to others" (Aquinas), perhaps in part encapsulates the practical difficulties of calibrating just coercive responses.[22] Given the difficulties of precisely judging and implementing appropriate responses, these thinkers suggest a binary practical standard for victims of unjust attack: a person must be given the respect and deference due a rational being or may be treated with the prudential, unilateral treatment of an animal.[23]

Thinkers considering defensive coercion sometimes distinguish what is just absolutely, considered from the "God's eye point of view" (taking into account all the information regarding the apparent offender's aims and power, which the defender would not necessarily be able to discern) from what is justified for the defender, given what he is able to know. Considered absolutely, Locke's and Aquinas's complete abnegation of the offender's rights is not consistently appropriate given that the offender may be acting under duress or temporary madness or that his intentions may only be to violate a relatively minor right or incur minor harm.[24] However, the two thinkers' claims can be partly redeemed if the matter is viewed from the perspective of what the defender is in the position to know and to do. The victim of a materially unjust action will often be unable to know the offender's intentions, mental health, hidden arsenal, and so on, and will also often be unable to respond precisely in kind and degree even if he did know these things.

So if we should reject Locke's and Aquinas's complete dismissal of the offender's rights when the interaction between offender and defender is considered absolutely, we can still draw two points of emphasis from their approach for an account of just coercion. First, viewed absolutely, the offender *has* ceded the otherwise legitimate expectation that others will defer to his general privilege against coercion to the extent necessary to halt and remediate his rights violation, by means of restrictions to his liberty on par with, or less valuable than, his original rights violation. In other words, the offender can be dealt with prudentially, "as he is useful to others," *within the limit set by the value of the right violated.* This, as opposed to Aquinas's and Locke's view that there is no limit.[25] Second, viewed practically, from the perspective of what the defender is in the position to know, we ought to give the defender a certain liberty to respond in ways that retrospectively would be judged as excessive or even mistaken (when the offender's intentions and

powers have been discerned). For example, shooting a mugger who is pointing a real-looking toy gun at his victim is excessive, considered absolutely,
but just if we ascribe to the victim the belief that he was being threatened by
a real gun. Considered absolutely, the offender has loosed the defender or
her proxy from the need to be *too careful* about observing his rights. Practically, most offenders, be they culpable or nonculpable, must be judged as
having loosed the defender in this way, since the defender cannot likely
know how far the aggressor intends to press the attack (or if he is indeed
nonculpable).[26] It is in order to capture this sense of the offender's action
partially *releasing others from self-restraint*, rather than completely forfeiting
the offender's rights, that I use the phrase "cede the otherwise legitimate
expectation" of a certain level of moral deference instead of "void" or "forfeit" a right. A further entailment of the offender's less-than-complete status
change will be addressed below in regards to third parties.

Third Parties

Explaining the role of third parties will be important for understanding the
role of police in society (discussed in chapter 2). To return to the previous
thought experiment, if Young steals Livingston's property, Young has ceded
the otherwise legitimate expectation others will refrain from coercion to the
extent necessary to restore the status quo ante. Since he seized more freedom than he is due, he is not wronged by coercive responses that push him
back to his previolation (and legitimate) level of freedom. One might ask if
it is only the offended party who has the right to exercise this just coercion.[27]
All other things being equal, a third party (call her Jones) is within her rights
to do anything in aid of Livingston so long as her aid does not violate other's rights (e.g., she cannot give money to Livingston she stole from Smith).
This is simply an expression of any person's freedom to do things she wishes
that are nonprejudicial to other's rights. In this case, Jones happens to want
to protect Livingston. Coercion exercised against an offender, limited in the
appropriate ways, does not violate the offender's rights—because he never
had a right to those unjust actions in the first place—so Jones may exercise
proportionate coercion against Young to aid Livingston.

Jones's action may be motivated by self-interest as well. In violating
Livingston's rights, Young wrongs more than Livingston; he indirectly wrongs
all other persons in the sense that Young arrogates to himself more freedom
than is consistent with universal exercise. He has abused a right and wronged
all others in taking a liberty he cannot extend to them; he is benefiting more
than they from the (supposedly) common self-limiting of each person's

freedom. He was able to get the jump on Livingston because Livingston was not readying a similar plan of assault and theft targeting him. In a practical sense, Young has identified himself as someone willing to behave unjustly; he is presently harming only Livingston, but Jones's fear that she could be next is not unreasonable if she lives nearby, fits the profile of Young's previous victim, is within range of his weapons, etc. At least in the moment of his rights violation, Young is indicating that he is a dangerous man.[28] For this reason as well then, Jones is within her rights to coerce Young to the point of reaching the status quo ante, limited in the appropriate ways. I will argue in the next chapter that police officers act in this third party role in restraining criminals.

TWO

The Liberal State and Police Powers

The Vallejo detectives' suspicion of Eugene Livingston changed things. Suspicion made his thoughts and actions *interesting* to the state of California. Livingston is now called to give an account; explain his motivations; and defend his choices. All that was banal about his life becomes a potential source of strife, a reason for the state to focus unwelcome attention on him and levy punishment. Once an abstract presence, the state now becomes alert, active, associated with particular human agents who bear the abstract power of the state in their questions, and in their expectation of answers, in their manacles and uniforms, and in their courts and prisons. The reason for this shift in attitude is not always clear: perhaps something Livingston did was perhaps wrongly interpreted, maybe the police heard a rumor, a lie.

The purpose of this chapter is to establish moral grounds for legitimate political coercion. By moral grounds, I mean grounds linked to a notion of autonomy which is expressed in rights and abstracted from any particular, real-world political setting (as discussed in the last chapter). "Political coercion" refers to a government's power to force people to do things, be it pay taxes, submit to business regulations, or refrain from harming one another. These moral grounds for political coercion will justify the specific police and prosecutorial practices addressed in chapters 3 through 5, as well as provide the context for determining the rights of non-state-based guerillas and terrorists in part 2. In this chapter, I will be operating in the "social contract" tradition of liberal political philosophy for several reasons. First, for the sake of brevity, a book with an applied focus needs to take certain points in fundamental theory as givens. I have chosen the starting points in liberal theory in general and contract theory in particular because they accommodate rights language and are oriented toward the protection and recognition of citizens' autonomy. These moral elements are salient to contemporary discussions of moral and political coercion, the rights to privacy and silence, the privilege against compelled self-incrimination, trial rights, police ethics, and other topics relevant to interrogation. This comment suggests the third point: contract theory is simply the one used or assumed by most of this book's interlocutors.[1] ("Liberal" political philosophy describes political systems oriented toward the protection and promotion of individual liberty; the term is not being used here in the sense it is used in contemporary politics, as an antonym to "conservative.")

In this chapter, I will defend a linkage of the possibility of political coercion with moral autonomy, abstracted from a specific political setting. I will argue that law-guided political governance is implied by the concept of a group of autonomous persons living in close proximity over time and fully enjoying their natural rights, such that the latter cannot be coherently conceived without the presence of the former. The "positive" freedom to plan out one's life presupposes a reasonable hope in a stable and secure future in which one's rights will be secure, and therefore, an overarching, law-guided power to foil the plans of potential rights violators. In many empirical settings, this power would take on the institutional features of a government. Governments, particularly liberal ones—designed to protect individual liberties—depend on broad legal compliance to function. Therefore, given governments' role in creating the background conditions for autonomous existence over time, complying with the laws of a basically just regime, or even the just laws of an unjust regime, is a moral duty, akin to the other duties involving deference to, or protection of, people's moral autonomy.[2] The legitimacy of a government's coercion in support of its laws is not dependent on a special right conferred on the government by the explicit consent of the governed, because legal compliance, provided a few caveats, is a moral duty, and moral duties are not determined by a person's explicit consent. Legitimate government actions, at least with respect to protecting inhabitants from rights violations, are those that inhabitants enjoying their rights could not rationally reject. Inhabitants could not criticize such actions in the name of more freedom without criticizing the very actions and institutions protecting their freedom.

A few words about the terminology in this chapter: "Political legitimacy" refers to the character a government must have to justly coerce its citizens or inhabitants. Unless otherwise stated, the use of the terms "autonomy," "rights," and "freedom" will be in the moral sense, abstracted from any particular political setting (e.g., present day Canada).[3] Much of what follows discusses states in a "conceptual" rather than "empirical" sense; in other words, the discussion will consider the implications of certain proposals for an ideal state, rather than the features of a particular, real-world state like Canada. It is important to isolate attitudes one might have toward a particular real-world government or police department as we discuss the police powers of a liberal state below in abstract.

Autonomy and Political Coercion

In this section I will argue that a coercive power capable of restraining rights violations—a government, in many real-world settings—is implied by the concept of a community of autonomous people fully exercising their rights over time. This conceptual implication in turn justifies the existence of certain real-world governments as well as certain types of government action. We begin with the assumption that all persons are autonomous, with moral rights as expressions of that autonomy, as discussed in the preceding chapter. We saw there that rights presuppose the legitimacy of coercive measures to protect those rights. Being able to fully exercise one's rights during the full, natural course of one's life implies two different kinds of freedom. As the terms are commonly used by philosophers, *negative freedom* means the absence of external impediments to one's actions, and *positive freedom* means the ability to plan and lead one's own life within the scope of one's rights. Negative freedom is a precondition for positive freedom.[4] One cannot consistently, freely plan and lead one's own life if externally impeded in ways relevant to one's plans and/or planning processes. Not only is it hard to make plans, say, while being punched in the head, one will circumscribe one's own designs if assuming that more assaults are likely in the future. Livingston is not going to buy a book if he suspects Young is going to assault him and steal it. Negative freedom implies the absence or suppression of effective rights violators in any arena that could affect the agent's rights. Therefore, continued existence as an autonomous person and untrammeled rights exercise implies (both freedoms and so) the absence or suppression of effective rights violators in the relevant arenas. For example, if Livingston has been living in the same place for an extended period of time, enjoying all his rights with no problem from anyone, we can infer that he has been lucky; that he lives in a safe neighborhood with law-abiding neighbors and a competent police force; that he lives in a neighborhood where the police presence compensates for the significant number of would-be criminals; or partial combinations of these.

The above argument does not assume that there will inevitably be rights violators in a community because people are inherently wicked, but simply follows the conceptual implications of the idea of wide-scale rights exercise.

Talk of autonomy presupposes a *community* of autonomous beings, so the rights exercise of one person has to be conceptualized against a background of other persons similarly making decisions and acting according to their own lights.[5] (It does not make sense to speak of autonomy, expressed in rights, if a person lives his entire life alone on an island, since rights are claims to limit others' freedom.) However, the concept of a community of autonomous beings does not necessarily entail effective and universal moral behavior, since people with finite perspectives may make choices they believe to be moral but which in fact materially infringe on other's rights.[6] For example, Livingston might want to listen to music in his apartment and chooses to do so at a volume he believes will not disturb his neighbors (because he recognizes that he implicitly gives leave to his neighbors to do the same if he listens to his music at a very high volume, and then no one would be able to enjoy his or her own music). Yet he could be mistaken about what his neighbors would be able to hear. He is not violating their rights if he is not intentionally trying to bother them or acting negligently, but rather, *materially infringing* on their rights—potentially causing them an undeserved harm. His neighbors could demand that he alter his behavior in deference to their rights in such a situation. In addition to well-intentioned errors, it is also possible that autonomous people will choose to violate their neighbors' rights. From the victims' perspective, a material infringement consequent to a mistake and an intentional rights violation may well appear the same. The music is just as loud if Livingston blasts his music thinking his neighbors cannot hear it as when he does so with indifference to his neighbors. Victims will also be just as likely to self-limit their plans if expecting inadvertent, material infringements of their rights (perhaps lacking some easy mode of remedy) as they would be if expecting intentional rights violations. So I will refer to "effective rights violations" below as an inclusive term including both inadvertent material infringements and intentional violations of rights. Rights violations per se are most relevant to our subject of police powers, but even material infringements are relevant to a state's police powers since conflicts over inadvertent infringements could easily escalate into violence without an impartial referee.

Any successful exercise of a right presupposes an absence of effective violations to that right to the extent that it is exercised for the relevant time period. Livingston's successful exercise of a right, say, to jog around the park, implies an absence of effective rights violations that would have directly affected his run.[7] He would not have been able to jog around the park had someone stolen his sneakers, much less assaulted or kidnapped him. This simply expresses the point that actions presuppose certain enabling conditions. The enabling conditions for rights exercise (relevant to social interactions) could be (a) a coincidental absence of all actors in the relevant arenas at the relevant times; (b) the effective, moral self-restraint of all actors in the relevant arenas at the relevant times; (c) the coercive restraint or deterrence of effective rights violators in the relevant arenas before, during, and after the right exercise; or combinations of these.[8] In other words, the fact that no one interfered with Livingston's run may have been a result of there simply being no one around when he ran, the presence of nice people uninterested in harming Livingston (who were also correctly able to judge which actions would violate his rights), the presence of villains intent on jumping Livingston who were fortunately restrained or deterred by Good Samaritans or police, or the presence of some good people *and* some effective rights violators who were restrained or deterred. Livingston might not have been able to finish his run had one of these variables been different.

Just as one instance of a person's rights exercise presupposes an absence of relevant rights violations in the proximate area and time period, a *full life* characterized by untrammeled rights exercise presupposes the enabling condition for both negative and positive freedoms in the relevant areas for the duration: a general absence of rights violations.[9] The relation of a general absence of rights violations to negative freedom is obvious. Regarding positive freedom, part of that freedom is the capacity to plan for the future and to choose from among all practically and morally possible options for present action. A reasonable hope that one's rights will not be violated in the future is a precondition for both present and future expressions of freedom, because prudence dictates that one self-limits one's options if one anticipates future rights violations.[10]

Given that it is *possible* that there would be rights violations perpetrated within a community of persons, one community member's *actual* autonomous life characterized by untrammeled rights exercise in the community over time[11] implies one or more of the three above-mentioned conditions: (a) solitariness, (b) morally upright neighbors, or (c) suppression or deterrence of effective rights violators.[12] *One instance* of a person enjoying his life and rights for a given amount of time does not necessarily imply any *one* particular condition. For example, Livingston's jog could have come about because the park was empty; because it was filled with morally upright people; or because the police presence scared away muggers. However, if he ran sixteen hours a day, seven days a week for his entire life, and never had a problem, it is no longer plausible to assume this was because there was never anyone else in the park nor ever any effective rights violators in the park. If we move beyond Livingston and include all people in his country and, in looking at all their activities, find that every person is able to live out his or her full life and fully exercise all his or her rights, it would be even more implausible that (a) or (b) were consistent causes for their good fortune. In any large community there will almost certainly be at least effective rights violators. Finally, if we abstract from real-world contexts and speak of the *concept* of a community of autonomous persons in which each enjoys his or her life characterized by untrammeled rights exercise—thereby considering what conditions could lead to this state of affairs *in all instances*, since a concept is an abstract and ideal property removed from all contingency—it must be that this concept implies condition (c), the suppression or deterrence of effective rights violators. This is to say, the consistent, conceptual precondition for a community of autonomous persons enjoying untrammeled rights for their full lives must be the suppression or deterrence of rights violators. This follows because conditions (a) and (b) are contingent causes—involving physical location and persons' choices, respectively—and so will not obtain in all possible instances affecting the lives and rights for persons in a community. Condition (c) acts as a kind of fail safe, creating the conditions for autonomy even when the other possible conditions fail to obtain. Even if there are people around, and some of them are effective rights violators, the suppression or deterrence of these rights violators will create the conditions for the community to enjoy untrammeled rights exercise.

The nature of the coercive power that suppresses or deters effective rights violators has not yet been determined; one might wonder if it too could exist contingently. Its nature need not be determined, because its existence is a mere function of the *actual* existence of something in all instances that, by its nature, could possibly *not* exist. Medieval theologians used the same argument to prove the existence of God: since the human species does not *have* to exist (its nonexistence is conceivable), but actually *does* exist, a nonhuman "creator of humans" must actually exist.[13] So the concept of a community of autonomous persons living lives characterized by untrammeled rights exercise over time implies the existence of a coercive power that in some form or other restrains, or could restrain, rights violators for the relevant period of time.[14] In order for the power to be efficacious with respect to community members' positive freedom, persons in the community would also need to be aware of the existence and scope of the coercive power.[15]

As with other implications or entailments of autonomy, the implicit, overarching coercive power does not necessarily need to be expressed in a given empirical setting.[16] For example, insofar as autonomy entails the freedom to plan and lead one's own life, autonomy entails the possibility of pursuing any number of morally permissible activities, such as going to grad school, marrying, bearing children, etc. This possibility does not necessarily entail that a person will decide to engage in any particular activity in a given empirical setting, but that instead, each would be a legitimate expression of her autonomy. The concept of a community of autonomous persons enjoying full rights exercise over time (from hereon I will mean this by "the concept of autonomy") implies the presence of an overarching coercive power that actually inhibits or could actually inhibit rights violations. In a given empirical setting, the conceptual implication would legitimate the *actual* presence of some kind of coercive power with a rights-protecting mission, be it a national government, a tribal council, or even a benign warlord in a stateless tract of land. The conceptual implication would also provide moral grounds for criticizing extant coercive powers that failed to play a rights-protecting role.

As we begin to get more specific regarding the scope of the coercive power implied by autonomy now, bear in mind the following fanciful thought experiment.

> Fed up with run-ins with the Vallejo police department, Livingston moves to presently lawless territory in western Afghanistan. Here he will experience real freedom, he thinks, with no government to push him around. He can do any drug he wants, own and shoot any kind of gun he wants, drive without a seatbelt, etc. Livingston realizes the land is rife with bandits, but he plans to hire some bodyguards and build a fortified compound. This project works well until his bodyguards are killed by opium dealers; as Livingston runs for his life, he ruefully wishes he could call the Vallejo police department. He avails himself to the protection of a local warlord, who provides rudimentary protective services in exchange for a monthly "tax." The difficulty is that the warlord is capricious and sometimes imposes strange edicts all must follow.

To the extent autonomy implies positive freedom, and so, confidence in the general absence of future rights violations, the coercive power in question must be of an enduring and consistent quality, and external to the person, rather than connected with any present empirical state of affairs relating to his own power (e.g., his present brawn, the ferocity of his Dobermans, the skill of his current staff of bodyguards, etc.). The power would need to be external to the person whose rights are being protected if it is to be enduring, because any given person will physically weaken, possibly lose allegiances, run out of money for guards, etc. In many empirical settings involving large numbers of unrelated people, this sort of overarching, institutional, constant, self-perpetuating power would likely need to take on the formal features of a government.[17] The need for the external power to be enduring and regular argues for coercion to be meted out through a legal system rather than the arbitrary fiat of a leader (like Livingston's warlord). If laws hew to this purpose of protecting people's rights, they would overlap with major moral duties, provide for general social order, and provide for the maintenance of that order.

There are at least four kinds of laws indicated for the portfolio of a governing body implied by the concept of autonomy. In other words, if Livingston's warlord was interested in good governance, or in formally establishing a state, there are four basic ways political power needs to be channeled into law. First, there would be laws overlapping with the basic moral rules directly related to persons' moral rights (prohibiting murder, assault, rape, etc.). Second, laws concerning general social order would function in empirical settings as general prophylactics (protectors) to rights, preventing their violation (e.g., a law prohibiting burning trash in one's yard eliminates the possibility that the fire will spread to one's neighbor's property); this category would be broad, including laws concerning private contracts, torts, traffic rules, regulation of pollutants, labor, food and drug purity, etc. Third, laws governing the fair implementation of laws such as those mandating that government will observe due process of law in exercising its power and apply the laws equally to all inhabitants. Fourth, laws governing the maintenance of the legal and political order would include its funding (taxation) and perpetuation (elections, appointments, etc.).

A system of law backed by force entails police powers, including the license to take steps to prevent and detect crimes, to intervene in criminal activity, and to arrest apparent law-breakers.[18] This entailment does not necessarily mean police per se, but a power of law enforcement. (By "crime" I mean a moral rights violation that is illegal in a state; I will therefore also sometimes refer to an environment free of rights violations as a "crime-free environment.")[19]

On the view of autonomy I am employing, Livingston's *anarchist* thesis that government coercion and autonomy are necessarily opposed is self-contradictory. Government power to coerce, channeled by law, is necessary for an environment relatively free of rights violations over the long term, and this environment is necessary for persons' continued autonomous existence and largely untrammeled rights exercise.[20] The government's power to coerce may not be necessary for a *particular* empirical community in a particular moment in time, because all the inhabitants are morally responsible and actually do nothing to trespass on their neighbors' rights. However, if this is the case, it would obviously be so by happenstance. As the potential for rights violations exists, so too must the potential for the government to exercise just coercion.[21] Further, as Locke, Kant, and Nozick point out, even morally upright people will occasionally disagree as to what justice demands in a given situation. Without an impartial referee, persons are free to assert their interpretations of justice unilaterally and this portends the possibility of unjust violence when the well-meaning asserters are in error or misjudge the appropriate level of coercion necessary to restore the status quo ante.[22]

Political Critique and Political Obligation

The purpose of this section is to establish the proper scope of government powers, including police powers, by identifying them with the rational grounds for inhabitants' dissent. I will argue politically legitimate actions are those to which inhabitants cannot rationally dissent. By "dissent," I mean the rejection of some state of affairs through critique. I do *not* mean disobedience, withdrawal of fealty, or other, more general relational state of affairs. In what follows I will refer to a specific form of irrationality called a "practical self-contradiction." This is an assertion made in a context that makes the speaker's stated or implied goals contrary to the actual end states his proposed actions will likely bring about. The general form of such an assertion would be: "In doing X, I want to achieve both Y and the opposite of Y [since X leads to the opposite of Y]." Kant's moral and ethical restrictions turn on practical self-contradictions. For example, Kant's objection to the consumption of mind-altering substances is based on the self-contradictory nature of freely choosing to consume substances that inhibit one's ability to make choices. One way lying can be shown to be immoral by Kant's lights is that universal lying will contradict the goals of all liars since no one would believe anything that anyone said. In short, such actions are irrational in the sense of "shooting oneself in the foot."

A person encounters a practical self-contradiction if he asserts that he could enjoy the full expression of his rights over time without the presence of a law-mediated government in a state where he is enjoying, or hoping to enjoy, the full expression of his rights (when he visits or immigrates).[23] The state of affairs demanded in his dissent (no political-legal regime and no police powers), presumably demanded so that he might be freer, would actually leave his freedom imperiled.[24] As Americans saw in the wake of

Hurricane Katrina, very bad things can happen in the absence of police protection and other government services. As police powers of a given state are necessary for the continued existence and full, or nearly full, rights enjoyment of inhabitants of that state over time, it is practically self-contradictory for residents or prospective residents to dissent to those powers, so long as the state's police powers are actually being used to protect the dissenter's life and rights. For ease of exposition, I will from here on substitute "irrational" for "practically self-contradictory," restricting the meaning of the former term to the sense of the latter.

It follows that it is *not* irrational to dissent to police powers that are not oriented toward the equal protection of all inhabitants' life and rights. This caveat creates both substantive and formal evaluative standards for police powers. If police powers are meant to protect inhabitants' lives and rights, police actions detrimental to both are substantively out of bounds. So, for example, it is an abuse of government power for police officers to use coercive means to benefit themselves alone, or a ruling elite, or even a majority of inhabitants at the expense of a minority (concrete cases will be addressed in the next three chapters). Similarly, there are rational grounds to dissent to activities *intended* by state agents to protect inhabitants' lives and rights, but which happen to have the same effect as substantive abuses of police powers. Such activities could be assessed by the formal standards of reasonableness, proportionality, efficiency, reviewability, efficacy, and reliability since they refer to the measures the state has chosen to use in conducting the substantively legitimate activity of policing.[25] These formal qualities describing means to an end derive their value from that end. We care about the tactics police use because we care about the purpose for which these tactics are employed: the maintenance of an environment relatively free of rights violations. Since the legitimacy of police power comes from the civic purpose of that power, police actions depart from their legitimate, "dissent-proof" role if they are not actually leading to such an environment—just as if their purpose had not been the maintenance of such an environment in the first place.

These substantive and formal standards are abstract and so only preclude abstract critiques of government. For example, it would be irrational for Livingston or a prospective inhabitant of Vallejo, California, to dissent to the city's *having* police powers, and irrational to dissent to reasonable, proportional, efficient, reviewable, efficacious, and reliable expressions of those powers (because rightfully having a power means the right to efficaciously use that power). However, there are rational grounds to dissent to *a particular tactic* on the grounds that it lacked one or more of these qualities;

for example, a person might argue that mounting a video camera in a high crime area will fail to lead to a reduction in crime. This follows simply because it is an empirical question (i.e., a question whose answer is evidence based) whether a particular tactic is effective, proportional, etc. So, for example, while it is legitimate in theory for the Vallejo P.D. to try to reduce muggings in a certain park, various approaches (patrols, cameras, better lighting, etc.) would need to be field tested to see which one was the most effective, proportional, etc.

The concept of autonomy implies police powers as such, political governance as such, a regulatory state as such, a regime of criminal and civil law as such, and the reasonable steps the government (or government-like power) takes to fund its activities, so it would also be irrational for any person to dissent to these general states of affair to the extent that they are expressed in her state where the government protected lives and rights by securing equal negative freedom for all inhabitants. Yet again, there are rational grounds in such contexts to dissent to *particular* laws or policies, such as particular taxation schemes or environmental regulations, since their reasonability, proportionality, efficacy, etc., depend on contingent factors.

I will refer to a government or de facto government (see the point about insurgencies below) that protects all inhabitants' lives and rights through equally applied legal mechanisms backed by force as "basically just." The modifier expresses the possibility that contingent events and personalities (e.g., biased judges, corrupt officials) will occasionally frustrate justice in a system that is just in its basic structure.[26] Excluded from the tag of "basically just" are governments that systematically exclude certain groups from legal protection or reserve unequal treatment for them, and governments that, while formally protecting all, effectively administer the law unequally, for example, by understaffing courts or police stations in minority neighborhoods. By "inhabitant" I mean a person who is currently inside the territory a government administers, be she a citizen, tourist, refugee, or legal or illegal alien. The focus on inhabitants rather than citizens will be explained below.

Rational grounds for political critique are not connected with limits on a political right to free speech or duties regarding democratic discourse. People have the right to criticize anything they wish. Not much is at stake if people wish to make claims putting themselves into practical self-contradiction; they are simply being irrational or are simply mistaken (as to whether a particular law or policy is effective). Rather, the rational grounds for dissent delineate politically legitimate government behavior. These grounds also delineate the scope of laws inhabitants are morally obliged to obey, a subject to which we will now turn.

The argument so far entails that it is rationally consistent to dissent to a particular law and, at the same time, refrain from dissenting to the overall political-legal regime of which that law is a part, the process by which it was formed, and the authority of those implementing and enforcing it.[27] In other words, someone like Livingston can agree to the idea of having a government with police powers while objecting to a particular law or a particular law enforcement tactic or while criticizing the sitting mayor of Vallejo or the governor of California. This acquiescence to the overall political-legal regime, its processes, and enforcement entails *obeying* laws he finds objectionable or unnecessary (even while criticizing them).[28] For example, if a baseball player agrees that Smith is the umpire of today's game, the player is bound to accede to Smith's authority with respect to the game. Therefore, it is rationally consistent for the player to obey Smith's orders regarding the game ("strike three; you're out"), even if disagreeing with the umpire's decisions in that case. Dissent to a particular law is consistent with obedience to it, because law-channeled state power is necessary to guarantee negative freedom over time, and states demand and need broad legal compliance—the great majority of inhabitants usually following most of the laws—in order to function.[29] Law as such is compulsory and universal in its application. When laws are redundant with moral duties like the duties to respect other's lives and property, their special purpose is not to communicate their content—they are *redundant* with moral duties everyone should know—but to compel those who refuse to observe their duties. Laws regarding general social order may appear purposeless considered individually (why drive on the *right* side of the road?). Indeed their content may be arbitrary (e.g., the right as opposed to the left side of the road); the purpose of these laws is only met insofar as they are compulsory and universal. They impose an orderly framework in society, a stable background, the absence of which would have a deleterious effect on people's moral autonomy (e.g., if there were no traffic laws).[30] Laws regarding the maintenance of a state such as those concerning taxation enable the state to continue to administer its laws. Disobeying all but egregiously unjust laws (explained below) in a basically just regime is irrational in the sense that that the state of affairs implicitly desired in acts of legal disobedience is freedom, but disobedience instead weakens the government's ability to protect freedom.

One is rationally and morally bound to obey all but the most egregiously unjust laws of a basically just state. This is the case even if, in a given instance, a person does not want to obey them or believes them to be purposeless.[31] More is at stake with obedience than one's own practical rational consistency (and ultimately perhaps, one's survival and freedom, insofar as the legal-political regime protects both). In addition to the role legal compliance plays in securing one's own rights, obeying all but the most egregiously unjust laws as well as contingent orders of state agents like police—barring strong evidence that they are unjust—is a moral duty owed others.[32] Legal compliance is a moral duty to the extent that some laws overlap with moral duties (banning murder, theft, etc.) or are secondarily associated with them (e.g., truth in advertising laws). Also, broad legal compliance is necessary for the support of political-legal regimes that are in turn necessary for the securing of inhabitants' negative freedom over time. Flouting the law weakens the authority of the government; stretches enforcement resources; and encourages others to disobey laws they find disagreeable (because they see their neighbors are no longer self-limiting their own freedom in deference to laws they dislike).The need for broad legal compliance is particularly the case in liberal states. Deferring to the same autonomy it protects by securing negative freedom, the liberal state affords its inhabitants a large degree of privacy; this privacy, and attendant host of political freedoms, is vouchsafed by the government with the implicit proviso that inhabitants not use this privacy and freedom to plot and commit crimes. The degree of control and surveillance in prisons gives us the image of what one kind of illiberal society is like where universal criminality is instead assumed or expected. Socialist East Germany provides another example, where it is often said that one in seven citizens was a paid informer for the secret police. For a liberal government to function and persevere liberally—in a manner respectful of inhabitants' autonomy—the majority of citizens must make responsible use of the freedom with which they have been entrusted. Since legal obedience is a moral duty, and moral duties are binding regardless of a person's explicit consent (e.g., one must refrain from assault even if one wants to commit assault), the duty to obey the law is independent of inhabitants' explicit consent to those laws. Therefore, just as the duty to tell the truth is both rational (i.e., self-consistent) behavior and a moral duty to others, the duty to obey the law is both rationally indicated and a moral duty toward others.

The grounds for disobedience to be discussed next will be relevant to the subject of police ethics, discussed in the next three chapters as well as the subject of insurgents' rights, addressed in chapter 6. Given the value of a political-legal regime as a whole for securing negative freedom—a dissenter would still likely find the vast majority of laws, policies, and powers of a given legal-political regime agreeable—a very high bar needs to be reached to justify disobedience to a law (and again, obedience is rationally consistent with dissent). I would tentatively say this is the case even in undemocratic states that are nonetheless successful at largely preserving all inhabitants' negative freedom. It is certainly the case in all regimes with regard to laws overlapping with basic moral duties as well as those oriented toward the maintenance of general social order. It is all the more the case in democratic states due to their procedures for reform, the practical necessity of accepting majority rule, and the possible shortsightedness of one dissenter's subjective point of view. Disobedience even to laws of apparent minor import is rationally inconsistent with acquiescence to a basically just political-legal regime.[33] It would then only be rationally consistent to disobey (i.e., there is a reason to disobey) a law or policy with all of the following qualities. The law is so unjust and deleterious to life and rights that it obviates the whole purpose of the legal-political regime;[34] reform is impossible because the system does not afford democratic legislative correction or the majority of the democracy supports the unjust policy (e.g., the Jim Crow laws);[35] the impact of the law is so deleterious with respect to life and/or rights that the time for legislative remedy or convincing the majority cannot be spared; and that its impact is so profound as to argue against a subjectivity limitation, meaning the individual has grounds to believe that her own dissatisfaction with the law is not idiosyncratic, but in line with major moral duties.

Citizenship and Political Obligation

To this point I have not explicitly addressed the issue of citizenship. The concept of autonomy implies acquiescence to political governance as such and to real governments that actually are effective at equally protecting negative freedom for all inhabitants in the territory within their jurisdiction. The preceding arguments for acquiescing to political governance were not linked to any sort of explicit or tacit sign of membership in a given polity. This is because they are linked to the concept of moral autonomy, abstracted from a particular political context.[36] Political-legal protection of persons' negative freedom is a basic human good, good for all persons, and therefore not linked to contingent factors regarding the person like citizenship or residential status.[37] It is a moral duty to obey all but the most egregiously unjust laws of a basically just regime (and even the just laws of an unjust regime), as well as the contingent orders of state agents, barring strong evidence that they are unjust. The scope of a state's reach then is not delineated by contingent factors associated with the person, each basically just state offering protections and structures good for all persons. Protection from robbery is just as valuable to a tourist as a citizen. The scope of a state's reach is instead limited by geography, its own effective power, and the power of other states.

This is to say that a state's borders are determined by the area in which it can effectively apply its political-legal regime.[38] This entails the possibility that a nongovernmental organization, perhaps an insurgent group, could take on the constitutive role of a state where an internationally recognized government failed to do its job (see chapter 6).[39] Tourists and aliens have a moral duty to follow the just laws of any nation they are visiting,[40] and private citizens of one nation are wrong to try to subvert the legal processes of another nation when those processes are basically just.[41] Just as one has moral duties to all other persons—to refrain from rape, assault, murder, etc.—regardless of their nationality, so too should one respect the institutions that help protect those foreigners from rights violations. It would be as irrational for tourists as it would be for citizens of a given nation to dissent to law-guided political coercion as such, and as irrational of the one as the other to dissent from the basically just and effective political-legal institutions of the government of the state in which they find themselves. Again, the tourist wishes to be safe from assault, theft, and rape when she is abroad as much as when she is home.

My argument has addressed what is irrational for inhabitants to criticize with respect to legitimate government functions. I mean to identify legitimate government functions with rational grounds for critique in the following way. Legitimate government powers and policies, at least with respect to the protection of negative freedom, are those that are irrational for inhabitants or prospective inhabitants of a state to criticize. The grounds for legitimacy are sufficient to direct police activities and guide inhabitants' potential critiques of these activities. The basically just state does not need to seek the explicit consent of its citizens to exercise police powers oriented toward the protection of their lives and rights, nor need it put up specific tactics to referenda prior to utilization, though it should accede to reasonable critiques of tactics once implemented. (Reasonable critiques are according to the substantive and/or formal grounds for critique discussed above.) Police need not obtain explicit permission from those members of the public with whom they deal prudentially in the course of their professional duties, though again, all their actions are subject to review and critique. Police need not obtain permission from apparent lawbreakers for the same reason that a Good Samaritan need not obtain permission from the apparent rights violator she restrains in the midst of an assault on an apparently innocent person. The attacker is apparently violating a moral duty to refrain from assault *and* the moral duty to obey all but egregiously unjust laws of a basically just state (or the just laws of an unjust state). (To be clear, these are moral duties owed to other persons, not owed to the state.) Whereas any person is within her rights to stop an apparent rights violator in the moment of his violation, police officers are simply those paid by the state to make themselves available for this protective role.[42] For a private citizen, acting as a Good Samaritan is a benevolent act—above and beyond the duty of justice—but a professional duty for police. The lawbreaker/rights violator's choices and preferences relative to this moment—if in fact the apparent rights violator is a rights violator—are not moral items to which others must defer, because the violator is pressing his choices and preferences in an arena where he is not free to assert them. In the next chapter, I will discuss how police are to proceed when they suspect but do not know a person is engaged in criminal behavior.

THREE

Plotting, Suspicion, and the Rights to Privacy and Silence

The court heard Dhiren Barot prepared meticulous plans for al-Qaeda figures on a series of synchronized attacks in the UK. "The central plan was for the construction and deployment in a basement car park underneath a building of an improvised explosive device using gas cylinders hidden in limousines," said Edmund Lawson, prosecuting attorney. Mr Lawson added it was to be launched simultaneously with other attacks including a dirty bomb, an attack on trains, and the hijacking of petrol tankers to be rammed into a target. In the document, Barot had written his primary objective of the project was to "inflict mass damage and chaos." . . . Barot's plans were found on a laptop computer seized during a raid on a house in Gujrat, Pakistan, in July 2004.[1]

Method and Scope

I will apply the earlier conclusions regarding just coercion to particular state actions in the criminal justice arena in this chapter and the two to follow. This chapter will address the rights to privacy and silence, and chapter 4, the privilege against compelled self-incrimination, often invoked by liberal political theorists and common-law jurists in reference to criminal investigation and interrogation. I will not be arguing that rights to privacy and silence and a privilege against self-incrimination are *logically necessary* entailments of a particular liberal notion of citizenship. (This would be a more complicated and lengthy approach than necessary here.) Rather, in response to legal scholars' calls for dismissing the right to silence and privilege for a dearth of plausible justifications, and to characterizations of suspects' rights as impediments to police investigations, I will be suggesting that there is at least one plausible scheme integrating rights to privacy and silence, the privilege against compelled self-incrimination, and police and prosecutorial efficacy. If such a scheme is judged favorably, it may argue for the protection of a robust political right to silence, a narrow per se privilege, and strong police powers. If the scheme fails, then the critiques accrue, and at least the recognition of the right to silence and the privilege may suffer for it.

This chapter will argue that rights to privacy and silence do not extend to concealing criminal plots, which I will define as serious, practical plans for criminal activity. Criminal plotting *would* cede the plotter's otherwise legitimate expectation that others defer to his rights to privacy and silence if plotting was as publicly obvious as is, say, assault. *Suspicion* that someone is criminally plotting gives another person the right to ask questions of the suspicious party that would otherwise be inappropriately intrusive. However, absent certain knowledge that the person is plotting (and so has abused his right to privacy), others should not *demand* he answer these personal questions, since a demand would imply that the questioned party no longer has a right to his secrets.[2] Since his plotting is covert, and one adult does not have a standing right to know another's thoughts, even a covertly guilty person (i.e., one who is not caught red-handed) can demand that he be treated like an innocent person, and innocent persons can choose whom they wish to address. As far as others know, he is innocent—he *looks* innocent.

The Rights to Privacy and Silence

Moral philosophers agree that privacy is to be counted among moral rights, or at least considered to be protective of such rights. Having a certain mental space of one's own is thought to be a precondition for moral autonomy.[3] "Privacy is the condition of having secured personal space, personal space is space required to reason, and individuals have a fundamental moral right to reason as a means of securing autonomy."[4] As Sissela Bok puts it, we would not be able to plan for the future; develop a sense of self; or control our interactions with others if every thought was exposed prior to our decision to share it publicly.[5] Bok's argument connects the two commonly used definitions of privacy: the moral space in which one may reason without interference and the power to control revelations about oneself to others. It can be seen that the latter helps protect the former. Even if there existed some mind-reading device that could be used without any physical harm to the target, the target's knowledge that it was being used or might be in use against her—knowledge that she was not in control of the release of personal information—would likely inhibit the free range of her thoughts.[6] In addition, certain integral human relationships are nurtured by confidences. One would not be a good spouse or friend if revealing everything she knew about intimate acquaintances.[7]

A *moral right to silence* is an entailment of the right to privacy (on both construals of privacy) in the event that one is questioned.[8] If privacy is construed as the power to control revelations about oneself, remaining silent would be a way of expressing one's right to privacy when one is being asked for personal revelations. While the right to silence is usually discussed in reference to criminal knowledge, we can see that because of the right to privacy and the moral autonomy it protects, a person usually does not have to speak to anyone she does not wish to address, regarding any subject besides others' criminality and perhaps public emergencies.[9] The force of claiming that there is a general right to silence means that the questioned party *does not wrong the questioner in refusing to answer his questions.* Put differently, the questioned party's silence does not conceal anything owed to the questioner. To understand this right, we can abstract from the issue of privacy and reflect on the underlying concept of autonomy. If one is in principle in control of her own actions and enjoys the freedom to decide what she will do with her own life, thoughts, and body, one ought to be able to choose whom to address and on which occasions.[10] The issue of privacy is additionally invoked, because divulging personal information to another can yield power to him even in instances when divulging other forms of information would not yield such power.[11]

Silence can be seen as a prophylactic to privacy if privacy is thought of as the moral space in which one is entitled to reason without interference. In the face of questioning, remaining silent is a way of resisting other's attempts to interrupt one's deliberations—to gain access into that mental space where plans of action are formed and considered. One has this right of refusal, because others lack a right to such interfering forays. The reason others lack this right is ultimately traceable to the impermissibility of one adult controlling another adult's actions, all other things being equal. Since one does not have a standing right to control another adult's actions, one lacks a right to interfere in the deliberations leading to those actions. Since *knowledge* of a person's deliberative process can amount to interference, one adult does not have a standing right to be party to another's deliberative process. In other words, all other things being equal, one adult is not entitled to know the thoughts of another adult.[12]

At first blush then, one is *not* within one's rights to demand that a stranger respond to questions about personal information, or put differently, one does not enjoy the legitimate expectation that a stranger will respond to questions regarding personal information.[13] The questioned party's silence is not concealing something owed to the questioner, and so she is not wronging the questioner by refusing to respond. One cannot justly coerce the questioned party in an effort to make her speak nor sue her in court to make her talk. To accost a stranger and *demand* personal information is disrespectful, because it assumes a paternal relationship in which one is automatically entitled to know the other person's thoughts, regardless of her desire to share or conceal them. Such disrespect infantilizes or objectifies the other (treating her like some kind of audio device).

The moral right to silence is in play even regarding a person's culpability in crime *if* she has done nothing to trigger suspicion. (I will unpack the complications regarding suspicion below; also, recall, I am using "crime" in a moral sense to mean a rights violation that is also illegal in a basically just liberal state.)[14] One is always obliged to act morally, and if one has committed a crime, one's moral obligation is usually to repent, confess, apologize, make restitution, and accept punishment. As will be discussed below, one does not have a right to criminal secrets per se, and one wrongs others by withholding criminal information. That said, one is wronged by others (be they private citizens or state agents) if they request personal information regarding possible criminal involvement without evidence the questioned party has relevant information. One is not always obliged to proactively prove to others that one is acting, or planning to act, morally, because one's neighbors do not have the right to demand a constant accounting of one's innocence. First, constant questioning about one's actions, criminal or otherwise, violates a person's privacy, burdening her time and thoughts with justifications and paranoia. Second, barring particular evidence of wrongdoing, it is disrespectful to treat a person as suspicious, in that it does not treat her as a free agent but as one whose relationship with oneself is set prior to any relational action she chooses.[15] Unwarranted, or prima facie suspicion is a form of prejudice, for example, as expressed in racial profiling.

Others do have a right to *request* personal information relevant to a suspected crime provided some evidence that the questioned party has such information. However, others are wrong to *demand* personal information if they only have weak cause for suspicion, because such a demand implies that the questioned party definitely abused his rights to privacy and silence and so cannot expect deference to them.[16] In many contexts, others would not be in a position to know this is the case and so their presumption is problematic. These matters will be addressed in more detail below.

Plotting

In this section, I will discuss criminal plotting, explaining the sense in which plotting is illicit and explaining how plotting diminishes plotters' rights. The prohibition of an illicit action such as assault surely includes all the components of the action: an attacker would still be in the wrong in some way if a passerby interfered and blocked his punch just before he struck his intended victim. If the components of the action include a definite plot to commit the action, intuition says that the plot should be illicit in some way too. If one planned to attack an innocent person such that one waited for him on his normal route home, hid in the bushes, etc., then the plotting is as much a part of the causal chain leading to the blow as is the clenching of the fist. It seems one is still in the wrong—at least in some sense—if in merely plotting to violate a person's rights, one has not caused the damage one causes when successful in an assault. One is also in the wrong if one is simply the plotter and not the assailant. If one's plot is in aid to another, the plot is akin to a weapon lent to an attacker by a knowing accomplice.

If these claims meet with some intuitive support, I need to further articulate the sense in which criminal plotting is illicit. A critic might point out that the plot in the foregoing example was presented as a necessary part of an assault, but in point of fact, not all plots terminate in criminal actions.[17] If we argue that plotting is illicit, are we committed by the same logic to call all private gun ownership illicit since some guns are used criminally? Are steak knives to be deemed contraband as well? While we might allow that plotting displays bad intentions and bad character, it is not clear that people's rights are violated merely by plotting against them. Therefore, on what grounds can we say plotting is deontologically illicit if people are not wronged by mere plotting against them?[18] Further, the critic might ask, since plots are not necessarily linked to criminal actions, how can we distinguish criminal plotting from fantasizing, prior to the commission of a criminal act? Finally, even if it is possible to distinguish plots from fantasies, one usually does not know what a stranger is thinking, so the distinction is moot apart from a confessional context where a person chooses to reveal his thoughts. In what follows, I will argue that plots as such can largely be distinguished from other mental items even absent a connection with a criminal act; that criminal plotting is unjust in the same way choosing to acquire contraband is unjust; and that there is a deontological presumption against criminal plotting since there is a moral, and not just a practical, reason for respecting persons' rights to privacy and silence.

Criminal plots

On my usage, four elements distinguish criminal plots from fantasies of crime, fictional plots, or other mental items.[19] "Criminal plots" are *serious, rational, and practical plans* to violate a person's rights. (For stylistic reasons, I will sometimes drop the "criminal" modifier without intending a change in meaning.) The modifier "rational" refers to rational calculation, to the exclusion of momentary emotional impulses. The plotter does not merely feel a momentary surge of anger in which he wants to strike an irritating person, or even a sustained angry mood in which he wishes another ill, but instead, coolly employs strategic, means-to-end reasoning to determine how to harm his target.[20] We can see this in the behavior of Dhiren Barot, mentioned in the epigraph to this chapter. He spent *eight months* scouting targets for terror attacks, generating fifty-one computer disks of targeting information. Investigators marveled that Barot's diligence extended to counting the number of chairs in the New York Stock Exchange boardroom.[21]

The modifier "serious" regards the plotter's intention to bring off some rights violation in the world. Plots are different from fantasies, games, or fictional criminal schemes a detective novelist might design. Only the agent knows whether her rational deliberation is in service of a plot or a fictional scheme until the plot is communicated to others, written down, or otherwise manifested in action.[22]

The real criminal plot's *practicality* further distinguishes it from a fantasy, both in the agent's subjective understanding and in the eyes of outsiders if the plot manifests in observable behavior. By being "practical," the plot involves the taking of concrete steps to meet the goal, including research and surveillance of the target as well as the marshalling of resources needed for the crime. These steps are a result of the sober choice the plotter made to cause harm to others and are a latter-stage application of the initial planning stage, which could have occurred "in the armchair." For example, in addition to conducting reconnaissance on targets in the United States and United Kingdom, Barot drew up detailed bomb recipes using common household chemicals and then determined how to deliver the bombs to various buildings' garages. The plotter has now done more than plan it out in his head, but has taken steps to make it a reality. I add this element of practicality to the rational element of plotting, because while it is conceivable that some plots are worked out theoretically and immediately implemented, many types of planning take the form of a feedback loop in which a tentative plan determines the course of early research and then is amended after initial research and field testing, giving rise to new courses of research, etc. True, the fantasist and detective novelist might engage in research and surveillance (the latter in service of a realistic plot for her villain), and anyone might innocently gather materials that could be used for criminal behavior, so again, the distinction between a real plot and a fictional one is ultimately determined by the agent's intention.[23]

Finally, a criminal plot is a *plan*, meaning it is indexed to a particular event in the world, such as to destroy *this* building at this time, to move *this* package of heroin from point A to point B. The specific real-life target does more to transform a general bad intention (e.g., to kill American and English civilians) and general knowledge of how to commit a particular sort of crime into a plot.[24] The plot now has discrete boundaries; even if it exists only in the words the plotter speaks to a conspirator, it is a determinate, complete thing, like a song or recipe, ready to be employed by anyone with the will to do so.

The agent's intention with respect to the particular plan remains determinative as to whether it is a real or fictional plot. While a given mental item's being other than a real criminal plot is less likely, the more rationally deliberate, practical, and particular it is, no preponderance of facts can objectively and decisively distinguish a fictional plot from a genuine criminal plot. However, the absence of a bright line distinction between a real criminal plot and a fictional scheme apart from intentionality does not lead me to believe that a mentally normal person would be unable to say if she intends to employ the mental item in her mind to commit a crime or not.[25]

The plotter employs strategic reasoning, devising the practical steps necessary to accomplish a goal with respect to a particular target, intending to actually bring the plot to fruition. The elements beside intentionality are objective features of the plot, or are reflected in the plot's objective features (in the case of rationality), and could be publicly discerned in the plot if it written down or communicated to another person. At this stage, the second person's intentionality determines whether what they have heard is now also "his/her plot" or "someone else's plot." If the second person also intends to commit the crime, s/he is a plotter too, whereas the hearer of the plot who does not intend to carry it out is not a plotter (e.g., I can learn about Guy Fawke's Gunpowder plot without being engaged in the activity of plotting). If the plot is the work of contemporary plotters and its execution is imminent, or it has been executed and the plotters were not punished, the innocent hearer of the plot has *criminal knowledge* she is in most circumstances bound to tell authorities (more on this below). If the plot is a historical artifact, the plotters dead or imprisoned (e.g., as with Guy Fawke's plot), then the plot is of no special significance.

Intentionality does the categorical work the critic relies on criminal action to do in ultimately distinguishing plots from fantasies. Yet the critic might also contend that a plot is only deontologically illicit to the extent that it is the efficient cause of an illicit action. Without illicit action, the critic continues, a plot is merely bad because of its bad intention; the plotter is "unethical," in a Kantian sense, and "malicious," in an Aristotelian sense, but he is not *acting* unjustly. Barot *plotted* to murder and destroy private property but was arrested before he could murder and destroy property. Yet as was discussed in chapter 1, not all rights violations produce a material harm, nor do all *abuses* of a right directly and immediately violate someone else's rights (for example, blindly shooting a gun from one's balcony, without actually hitting any person or thing). I need to show now that plotting has the nonuniversalizable profile of rights violations or abuses of rights in order to argue that mere criminal plotting is unjust, ceding the plotter's otherwise legitimate expectation against coercive treatment.

All other things being equal, persons conceived of as autonomous can expect and demand others defer to their privacy by not demanding answers to personal questions. People have a moral right to formulate their own opinions and plans; protect personal confidences; nurture memories key to personal identity, etc., and all these mental activities are potentially up-set by being questioned, much more by being compelled to disclose these thoughts to strangers. As argued in chapter 1, all moral rights must be lim-ited to a level of expression consistent with universal exercise. Given this moral horizon, it is hard to see how *any* activity protected by my rights to silence and privacy (insofar as it is expressed and protected by silence)[26] would offend yours, similarly protected. My right to speak freely infringes on your right to speak freely if I slander you (people won't listen to you with the same respect they listen to me) and my free exercise of religion could inhibit yours if mine requires killing infidels, but it seems my think-ing *anything* would be consistent with *your* thinking anything. Further, your concealing your thoughts and controlling their revelation does not prevent me from doing the same. This is the case even if we are both engaged in criminal plotting (while not having yet enlisted accomplices or expressed physical manifestations of plotting), as your standing beside me mentally planning my demise does not physically interfere with me plotting the same for you. Our thoughts don't bump up against each other in the world in the way actions sometimes do.

The proper comparison for abuse of the rights to privacy and silence is abuse of the right to private property, notwithstanding the material differ-ences between thoughts and property.[27] The right to private property entails the right to own property and use it as one sees fit so long as the use is consistent with others' enjoyment of their property as well as the exercise of their other rights. Certain items, like cars, can be used both responsibly and irresponsibly—I can drive my car on the highway or through your living room—and other items, such as machine guns, cocaine, tigers, nerve gas, etc., are very hard for most people to use or own responsibly in most settings. (Even if I have done my best to train my pet tiger, it's a *tiger*.) What could be morally designated—and is legally designated in most jurisdictions—as "contraband" is material that perhaps can be *held* without offense to others, but which can rarely be *used* without having deleterious effects on others. One does not have a moral right to own contraband, because a right means the freedom generally to use it as one sees fit, and contraband in most circumstances does not admit of such broad, responsible use. Similarly, a criminal plot could be "held" in one's mind without offense to others, but cannot be employed *as a plot* without doing others injustice.[28]

The comparison to contraband meets three of the above critiques: (1) that criminal plots are not plots unless actually connected to criminal actions; (2) because of this indeterminacy, it cannot be said that all plotting is illicit; and (3) plotting is only a matter of virtue rather than of justice. Contraband is not prohibited because it will inevitably be used for ill effect, but because its typical use has such grave effects that its use by most persons cannot be risked. Since contraband is inherently dangerous, universal ownership of contraband—with attendant rights of use—cannot be coherently willed by a person who may wish to acquire it. In *choosing* to acquire it, one is arrogating to himself a right he cannot coherently grant others. So too for criminal plots; like contraband, plots could be universally *held* without contradiction, but a right to have, and so employ the plots, could not be coherently extended to all persons.

Even if there is a moral argument for considering criminal plotting illicit in a deontological sense, deontology also presupposes the possibility that others can coercively protect their rights from violations. This implies that others can perceive that their rights are being threatened or violated at least some of the time, *and* that there is something they can in principle do about it. Yet it is unclear how to perceive or regulate the mental activity of other people.[29] Surely it is easier to speak of illicit mental activity using the religious language of sin, inasmuch as such language may presuppose a being who can actually discern secret thoughts. So the analogy between contraband and plot seems to fail when it comes to coercive responses.

To respond to this critique, we first need to note that privacy has moral dimensions independent of its practical dimensions. It is not simply that I am unable to read your mind and so have no choice but to defer to your right to privacy. If people should have their privacy respected—given the mental space to think freely—it is wrong, all other things being equal, to *try* to interfere with the free play of their thoughts. This rule has concrete implications when we say that it is on account of your right to privacy that I must refrain from reading your diary or listening to your conversation with an intimate. These are moments when your thoughts are effectively externalized and so I *am* able to know your thoughts. If the only reason to respect people's privacy was the relevant practical impediments, we would not criticize the reading of people's diaries as invasions of privacy.

The privacy of others is respected in order to respect their autonomy; their autonomy should be respected to the extent that their chosen expressions of autonomy are in turn consistent with equal universal respect for other people's autonomy. It makes no sense to say that others defer to one's privacy so that one can fine-tune plots to harm them because criminal plots are plans for actions prejudicial to the autonomy that gives moral salience to privacy in the first place. In other words, just as the justification of the right to bodily autonomy assumes people will not be using that autonomy to commit assault, the argument for the value of rights to privacy and silence assumes that people are not using this privileged space to plot other's harm. Since the reason for deference to the rights of privacy and silence is independent of practical limitations, the reason for refraining from plotting and the grounds for calling plotting illicit are independent of practical limitations too. The material differences between contraband and plots—differences that allow for the former to be more readily detected by outsiders—therefore are not germane to the analogy I drew between the two.

If various forms of coercion are in some cases justified to prevent rights violations, we might ask if some form of coercion is also justified to interrupt criminal plotting. Suspend for a minute the practical question of how one might do this, given that one usually cannot know what a stranger is thinking. Dhiren Barot put his blueprints, bomb recipes, and attack plans on CDs and sought to disseminate them to fellow jihadis. Would not an investigator be justified in trying to seize these disks if informed of their existence? If some kind of coercive interdiction is justified when a plot takes physical form, our discussion will have to turn to the less than obvious means one would use to elicit from the recalcitrant plotter the illicit knowledge he carries in his head like contraband in his pocket.

I will evaluate the interrogation methods designed for this purpose in chapter 5, but now need to further address moral restraints on investigators created by criminal suspects' rights to privacy and silence and privilege against compelled self-incrimination. One lacks the "right" to plot an innocent person's harm, but one does enjoy rights to think freely, to privacy, and to silence. The first right could be abused to plot, and the second and third right could be abused to conceal the plot. On account of these rights, we cannot move directly from the impermissibility of plotting to the permissibility of others suppressing such activity, as we can in the case of physically doing harm. While there is no right to assault innocent people, there is a right to control the revelation of one's thoughts or information about oneself, and this right could be used to protect possible criminal plots.[30] Another way of expressing this idea is that while one does not have a right to criminal secrets, one does have a right to secrets in general, and an outsider does not know which, if any, of one's secrets are criminal.

Two Conceptions of Autonomy and the Limits of State Power

Distinguishing two theoretical conceptions of autonomy, and two practical ways of employing these conceptions, will help determine who is entitled to probe a person's secrets for the purposes of crime detection and prevention. This section is somewhat technical, but clarifying these matters will allow us to resolve a number of debates in the literature regarding privacy and the privilege against compelled self-incrimination. I will first address the two practical ways the conceptions of autonomy are employed. For the purposes of this argument, an account of a person can be treated as an *authentic account* of how people really are (e.g., a philosophical or theological account of human nature) or it can be taken as what I will call a "practical model," which is temporarily *treated* as true for the purpose of guiding practice in a particular arena.[31] For example, a boxer might treat his opponent as his "enemy" during training and the bout itself, motivating himself with the idea that this man truly wishes him harm, even while aware that the opponent is not really his mortal enemy but merely playing a professional role that terminates at the end of the bout. Practical models can also be morally useful, because people's epistemic limitations may prevent them from determining what other people deserve morally in an absolute sense. (As suggested in chapter 1, there can be a disparity between what someone deserves absolutely and what a bystander is in a position to judge him to deserve.) So practical models can serve as "default settings" for social interactions, guiding people to act in ways that will usually produce moral effects even if the people are not consistently in the position to judge the moral desert of their neighbors—most rules of etiquette qualify.

Having addressed their practical modes of employment, I will now address the different theoretical conceptions of autonomy relevant to our subject. Philosophers have taken the term "autonomy" to mean different things. There is a useful distinction to make between two common usages of the term: what I will call a "moral conception of autonomy" and a "political conception of autonomy."[32] The moral conception conceives of autonomy as constituted, or undermined, by the agent's judgments and treatment of others (e.g., the model explained in chapter 1). The political conception conceives of persons as self-sufficient atoms, who may interact with other "atoms" based on calculations of self-interest, but whose interactions have no effect on their respective makeups —only on the recognition or revocation of conventional rights by the state or on a private citizen's restriction of another's freedom at an interpersonal level.[33] The moral conception of autonomy links freedom constitutively to moral obligation (the "slavery" to which it is opposed is chiefly the yoke of irrational desires) abstracted from any particular political setting. On this understanding, an immoral person has made himself unfree, even absent physical restraints. The political conception can, by contrast, conceive of freedom and moral obligation in tension—the morally appropriate action might be thought of as at odds with one's freedom—and mainly uses a conception of autonomy to delimit a state's power with respect to the citizen or inhabitant. The political conception is not chiefly concerned with private citizens' positive duties toward one another, nor toward themselves, and does not focus on what makes persons worthy of deference. On this view, even an immoral person is free if not externally restrained. Based on a political conception of autonomy, the full privileges of moral autonomy are recognized wholesale by the state, effectively treating all its noncriminal citizens as fully rational and responsible. The state restricts only irreconcilable public actions and formally limits political autonomy only following observed or proven criminality.[34]

The two conceptions of autonomy have different understandings of rights associated with them as well. As discussed in chapter 1, *moral rights* can be thought of as being abstractly created by morally autonomous persons' reciprocal recognition of rights on the part of others. Discussions of moral autonomy assume a "God's eye view" inasmuch as one speaks of the rights one is owed absolutely, based on hidden, subjective judgments as well as publicly observable actions. By contrast, *political rights* are those conventionally conferred or recognized by the liberal state on citizens in self-limitation of its own power and through limitation of citizens' interactions. Political rights can be curtailed in response to the observable criminal behavior of citizens or inhabitants. In some cases, political rights are unique to a political context, such as a right to vote, a right to run for political office, etc. Beyond those sorts of rights, political rights often overlap with moral ones, differing only in regard to the actors whose behavior is restricted, and the impetus for recognition or curtailment of the rights. For example, it is wrong to physically control another adult's bodily motions, all other things being equal, on account of the *moral* right to bodily autonomy. The *political* right to bodily autonomy entails that *state agents* are wrong to physically control an inhabitant's bodily motions, all other things being equal, and wrong to refuse to halt one inhabitant's attack on another. Both moral and political rights to bodily autonomy can be curtailed if a person is apparently using that autonomy to violate another's moral or political rights, as in cases of assault. In this context, a Good Samaritan (a private citizen) who intervenes is interacting with the offender on a level to be examined in reference to moral rights. A police officer who restrains a violent offender violates neither his moral or his political rights, though it would usually only be the latter that would be relevant to discussions of police ethics.

Having introduced the two conceptions of autonomy as well as the modes of employing these conceptions, I will now address when and how these conceptions should be employed in the criminal justice arena. I argued in chapter 2 that law-mediated political governance is implied by the concept of moral autonomy, so there is a moral duty for persons who are fully enjoying their rights to comply with all but egregiously unjust laws of a basically just state. Such a state acts legitimately when it acts to protect all its inhabitants' lives and rights equally through reasonable means. However, state officials will encounter practical difficulties in trying to protect inhabitants' rights if conceiving of them in the sense of moral rights, because epistemically limited in determining inhabitants' moral desert (such desert is partially dependent on internal mental states and judgments).[35] It is therefore more sensible to conceive of the rights a liberal state should protect as political rights, which can be curtailed based on observable behavior, without reference to inhabitants' or citizens' internal states. The associated political conception of autonomy would therefore seem a good candidate for use in assessing the coercive behavior of liberal states. The atomistic quality of the political conception further recommends it for the assessment or design of liberal states since the robustness of the conception places correspondingly heavy restrictions on government coercion. Such restrictions are desirable since one can imagine states overreaching in their attempts to prevent wrongdoing or enforce good behavior,[36] to say nothing of worse abuses consequent to (potential) government corruption.[37]

This conception should be employed by state officials *as a practical model* rather than as an authentic understanding, at least in the criminal justice arena (where people's rights might be curtailed).[38] Even states with extensive surveillance and patrol assets cannot see everything their inhabitants may be doing possibly meriting restriction of political rights. So states cannot practically tailor their behavior toward citizens or inhabitants in reference to the political conception of autonomy in the precise way a political theorist can when speaking in the abstract. A theorist can say in the abstract that citizens with such and such a profile merit such and such treatment by government. Yet states lack the means of consistently determining the status and merit of every inhabitant (even in regards to a political conception of autonomy) and so must effectively make an *assumption* about inhabitants' status, an assumption that in turn serves as a basis for the state's ordinary treatment of inhabitants. This is to say, the state is often going to have to effectively err on one side or another in its dealing with inhabitants.[39] Whether the state "errs" with more or less deferential treatment of inhabitants than is actually deserved is determined by the model of the citizen state officials use in crafting policies. For example, by engaging in nearly omnipresent and intrusive forms of surveillance, illiberal totalitarian states (e.g., Stalinist-era USSR or contemporary North Korea) in effect assume their citizens are always guilty with respect to the interests of the state, or guilty until proven innocent. In such states, there is no baseline assumption that citizens are to be left alone or are entitled secrets from the state.[40] By contrast, liberal states ought to effectively assume that their citizens or inhabitants are innocent until proven guilty of any crimes and should consider them adequately rational and responsible to ford their own way through the world with minimal state oversight.[41] Liberal states do this by affording citizens or inhabitants broad deference to lead their own lives and retain large zones of privacy from the state.

A practical model is not a substitute for more specific and formal principles for policymakers and judges such as due process and equal protection of law but might add a substantive lesson from the nation's (or similar nations') political history sufficient to direct the content of the laws to be equally applied to all as well as the mode of their application by the police and the courts. It is a kind of colloquial version of a political philosopher's account of the citizen, simple enough for legislators to bear in mind, but substantive enough to produce outcomes distinct from outcomes produced by different models. It may even be possible to have multiple models of citizenship at work in a single government, apt for different policy arenas, with each one geared to avoid a specific historical problem.[42] For instance, a liberal state may err on the side of assuming more people are interested in crafting the face of their government than is empirically supportable when developing suffrage policies, because of the historical negative effects of implementing alternative models (e.g., the use of poll tests to disenfranchise minorities). Similarly, states may assume consumers are savvier than empirically warranted due to concern that excessive, paternalistic commercial regulation will stifle economic activity.

There are three practical models relevant to the criminal justice arena. First, there is the default, baseline level of interaction in which the state assumes the inhabitant is innocent of crimes: *apparently innocent.* When they have been convicted of a crime, inhabitants are treated according to the practical model of *proven guilty,* with an associated diminution of recognized rights. It is appropriate to think of practical models here, because while a conviction is the state's epistemic equivalent of "knowledge" of guilt, trial procedures are fallible—only the convict really knows if he is guilty. Further, state officials must treat a convict as guilty even if personally believing him to be innocent. Third, there is a transitional phase in which a suspect is paid special attention in order to determine which of the two extreme categories applies: *suspicious.* In international contexts, there is another model that will be addressed in part 2: *enemy of the state.*

The Political Conception of Autonomy and Suspicion

The purpose of this section is to articulate a basic framework of police ethics, given the moral justification for political coercion defended in the last chapter. This framework will serve as a backdrop for the more detailed discussion of the proper limits of police investigations and interrogations to follow in chapters 4 and 5. Specific questions of application will therefore be put off until those chapters in favor of the present broad and contextualizing overview.

Some philosophers argue that contractarian liberal accounts of human nature can overemphasize or mischaracterize autonomy, erroneously atomizing the individual and ignoring the social relations and obligations necessary to develop and express selfhood.[43] Such atomization can yield an overly circumscribed account of one's *positive* moral duties toward others (what one is bound to do to others).[44] I just argued that a rigid and atomistic conception of autonomy is an appropriate practical model when considering a liberal state's interactions with inhabitants of the state in the criminal justice arena. In an empirical setting, it is also an appropriate practical model when considering *all* persons' basic negative duties toward others (what one must refrain from doing), as a means of preventing various forms of social and political oppression.[45] Practically, one can see that society would witness an intolerable level of privacy violations if neighbors, pedestrians, and subway occupants interfered with others' affairs every time they saw or suspected some minor behavior they found objectionable. We may "know" most in our society do not meet the robust visions of autonomous agents rationally negotiating an independent life path described by Enlightenment thinkers. Yet we can perceive that a society in which individuals *act* as if the robust and atomistic, "men as islands" account of autonomy were universally true is preferable to a society in which social and political deference was minutely apportioned based on individuals' actual capacities and level of moral responsibility.[46] Even if one entertains notions of a desirable society—good for all, privileges commensurate with abilities—in which one played Calvin to Geneva and minutely prescribed right from wrong, art from trash, one can see, formally, that one would not like Geneva if one's benighted neighbor played Calvin.[47] Therefore, one tolerates the "backward" lifestyle of one's neighbor in exchange for her reciprocal noninterference in one's own affairs.

As a matter of course then, neighbors and state agents in a liberal state properly give one the benefit of the doubt, as it were, to the effect that one is making responsible use of the liberties politically afforded her (and socially recognized). Usually, only when one is flagrantly not acting responsibly, committing some kind of crime, can one's political autonomy be forcibly curtailed, and the social and political deference that a robust conception of autonomy demands, be partly foresworn.[48] As argued in chapter 2, any person can accost, question, and if need be, restrain the apparent offender, but the police are paid by the state to perform this role full time.

There should properly be a sliding scale of coercive responses pegged to the apparent severity of an offender's mischief and the relative certainty that he is culpable. (As mentioned in chapter 1, "coercion" includes a spectrum of actions that treat a person prudentially, as a means to an end, including demands for personal information, threats, emotional manipulation, lying and other forms of deception, extortion, and varying levels of physical force.) This is because just coercion is indexed to the restoration of the status quo ante, and disproportionately severe coercive responses would create a newly unjust asymmetry. Therefore, if the person apparently engaged in criminal behavior is not using force, or apparently threatening force (including, for example, physical resistance to lawful state confiscation of property or trespassers' refusal to leave a building), authorities ought not to use physical force against her, and barring criminal conviction, they should not restrict for an extended period of time those liberties that are normally restricted as a way of punishing a criminal and isolating her from society.

How may police prevent and detect crimes besides forcibly restraining and possibly arresting persons caught in the midst of apparent criminal activity? A state agent's suspicion that a person is improperly using the thick and largely opaque walls of her political autonomy to plot crime(s) properly puts into motion an investigation aimed at proving this is the case. One cannot abstractly determine what constitutes "reasonable grounds of suspicion," because the quality of being suspicious is inherently contextual and subjective (more on this below).[49] Yet the police officer or other state agent should be able to produce reasons for his suspicion; this is to say he ought to have publicly\defensible reasons for beginning to treat a person prudentially, lest he be applying his police powers arbitrarily. I will argue in the next chapter that many of the political rights properly afforded a criminal suspect stem from suspicion's indeterminacy.

It would be irrational for inhabitants of a state in which they are enjoying their lives and rights to dissent to criminal investigations consequent to police officers' reasonable suspicions of criminal activity, because a relatively crime-free society is a precondition for the enjoyment of inhabitants' rights. State agents must sometimes act on suspicion rather than certainty, because restricting action to a certainty threshold would fail to effectively prevent crimes even if the state utilized omnipresent surveillance technology and highly intrusive intelligence networks.[50] Inhabitants could dissent to the governance of a regime unable to secure a relatively crime-free environment.

An investigation will likely infringe on the robust political autonomy prima facie conferred on all adult inhabitants in a liberal regime for practical reasons to be discussed below.[51] Until guilt is proven however, authorities should still hew as closely as possible to the robust political autonomy normally owed apparently innocent persons, which is to say, be as deferential as they can to inhabitants' normal maximum complement of political rights. Again, this is due to the protective obligation of police.[52] Given that the prudential measures often necessary to investigate and prevent crime are also in tension with inhabitants' rights, police properly ought to always employ the measures least in tension with those rights that are still effective at preventing or solving the crime in question.[53] This imperative places constant pressure on authorities to use the most efficient, most effective, most minimally prudential measures possible (efficiency and efficacy serve to minimize the degree and duration of the prudential activities).

As the probability of guilt increases with the discovery of evidence, authorities should be allowed to depart farther from the broadest levels of deference and treat a suspect in increasingly prudential ways in order to determine if he is engaged in criminal plotting or criminal behavior. For example, given cause, they should be allowed to disturb a person's privacy with noncustodial questioning and his bodily autonomy by requesting a return to the stationhouse or by arrest him. In the stationhouse, his privacy may be further disturbed with increasingly personal questions, and his right to honest-dealing, offended if police try tricks and deception to get him to confess. In the trial phase, the state has effectively announced its intent to make his partially prudential treatment in custody a semipermanent or permanent condition by depriving him of his liberty or life.

The foregoing discussion suffices for the broad overview; now to focus on politically legitimate police responses to suspicions that a person is engaging in, or planning to engage in, criminal activity. The reason authorities cannot switch from complete deference to complete prudential behavior on mere suspicion of wrongdoing or of withholding criminal knowledge has to do with the nature of suspicion and, ultimately, with the limits of a liberal state's power. A person's appearing suspicious is largely contextual—she may simply be in the wrong place at the wrong time—there being no act that is inherently suspicious, and so, entailing of privacy forfeiture in the way that assault cedes the legitimate expectation others will defer to one's bodily autonomy.[54] Similarly, thoughts are hidden to outsiders, so it is not immediately clear if someone is *plotting*—as it is usually clear, or relatively clear, if one is *committing*—a crime. The authorities act properly in these cases if there are good reasons to believe a particular person has information relevant to a crime.

Police must proceed in a manner consistent with the suspect also possibly being innocent, because suspicious behavior is not identical with criminal behavior. Imagine a police officer who shot at armed robbers but also shot at nervous-looking people standing in front of banks. A person could rationally object to police responses that made no distinction between suspicious behavior and criminal behavior since the whole purpose for police power is to protect inhabitants' lives and rights. The police are exercising coercion arbitrarily if they operate prudentially without means of distinguishing guilty from innocent persons, and it is obviously reasonable to object to arbitrary coercive treatment. A state's inhabitants would effectively be subject to a reign of terror if police acted as aggressively with people they consider suspicious as with people they witness committing an apparent crime. Inhabitants could also legitimately expect that there be ways for wrongly suspected persons to exonerate themselves and that interrogation and trial procedures reliably distinguish the guilty from the innocent.

In a basically just liberal state, where all inhabitants can enjoy their lives and rights to an equal extent, it would be irrational for inhabitants to dissent to reasonable and reviewable crime detection and prevention procedures including the questioning of suspicious persons. To assert that one wishes police to question suspicious persons but never to question oneself (if one appears suspicious) is to assert a parasitic "private right." So it is inappropriate for inhabitants in a basically just state to object to the police practice of questioning suspicious people in general and to object to *particular* instances of questioning, including questioning of oneself, provided the police are acting on reasonable grounds for suspicion. The question of what constitutes reasonable grounds for suspicion will provide grounds for objections to police questioning in particular situations and will be discussed in the next chapter.

The Duties of Those Living in Liberal States

What is a person morally obliged to do when police ask questions about crimes or public hazards? At first blush, a person's moral and political rights to privacy and silence would seem to indicate he need not speak to any person he wishes to ignore.[55] However, like all rights, these rights are not absolute and are overridden in cases where it would be irrational to dissent to authorities' infringing on privacy in the course of their protective duties. In other words, even though police materially infringe on a person's privacy by accosting him and asking him questions, say, about his activities on a certain morning, these actions do not *violate* his moral and political rights to privacy, because it would be irrational to dissent to such proportionate measures by police when necessary to detect or prevent crimes. Infringement, on this usage, means materially operating in a zone usually reserved for the holder of a right, and as such, standing in need of special justification.

Is the person obliged to truthfully answer police questions, given that the person's political rights are not being violated when police question him (i.e., the police are not exceeding their mandate)? It is irrational to both demand a relatively crime-free society and to assert that inhabitants are entitled to keep criminal secrets, because criminal plots and criminal knowledge facilitate criminal behavior. Also, it is incoherent and parasitic for a person to hold that *all other* persons with information relevant to criminal activity should divulge it, but one should be able to conceal one's own criminally relevant information. Thus, there is a moral obligation for inhabitants to tell police information pursuant to the solving or prevention of a crime in situations where there are reasons for police suspecting the person has relevant information,[56] but inhabitants are not obliged and police have no right to ask for information that is not pursuant to solving or preventing crime or preventing a public hazard.[57] This caveat is linked to the foundations and limits of police authority, discussed above.[58] (It should be noted that the justification for police authority does not practically rule out any set of questions or situations in which questioning may be justified, but simply links the standing right of police to question people to the protective obligation of police. In a basically just state, if an inhabitant has no reasonable grounds to suspect authorities are acting beyond their official capacity, he most likely ought to assume that they have a legitimate reason for questioning him and as such should cooperate.)

While one has a duty to keep confidences of friends, relatives, and associates, Bok rightly argues that some confidences should never have been promised, such as those involving criminal plots.[59] If one lacks the right to criminally plot, one lacks the right to do those things necessary to bring the plot to fruition like keeping the plot and the identity of coconspirators secret.

By this same argument, self-incriminating responses would also be required, given probable cause for inquiry. It would be incoherent and parasitic to assert that all other criminals should confess, but one should be able to conceal one's own criminal secrets. Yet there is a privilege against compelled self-incrimination in the common law tradition, which in the United States entails a suspect's right to remain silent during police questioning; his right to counsel in police custody; to refuse to take the stand (where he would be subject to cross-examination); his refusal to respond, while on the stand, to questions when the answers would incriminate himself; and the prohibition of the judge's negative characterization of the defendant's silence to the jury.[60] Commentators have noted that the privilege has been invoked and defended for various reasons in its four-hundred-year history.[61] The modern reasons can be usefully grouped into objections concerning the nature of the self-incrimination itself and concerning the circumstances involved with the state compelling confessions.[62] Both reasons are expressed in the U.S. Supreme Court's majority opinion in *Chambers v. Florida* (1940): "To respect the inviolability of the human personality, our accusatory system of criminal justice demands that the government seeking to punish an individual produce the evidence against him by its own individual labors, rather than by the cruel, simple expedient of compelling it from his own mouth."[63]

An objection to compelled self-incrimination related to the act itself is rooted in the perceived cruelty and perversity of forcing a person to testify against himself (fracturing "the inviolability of the human personality"). The second objection is related to the limits of government power. The state must *labor* to deprive a person of his liberty, having no automatic prerogative to do so.[64] A citizen is assumed innocent so the state must first gather evidence and fashion a rational argument that he is guilty compelling to a jury of the accused's peers before he can be deprived of his liberty. The connection of the state's burden to prove guilt with individuals' liberty is made directly by Justice Goldberg in *Murphy v. Waterfront Commission* (1964). The preferred balance of power between state and individual in a liberal society is protected by "requiring the government to leave the individual alone until good cause is shown for disturbing him, and by requiring the government in its contest with the individual to shoulder the entire load."[65]

Above, I argued prima facie moral and political rights to privacy and silence do not apply to criminal plots or behavior. A person's privacy is justifiably infringed by neighbors or by state agents given reasonable suspicion that the questioned party has criminal knowledge or information otherwise relevant to public safety. Generally speaking, one is morally obliged to proactively confess to wrongdoing and to reveal criminal confidences, even absent an outside inquiry. The inhabitants of a basically just liberal state are also *morally* bound to reveal information relevant to criminal activity when questioned by police acting on reasonable suspicions, even if this information is self-incriminating. However, in line with Justice Goldberg, and the state-related objection in the *Chambers* decision, I will argue in the next chapter that a *political* right to silence and (in one narrow context) a *political* privilege against compelled self-incrimination are appropriately recognized by the state (even for the secretly guilty) to maintain the state's recognition that suspicious persons are still possibly innocent.

The Privilege against Compelled Self-Incrimination

Whether the privilege against self-incrimination rests on *any* principled foundation has been debated at least since [the mid-eighteenth century].[1]

Elements of the Bill of Rights are usually not treated with such skepticism.
The counterintuitive nature of the privilege is apparent when considering
the case in Vallejo. The detectives believed that Eugene Livingston was involved in a robbery. They brought him in for interrogation; accused him of
the crime; and informed him of incriminating evidence. They *demanded* a
confession but were also forced to tell Livingston he had the right to *refuse*
to confess. Further, Livingston could not be legally punished in any way if
he refused to cooperate, even if his refusal impeded the investigation, potentially allowing coconspirators to flee or to destroy evidence.

There is much debate in the legal literature over whether this putative privilege is morally or politically important, rather than some strange
holdover from English legal history, now better abandoned. Scholars ask:
why do criminals get a special right to protect their plots?[2] Why is such a
broad right (to silence, about *all* matters) afforded suspects if only for the
sake of protecting self-incriminating statements? Are the privilege and right
to silence not redundant with due process guarantees if they are meant to
guard against interrogatory torture?[3] Why should police be denied the opportunity to question criminal suspects, or why must they hobble themselves by informing suspects that they are not obligated to confess?[4] Despite
the volume of scholarship on the subject, there has been very little construc-
tive *moral* analysis of it—a deficit this chapter means to overcome. Given
our subject of interrogation ethics, it is obviously important to ascertain if
police are wronging suspects by demanding confessions, and if even guilty
suspects are blameless in refusing to confess. To be clear, I will be discussing

possible moral bases for a privilege against compelled self-incrimination, rather than arguing for a particular interpretation of the U.S. Constitution or other legal documents.[5]

I will argue here that confusion regarding the purpose and acceptable implementation of the privilege has come from vacillating between the atomistic political conception of autonomy and the more intersubjective moral conception of autonomy. ("Intersubjective" refers to the interdependence of autonomy and moral behavior, as defended in chapter 1.) Many of the questions asked by legal scholars concerning the implementation of the privilege can be further resolved if we consider the *political right to silence,* rather than the privilege, as being of primary importance, and the privilege in fact being *based on* the right to silence. I will argue there is only a de facto privilege in police custody since the foundational political right to silence is comprehensive of all statements a suspect might make. (A distinct privilege with a unique function is pertinent to the trial stage when witnesses in other people's trials may refuse to give self-incriminating questions.) My proposed views of the privilege and right to silence contrast with the traditional understanding of the right to silence as a more or less nominal expression of the privilege when a suspect is in police custody. Rather, the political right to silence should be recognized as an important component of the raft of political rights afforded an inhabitant of a liberal state, important inasmuch as it helps maintain the deference the state should show criminal suspects prior to conviction. On a more profound level, the recognition of the right to silence admits the state's fallibility, denying the state the power to unilaterally and invidiously determine a person's status in the criminal justice arena, with an attendant revocation of liberties.

The argument in the last two chapters was in reference to a generic liberal state. This chapter will focus on literature written about the constitutional protection of these rights in the United States in order to assess certain candidates for liberal rights. As mentioned in the introduction to chapter 3, my argument is correlative rather than deductive. It draws its strength from its ability to account for rights traditionally recognized in the common law tradition (for different reasons throughout the years) in a manner that integrates them into a coherent whole; meets critiques commonly leveled against the rights and privilege; answers questions regarding proper interrogation standards, and does so better than the alternatives available in the literature. In seeking to formulate a coherent and systemic understanding of the privilege and associated rights in an American context, I will defend an understanding of the privilege and associated rights that could be modified according to the legal conditions of other liberal states and then used to support or criticize the expressions of the privilege and associated rights in non-American milieus.

Two notes on terminology: some scholars distinguish "privileges" from "rights" by saying the former are conferred on citizens by the state while the latter are natural human features recognized by the state. I will defer to this usage in the case of the privilege against compelled self-incrimination as conventional usage without necessarily endorsing the distinction. Also, some scholars refer to the "privilege against self-incrimination" rather than a "privilege against *compelled* self-incrimination" without making it clear if this is an abbreviation or a substantive distinction. It is properly "compelled self-incrimination" since the issue is whether or not the state may take steps to compel a person to incriminate herself, holding her legally liable if she refuses.

What the Privilege Does Not Protect

This section will argue there is no moral privilege against compelled self-incrimination. Compelling people to incriminate themselves is therefore not in principle unjust or perverse. I have found only two contemporary philosophical—as opposed to legal—treatments of the privilege, by Kent Greenawalt and Robert S. Gerstein. Both seek to limit the state power to compel self-incriminating confessions based on respect for autonomy. Greenawalt tentatively endorses a right of self-preservation that is maintained even when one has committed a crime, and Gerstein, a right to come to terms with one's guilt privately and voluntarily—an extension of the right to conscience. I will argue here that they make a common error in conflating moral and political conceptions of autonomy.

Hobbes wrote that natural law compels people to avoid self-destructive actions.[6] It follows that no man could be imagined to consent to a regime that might order his suicide or self-incrimination.[7] Greenawalt seems to have this inherent right to self-preservation in mind in "tentatively" endorsing the idea that a wrongdoer cannot be expected to own up to his misdeed when such an admission would lead to termination of employment or incarceration.[8] Such an admission seems to split the personality by making a person his own adversary.

Greenawalt writes of "the cruelty of forcing people to do serious harm to themselves, even when infliction of the same harm by others is warranted."[9] It is not the harm itself, but the external force and the self-infliction of harm he finds objectionable; it is because harm is nonetheless deserved that Greenawalt bases the privilege in compassion.[10] Yet for a guilty person, self-incrimination is not analogous to self-annihilation, because suicide is destructive of a good (life) whereas truthful self-incrimination *restores* a good by remedying its reciprocal evil (crime, deceit). Further, self-incrimination cannot be evil unto itself, if it is indeed appropriate to urge a wayward friend to turn himself in, or to praise the wrongdoer who voluntarily confesses out of remorse.[11] The reason these actions are appropriate is that the confessor's social responsibilities, and not only his material well-being, are at stake in a self-incriminatory confession. These responsibilities are violated when a person criminally transgresses, and these responsibilities met when he partly rectifies his crime through confession. By contrast, a criminal's desire to avoid punishment, while perhaps understandable, is not reflective of a moral right.[12] The criminal has already ceded his right to self-preservation (broadly construed) to the extent that he has imperiled other's rights and ceded the legitimate expectation that others fully defer to his autonomy regarding choices about his interpersonal behavior.

A state may use coercive measures to make inhabitants comply with at least their major social duties (i.e., those the violations of which are criminal), regardless of the offenders' wishes, so long as the means it employs are proportionate; undertaken with probable cause; and can reliably distinguish between those deserving of coercion from those who do not (discussed further below). To argue otherwise is to limit government's role in maintaining law and order to instruction and exhortation, which would seem inadequate given administration of something other than a race of angels. Therefore, the fact that pressure to confess comes from the state rather than the criminal's own conscience is not in principle problematic, provided compliance with the three conditions listed above.

Political unity is possible, on Hobbes's view, because self-preservation is consistent with deference to other's rights. To escape the perilous "state of nature," he conjectures, individuals would be willing to cede their natural right to do anything they wished—*now* respecting other's lives, bodily integrity, property, etc.—if others agree to do the same. Importantly, however, on Hobbes's conception, self-preservation is prior to rights observance; "natural" man is self-sufficient and enters political society only as a prudential calculation that life is safer there than in the wilderness. He never loses the inherent right to preserve himself. This right trumps what Hobbes presents as *conventional* (i.e., man-made) obligations to fellow citizens when the state treats a man as an adversary, even if by virtue of his own wrongdoing. So a citizen is under no obligation to cooperate in the state's executing or imprisoning him.[13] Similarly, Greenawalt is reluctant to say that the citizen is obliged to cooperate in his own demise, even while allowing that a citizen does have an obligation to help authorities solve crime, and an obligation to respond to questions prompted by probable grounds for suspicion.[14]

The Hobbesian, and perhaps Greenawaltian, characterization of the person is too atomistic, running together the political and the moral conceptions of autonomy. The authors improperly assert that moral actors retain the expectation of broad deference, proper to an atomistic political conception of autonomy—a quasi-adversarial relation of equals—in a moment brought about by their relations with other moral actors, when they have real intersubjective commitments. Political autonomy is properly observed when a citizen is apparently innocent from the perspective of the state but can be proportionately infringed (the state transitioning to a more paternalistic/prudential attitude) when there is cause to believe that the thick walls of the citizen's political autonomy are not protecting a moral self innocently and responsibly fording its way through the world, but rather, barreling around at other's expense. Justifiable grounds of political critique would be related to the state's reasons for departing from the benign indifference equals or quasi-equals owe one another. A person's complaints could include the following: that he presented no publicly discernable grounds for suspicion justifying the state's infringing on his privacy or that the state failed to prove misconduct (and so must hastily retreat to its former deference). However, he could *not* object that he has the (moral) right to barrel around with impunity. If rights talk is coherent, moral obligations are constitutive of, rather than secondary to, moral autonomy and so cannot coherently be opposed to the self-preservation of autonomy. The criminal cannot object that he would rather not meet his social obligations (revealing his plot), simply on account that he will be punished. He cannot complain that his freedom (which is unnaturally expansive now because of the "extra" liberty he seized at other's expense) is being limited after he has done something triggering coercive protection of others' freedom.

Hobbes and Greenawalt improperly assert the prerogatives of an atomistic citizen in a moral context (brought about by the actor's treatment of others) where people have real social duties. Robert Gerstein errs in the opposite manner, by objecting to compelled self-incrimination on grounds related to a moral conception of autonomy when a political conception of autonomy is instead germane. He feels that the compulsion of self-incrimination is cruel because of the process leading to the self-destructive effects lamented by Greenawalt. It is good if remorse moves a guilty person to confess, Gerstein grants, and is in fact a profound self-realizing act of the autonomous will when it judges itself, controlling self-preservative instincts enough to force an action in keeping with moral convictions.[15] However, by compelling a confession, the state bastardizes a process that is only authentic and psychologically restorative if chosen autonomously. The state humiliatingly makes public an inherently private judgment of self-condemnation. It is not the revelation of criminal facts to which Gerstein objects, nor the criminal's "self-destruction," but the "mea culpa," or the "coming to terms with one's guilt" that may be involved in the facts' disclosure.[16] It is degrading to intrude in the mental space where a person makes moral decisions to take away his freedom to decide to confess.[17]

Gerstein is right that the moral worth of coming to terms with one's guilt is voided if doing so is not a personal decision.[18] A gift is not a gift if its giving is coerced. We should first acknowledge though, that if this voiding occurs, it is not a deliberate effect of the state's attempt to punish rights violations, prevent on-going violations, and facilitate restitution. A penitent criminal's process of recovering the dignity he surrendered in violating his duties is something that takes place out of the state's purview. The state's purview includes political rights, the limiting of which is consequent to the public appearance and legal provability of criminal actions. In addressing rights violations, the state at best *dimly* sees, and inexactly treats, inhabitants as moral actors, because it never really knows the extent to which an inhabitant has abused (and so compromised) his rational freedom. It is not in the state's power to assess the extent to which a criminal's moral freedom is *really* compromised by his immoral actions and plans, the extent to which he has made himself, say, a slave to his inclinations or external stimuli, thereby debasing his dignity. Such things take place internally, at the level of the person's conscience, and are only visible from the "God's eye point of view" of theory where hidden thoughts and judgments are on display. Similarly, the state cannot assess, and so cannot care, whether a criminal has partly regained some of his innate dignity by resubmitting his will to the moral law demanding confession for crime. It can only assess, and only wants to know, what the person *did* to affect other people.[19]

Gerstein allows that the state has a right to know about criminal activity and that a criminal does not have the right to criminal knowledge.[20] However, he wishes to preclude compulsion or the use of confessions where evidence of sufficient guilt did not already exist, because a confession may be a humiliating revelation of self-condemnation. He would thus check legitimate state activity, properly indexed to an inhabitant's *political autonomy*, because of a possible attendant event occurring on the level of the person's *moral autonomy*. I assume he rules out compelling self-incriminatory testimony even while admitting that many criminals feel no sense of self-condemnation, because of the inability of the prosecution to know beforehand which criminal defendants are capable of an unperturbed recitation of self-incriminating facts and which defendants will express a wrenching avowal of moral failure when doing the same.[21]

To assess a justified, prudential state action with unintended negative effects on an inhabitant, political theorists usually ask if the negative effect overrides the good done or if a significant negative effect is widely experienced as opposed to idiosyncratically felt by a few. On the first point, the good done in most criminal cases probably offsets the degradation done to one who has made himself vulnerable to some prudential manipulation by committing a crime. On the second point, if the practice is otherwise just and proportionate, the state does not have the luxury of inquiring what may subjectively occur beyond the boundaries of political autonomy for (only) some criminal defendants. A common principle of law is that exceptions are not made for unique characters.[22] If anything, Gerstein's point would have the most force in the situation in which he allows use of self-incriminatory testimony. If the state already has the evidence to convict the defendant, it could be considered gratuitously cruel to force him to admit his guilt as well.

To summarize this section, Hobbes and Greenawalt commit something like a category mistake by using an adversarial, self-sufficient element from a political conception of autonomy as a basis for a quasi-moral right to self-preservation. They do so when a person has exposed himself to non-preservation (broadly construed) through a rights violation he perpetrated with his own hand. I say a quasi-moral right, because the putative rights to self-preservation is meant by the authors to take the place of a moral right in limiting state action, yet it cannot meet this role since it is nonuniversalizable and parasitic. Gerstein asserts a form of the legitimate moral right to privacy (as a prophylactic to conscience) in a place where the right is not under direct threat. This is because the state is within its rights to ask inhabitants questions regarding the exercise of their political autonomy with cause, and, to comply, a person only need answer with respect to the external facts, not with respect to his internal, quasi-affective moral assessment of those facts. A person being questioned only needs let authorities into the foyer of his political autonomy, as it were, not the den of his moral autonomy.

There is no *moral* ground against compelled self-incrimination (apart from separate complaints about the type of compulsion), because one does not have a moral right to conceal one's crimes, nor to self-preservation (broadly construed) following forfeiture of that right through criminal behavior. To assert the lack of such grounds is not to justify torture, but to say that the rights violator does not enjoy the legitimate expectation that others will defer to his possible preference to keep self-incriminating secrets to himself. He has abused his right to privacy, and so lacks moral grounds to object to other's *demanding* self-incriminatory information, provided clear evidence of wrongdoing, such as when he is caught red-handed or admits to a crime (while perhaps withholding the particulars). The self-incriminating knowledge he has is not something morally precious he is entitled to keep secret. He in fact wrongs others by remaining silent and not confessing of his own accord as well as by refusing to truthfully answer their questions. Nor is there a moral right to therapeutically come to terms with one's guilt in one's own time, in one's own way, as there is a right to therapeutically come to terms with some self-evaluation in most noncriminal matters. One's moral (and political) autonomy is justifiably infringed when his actions have made proportionate infringement necessary to render justice, prevent harm, and make restitution. Further, the putative right of coming to terms with one's guilt is not even directly threatened by state action. Finally, the fact that self-incrimination is compelled is not in itself problematic as a state can use proportionate forms of coercion to make people meet their major social obligations in moments when they refuse to do so voluntarily. The level and kind of coercion may be problematic and will be addressed below.

What the Privilege Does Not Protect: Constitutional Arguments

Most legal scholars do not articulate independent moral bases for the privilege like Greenawalt and Gerstein but take the relevant Supreme Court rulings as starting points for the development of practical standards they urge police and judges to implement. Scholars assess controversial police and prosecutorial practices by triangulating them with the justificatory concepts invoked by the Supreme Court like "privacy," "autonomy," and "voluntary choice" and the concrete practices the Court has sanctioned in the past.

Commentators point out the inadequacy of the concept of privacy to justify the privilege (at least in the United States) given that noncriminal, but damaging, information and information concerning some intimate relationships can be compelled, as can the procurement of potentially incriminating evidence like fingerprints or private papers.[23] Writers focusing on the privilege's putative protection of autonomy worry that the deceptive interrogation tactics allowed by the Supreme Court, in addition to the rejection of mandatory counsel during interrogation, seriously erode the state's respect for citizens' autonomy so eloquently invoked in the *Murphy* and *Miranda* rulings.[24] Many acknowledge that almost all police-procured confessions are involuntary in the sense that the suspect would not have confessed absent the psychological pressure of interrogation.[25] Some, allowing that most confessions are involuntary in this sense, but acknowledging that the courts have sought a pragmatic balance between respect for autonomy and criminal prosecution,[26] suggest that tactics an ordinary person could not withstand,[27] or that overbear regular, preinterrogation preferences alone, be prohibited.[28] Questions regarding how volition is to be measured, given the variability in human psychology, have left some suggesting that only obvious instances of coerced confessions involving torture be excluded;[29] that only public, court supervised interrogations be allowed (i.e., all police-procured confessions be excluded);[30] that police interrogation techniques that risk overbearing the suspect's will should be prohibited on a per se basis;[31] or that the "voluntary standard" should be scrapped all together.[32]

I suspect that confusion regarding the purpose and acceptable implementation of the privilege has come again from vacillating between the atomistic political conception of autonomy and the more intersubjective moral conception of autonomy. If one considers the privilege as an entailment of the moral conception, a conception that takes into account what a person deserves absolutely, on the basis of private judgments as well as public actions, the privilege appears to involve a counterintuitive right for a criminal to protect his criminal secrets or to protect his autonomy over and against that of his victims. This construal would seem to put criminal secrets in the same category of morally precious things properly protected by privacy as lovers' confidences. Yet there is nothing wrong with expecting a rights violator to abide by his social obligations (in this case, confessing and making restitution), nor in principle in compelling him to do so by proportionate means if he refuses and his refusal presents a danger to the community.[33] It is incoherent to talk about his moral autonomy over and against the legitimate demands of those whose rights he has violated. It follows then that the question in assessing various investigatory or interrogatory methods used by state agents should not be whether the suspect volunteers incriminating information himself, nor whether his will is being overborne.[34] The respect others must show to one's own decisions and will is contingent on one's acting in a morally upright manner deserving of respect, and a rights violator has failed to act in this manner.

However, proportionate coercion is appropriate in some measure against only those who actually are violating, have violated, or are obviously bent on violating other's rights; if the state is going to exercise this coercion against criminals, there must be procedures for determining who is a criminal. All inhabitants of a liberal state, even those covertly guilty (i.e., those whose crimes are undetected), have certain political rights—distinct from moral rights consequent to moral desert—pegged to outward actions of which the state is, or could be, cognizant. In the criminal justice arena, these rights are aimed at ensuring that the state is judicious and deferential in its efforts to identify and punish guilty parties and also at treating inhabitants in a manner commensurate with what the state has cause to know about them. Except in cases of (apparent) criminal action observed by a state agent, or when it has been proven in court, the liberal state is mostly ignorant of its inhabitants' moral characters and must treat them in accord with the political conception of autonomy.[35] This means treating them as if they were morally innocent, responsible, and robustly competent. The grounds for these claims are detailed in chapter 2: the liberal state would be acting arbitrarily if it randomly revoked inhabitants' or citizens' rights, absent evidence of wrongdoing. As we will discuss further below, a (de facto) *political* privilege against compelled self-incrimination, along with a political right to silence, is entailed by a political conception of autonomy as an expression of the deference the state must show its inhabitants, while it is investigating whether they have broken the law, which is to say, prior to the state having cause to know they are guilty.

Having clarified how scholars' intuitions regarding the privilege correspond to moral or political conceptions of autonomy, I will now argue for the importance of the political right to silence and its primacy to a political construal of the privilege. Whether the privilege is understood in a moral or political sense, casting it as the basis for the right to silence in police custody (the conventional view) conflates moral and political conceptions of autonomy, prompting the confusions expressed in the critical questions at the start of this chapter. By contrast, I will show below how viewing the privilege *as based on a political right to silence* successfully answers many of these concerns.

What the Privilege Protects: The Shortcomings of Construing the Right to Silence as Based on the Privilege

In this section, I will criticize four versions of the conventional view of the right to silence as based on the privilege; these critiques could also be directed at a stand-alone privilege. Conceiving of the privilege as the basis for the right to silence under a *moral* construal of the privilege prompts the question of why a criminal has a special right to conceal just his *criminal* secrets from police. As already argued, there is no such moral right. More confusion follows if the privilege is thought of as the basis to the right to silence under a *political* construal. A political construal would be concerned to limit the power of the state based on the amount of information it has about an inhabitant's status. In this case, basing silence on the privilege introduces an awkward conditional justification for the state's self-limitation of its own power. Talk of compelling self-incrimination is presumptuous because the state does not "know" that a suspect is guilty when he is in police custody. A privilege against compulsion, strictly speaking, would then have to be understood in the subjunctive mood: the suspect cannot be compelled to incriminate himself *in the event that* he happens to be guilty. Yet critics are right to point out the incoherence of asserting that the suspect retains the legitimate expectation the state defer to his privacy *just in the event* that he is guilty of criminal behavior. The scheme of political rights are afforded an inhabitant on the assumption that he is *not* behaving criminally; the rights afforded him in the criminal justice arena are not to protect him insofar as he is a rights violator, but insofar as he is possibly innocent. Further, the breadth of the prophylactic right to silence, covering far more than potentially incriminating information, is also properly criticized as an embarrassment if self-incriminatory information alone is privileged. Rather, if a person has the legitimate expectation that the state defer to his privacy, it has to do with what the state *has cause to know* regarding his possible criminal status. (The standard is not what the state *knows* about the person, since the state does not have the epistemic equipment to ever really "know" a person's guilt or innocence. A criminal investigation is the state equivalent of a person's discernment process; a trial, a person's decision-making process; and a legal verdict, as close as the state comes to certainty about a person's status in the criminal justice arena. A verdict is sufficient to direct the state to treat a person either as an innocent person or as a guilty person. Incriminating evidence is cause for the state to know a person is suspicious and a conviction is cause for the state to know the person is guilty. As mentioned before, since juries and judges are fallible and convicted people might actually be innocent, it is appropriate to consider a guilty verdict as "cause to know" rather the equivalent of knowledge, and to consider the tag *proven guilty* as a practical model the state *treats as true* rather than an authentic identification of a person's status.) Therefore, the political right to privacy is in play before guilt has been legally determined, not in the event that he really is guilty (which is only "known" from the God's eye view).

If the privilege is not pegged to some quality on the suspect's part, and is in the political rather than the moral realm, the logical alternative for its purpose would be something related to state power. Indeed, it has been suggested by some that the privilege is not related to the suspect's guilt or innocence, but is instead meant to put the entire burden of proving guilt on the state's shoulders.[36] On this view, the privilege and its attendant rights to silence in interrogation and at trial are assigned to the suspect/defendant merely so he is equipped to "play" an adversarial legal "game" with the state. The idea is that in those liberal states that prosecute criminals in an adversarial rather than inquisitorial manner, where the burden of proof is on the government rather than the defendant, rights, privileges, and powers related to defense are assigned to the suspect/defendant to help insure that the government proves its case. This characterization of the privilege would at least remove the question of why a criminal gets a special right to conceal his plot. Yet others have noted this characterization of the privilege makes it redundant with due process and is further unsatisfactory in an American context, because the American legal system is not completely adversarial.[37] Continuing this line of critique on a philosophical level now will set the stage for a defense of a robust political right to silence.

If the privilege is related to state power, its role could be negative or positive: inhibiting abuse or promoting good practices. We need to consider what evil(s) is avoided if the privilege is meant as a check on state power. The following elements of state compelled self-incrimination might be considered objectionable: the form of compulsion, the origin of the compulsion (the state), the purpose of the compulsion (self-incrimination), or the grounds for compulsion. If the privilege is meant to have a unique function in a liberal system, its purpose cannot simply be to prohibit police torture, for reasons of redundancy with due process. In searching for the purpose of the privilege, we must bear in mind it presupposes a legal milieu in which compulsion could occur through nonphysical means such as fines, incarceration, and/or the judge's instructions to the jury to consider the defendant's silence in a negative light. These sanctions could be used both to compel testimony in court and to punish silence in police interrogation. There is nothing inherently objectionable about these forms of compulsion unto themselves, at least not on the order of torture, so the issue in this context is not the form legal compulsion takes. State compulsion per se is also not the relevant issue, because the state may justly compel inhabitants to adhere to their major social duties, and revealing criminal plots or misdeeds qualifies. As discussed above, self-incrimination per se is not objectionable. These exclusions leave the grounds justifying state agents efforts at compulsion as possible cause for concern.

What is meant by justifying grounds? A person assaulting another has ceded the otherwise legitimate expectation that others will respect his bodily autonomy; his behavior has created the moral grounds for a bystander or police officer to forcibly and proportionately intervene without doing him any injustice. If the state has the grounds to compel a suspect's speech, this implies that the person no longer enjoys the right to keep personal secrets from others, including state agents. It must be explained how such an occasion could arise. While a defining characteristic of a liberal state is respect for its inhabitants' privacy, including a respect for secrets they choose to keep, a person does not have a right to criminal secrets per se. It would therefore seem to be unproblematic if the state revokes an inhabitant's right to silence with respect to criminal matters, be they self-incriminatory or incriminating of others, as these are not secrets to which he has a right. The difficulty however, is that prior to conviction, the state does not have cause to know that a given person has criminal secrets, and so it is presumptuous for the state to revoke a right to keeping secrets (i.e., a right to silence) in their regard.

This presumptuousness is also present if the privilege is construed to promote good government practices. If the privilege's salience is limited to the state's solo prosecutorial effort, this construal could still imply that suspects are assumed guilty until proven innocent and that the state proposes to prove their guilt on its own for reasons relating to its own professional standards, rather than deference to the suspect's political rights. The implication of this construal is that the state could compel suspects if it wished, since it already considers them guilty, but chooses, in a self-assigned test of its own fitness—like a magician working with a blindfold—to prove guilt strictly through its own labors. Yet lest it act arbitrarily, the state's actions toward inhabitants apart from the regular, baseline behavior indicated by the "apparently innocent" practical model must be indicated by what the state has cause to know about them; and again, prior to a guilty verdict, the state does not have cause to know suspects are guilty. It cannot revoke their political rights to remain silent (about criminal matters)—because the state does not have cause to know they are concealing criminal information. The state operates with an illiberal, baseline assumption of guilt rather than of innocence if it assumes that its inhabitants all have criminal information and are therefore not entitled to a right to silence. It *would* follow that inhabitants could be compelled at the state's discretion if the state *did* operate with this illiberal assumption. Instead, inhabitants' default status of *apparently innocent* ought to direct the liberal state's treatment of them in the criminal justice arena until or unless there are grounds for curtailing it.[38]

The state may properly make forays against a suspicious person's privacy by accosting, questioning, arresting, and interrogating him—this prudential behavior is oriented toward the possibility that he is guilty of a crime or has criminal information. Yet since the suspicious person is still possibly innocent, there should also be a way of respecting at least a portion of the political autonomy due an apparently innocent person lest the liberal state overstep the bounds of its power and treat suspicious persons as if they were guilty. Therefore, the suspect's assumed innocence should not be thought of merely as a conventional legal status bestowed by the state to meet the requirements of an adversarial legal system. Rather, his status should be seen as a feature of a liberal state's political relationship with its inhabitants as well as an entailment of its epistemic limitations. Therefore, this status is entailed in liberal states with adversarial as well as inquisitorial legal systems.

One might still contend that the privilege is relevant to the state's solo prosecutorial effort, while rejecting the contention that the suspect is presumed guilty, by arguing a state agent has the right to demand an answer to *any* question she asks, regardless of the questioned party's status in the criminal justice arena. Above, I granted that police have the right to *ask* inhabitants' questions in service of the state's protective function. Yet the argument under consideration implies that the state may *demand* that the person answer, on pain of legal liability (e.g., fines, incarceration). I will now argue that state agents may not demand self-incriminating information due to the fallibility of state agents and the generally onerous nature of criminal investigations to the person under investigation.

State agents in liberal states are fallible in three ways. First, state agents, like all people, are vulnerable to error and prejudice. Second, they are epistemically limited in the sense that the suspicious behavior they see or hear about is not necessarily linked to criminal behavior on the part of a particular suspect. Third, the liberal state they represent is fallible in the sense that state actions are not just simply for being state actions. Inhabitants of a liberal state enjoy the right to assert state actions are unjust (without being punished for it) and contest their prudential treatment by the government as unmerited.

In further explaining why this fallibility has bearing on the political right to silence and the privilege, I will now defend an understanding of the privilege as *based on* the political right to silence. To this point, I have argued that the alternative understanding of the right to silence as an expression of the privilege in police custody is unsatisfactory for several reasons. This ordering could suggest that a person has a moral right to conceal criminal information. It could presumptuously imply the suspect is considered a criminal before police are in a position to know he is a criminal. The breadth of the right to silence (effectively regarding all matters) far exceeds the self-incriminating information putatively privileged. Finally, the primacy of the privilege could imply that the liberal state may unilaterally revoke political rights at the start of an investigation that are properly revoked only after a conviction.

The Significance of the Political Right to Silence

The political right to silence needs to be understood as an important component of the political conception of autonomy if it can be viewed as the basis of the privilege. I will argue here that a political right to silence in fact does all the work traditionally ascribed to the privilege in police custody.

A liberal state properly treats its inhabitants with benign indifference in the sense of leaving them largely alone to run their own affairs. Even in regards to the many state regulations to which people conform their behavior, the state is a largely passive presence, shaping the background conditions for a person's behavior but usually not producing a set of circumstances that actively interferes with her conscious deliberations. The state interferes more dramatically with a person's life when authorities question her, particularly in police custody. These forays into an inhabitant's zone of privacy are legitimate if state agents have cause to suspect the person has criminal information. Yet, this said, there is still a mismatch between the state's quasi-prudential treatment of suspicious persons—materially infringing on what would be the maximum possible expression of their privacy by questioning and/or arresting them—and the treatment innocent inhabitants deserve qua innocence. (The mismatch of treatment is inevitable given the epistemic limitations of state agents. They cannot consistently question and arrest only guilty people.) This mismatch can be particularly onerous as frequent police questioning can have the effect of harassment—especially if the questioned person feels that authorities are so biased or incompetent that she is vulnerable to arbitrary harassment.

The political right to silence can be thought of as organically integrating the opposing pressures of the state's prudential actions with the baseline rights of the inhabitant of the liberal state. This integration allows us to see certain police and prosecutorial practices as in keeping with inhabitants' rights, rather than as the unhappy combination of practical necessity and rights infringement.[39] Evidently unable to reconcile these opposing pressures, some scholars find themselves at once arguing for the protection of suspects' rights during interrogations and hoping the same suspects' are ignorant of their rights,[40] or actually characterizing guilty suspects' invocation of their right to remain silent as "regrettable."[41]

The right to silence mediates the following tension, thereby reconciling suspects' rights with police efficacy. It is irrational for an inhabitant enjoying his life and rights to dissent to police questioning him if he appears suspicious. Yet he has not ceded the legitimate expectation that police will respect his privacy in the same way he has ceded the legitimate expectation others will respect his bodily autonomy when he commits assault. This is because appearing suspicious is contextual and subjective, there being no quality that is inherently suspicious, and no witness whose testimony is necessarily truthful instead of mistaken or slanderous. There is no necessary connection between appearing suspicious to a given observer and actually being guilty. One *chooses* to commit assault but does not choose to appear suspicious. All other things being equal, apparently innocent persons should not be questioned by others and do not have to speak to those they wish to ignore. Suspicious people, or those implicated by others, can be questioned and generally ought to aid in crime detection by cooperating. However, they do not *have to* cooperate, because they can insist that they belong in the default class of apparently innocent people—to be left alone—since there is nothing about their public behavior necessarily making them liable to privacy infringement or prudential treatment in the way assault does.[42] The average person might well comply with a policeman's intrusive requests for information even if confused as to why he deserves the officer's attention—assuming there must be some good reason—but be less solicitous the third or fourth time this occurs, suspecting that inept police tactics or prejudice are behind the intrusions.

Police or other state agents are justified in questioning someone who appears suspicious to the questioning agent or someone reporting to that agent. The questioned person's refusal to respond is tantamount to rejecting the contention that authorities have cause to consider him suspicious. If a liberal state sins by assuming its inhabitants are always effectively guilty (e.g., as in a Stalinist state), it also sins (though less egregiously) when starting with a baseline assumption of inhabitants' innocence but then too quickly suspecting them of crime, as in racial profiling. A person who is not committing an apparent crime or has not been criminally convicted deserves to be treated by authorities in large measure as innocent, *even if actually guilty*, because no one would consent to the state arbitrarily bothering people or treating them as guilty without cause. Acting arbitrarily is precisely what the state is doing if it treats an inhabitant prudentially without public evidence of wrongdoing or of criminal knowledge.[43] Therefore, even the covertly guilty suspect can assert that the state is wrong to *demand* he speak, because as far as the state has cause to know, he is innocent—*he looks innocent.*[44]

Yet we can also say it would be irrational for an inhabitant of a basically just state to dissent to being treated prudentially by authorities given cause, because he legitimately expects to be protected from criminals, and prudential behaviors such as questioning, arresting, and interrogating suspicious people are legitimate means of detecting and preventing crime. These contending expectations force authorities to adopt a hybrid approach, treating suspects at once as apparently or possibly innocent and apparently or possibly guilty—simultaneously deferring to their political autonomy and infringing on it in a prudential, perhaps manipulative manner. The authorities' actions are not contradictory, because crime detection and prevention is necessary to ensure innocent people their liberty.[45] To be clear, a suspect's "hybrid status" is not meant in the logical and trivial sense that *anyone* is possibly innocent, and so also possibly guilty, of criminal activity. Rather, a *suspicious* person is one whom evidence suggests is guilty (with greater or lesser certitude). There may also be countervailing evidence indicating innocence—or the incriminating evidence may be so overwhelming that innocence may only seem like a mere logical possibility to investigators. Authorities must nonetheless respect that logical possibility, no matter how remote, because full prudential treatment by police is politically illegitimate when based on fallible evidence or on some person's suspicion, which is usually subjective and contextual. A political right to silence ought to be recognized as an expression of the person's hybrid status when under suspicion; respecting it is a way of ensuring this hybrid status is not dissolved into a status of guilty-until-guilt-is-disproved. From a moral point of view, plotters, and those who have committed or are committing crimes, cede the legitimate expectation that others will defer to their possible preference to remain silent about their crimes or plots once there is some public evidence that they have criminal knowledge. Yet prior to criminal conviction, the liberal state does not have cause to know a person is plotting or has committed a crime. Revoking the *political* right to silence prior to criminal conviction, in custody or court—which means refusing to defer to the person's possible preference to remain silent and holding him legally liable if he does remain silent—amounts to rendering a person guilty by fiat of the state. The state treats him partly in accord with the diminished rights of a criminal before it has cause to know he is a criminal.[46]

If a state agent thinks an innocent person is suspicious, it is unfortunate that his privacy is materially infringed through questioning and possible arrest. The real Eugene Livingston, suspected by Vallejo police of robbery, was innocent but was arrested and brought to the stationhouse for interrogation—one can imagine his frustration and anxiety. Yet there is likely no practical way for police to fully and simultaneously defer to his expectation of privacy, on the one hand, and his expectation of crime detection, on the other, at least if the latter sometimes includes questioning suspicious people. In this context, silence can be understood as protecting a final zone of privacy authorities cannot practically breach, and so serves as the next best condition to that robust privacy the person normally enjoys. The suspect who invokes his right to silence is effectively objecting to his being disturbed—even though there is no putting the genie back in the bottle, his privacy has been materially disturbed. The detectives interrupted Livingston's day; insulted him by asserting that he was a criminal; and presumptuously asked personal questions. There is no undoing all this. Yet through silence, the suspect can assert some agency and reassert the distance between himself and the state: there is a practical limit to what investigators can learn about the citizen's personal life because his thoughts are protected by his silence.[47] Livingston does not have to cooperate; he does not have to reveal his personal confidences; he need not tell the detectives anything at all. He can sit in the interrogation room with his mouth shut ignoring them and cannot be punished for it.

The right to silence grants the suspect a good deal of privacy normally afforded apparently innocent people and also provides a way to stubbornly object to the whole investigation and prosecution process, which partly objectifies him even when it meets due process standards, an investigation that may after all have been triggered by state agents' error or prejudice.[48] State agents are epistemically limited in determining who has information relevant to criminal plans or criminal activity; silence is a way of arguing that this limitation has actually brought the state up short in this instance. Therefore, the right to silence again need not be understood as bestowed *within* a conventional legal game—bestowed by the state to enable suspects/defendants to "play" in a contest with the state—but as existing "outside" the game, as part of all inhabitants' ordinary civic profiles. The suspect can object to his forced introduction into the legal game from the vantage point of a quasi-equal with the state. As such, the right effectively recognizes an even more robust claim of the inhabitant's value than is recognized by his conventional legal status: he can refuse the state the right to summarily and unilaterally designate his political status, with all that status's associated rights and liberties. The right to silence reflects an essential trait of the liberal state—it is fallible—and an essential right of the inhabitant of a liberal state, to assert that the state's actions are wrong.

I do not see a privilege against compelled self-incrimination apart from, or in addition to, the political right to silence in police custody. To say authorities have to respect a suspect's right to silence is to say they cannot compel him to say anything, self-incriminatory or otherwise. (Below, I will therefore refer to a de facto privilege against compelled self-incrimination in police custody.) This deference acknowledges that the state still considers the suspect possibly innocent and so extends to him the respect for his secrets normally granted apparently innocent persons.

While I do not think a privilege adds any substantive protections for the suspect in police custody in addition to the right to silence, I accept that it can have further rhetorical value in discouraging police brutality, laziness, and incompetence.[49] If the suspect cannot be forced to incriminate himself, police cannot use physical force in interrogations and must be prepared to conduct skillful investigations if the suspect does not confess voluntarily.

I only have the space here to briefly address the relevant trial rights. At the trial stage, the political right to silence can be understood as grounding the right to refuse to testify in one's own defense and the prohibition of the judge negatively characterizing the suspect/defendant's silence in interrogation or at trial. The right to silence also grounds a distinct privilege against compelled self-incrimination when testifying at another person's trial and asked a question the answer to which would be self-incriminatory. A defendant's expressing her political right to silence is a way of protesting that the grounds for the state's suspicions against her are flimsy; asserting that she should be left alone; and should not be any more inconvenienced or embarrassed than she already finds herself by being asked for personal information by police and prosecutors. Presumably, a defendant would express this diffidence by refusing to testify all together. Until the question is asked though, a witness in another party's trial does not know if the prosecutor's question is oriented toward the incrimination of the defendant, the witness, or a third party. Hence, there is properly a right to refuse to answer self-incriminatory questions on a per question basis. Therefore, we can say the privilege against compelled self-incrimination per se can properly apply to this specific instance in the trial phase as an application of the right to silence, whereas all other associated pretrial and trial rights can simply be viewed as direct applications of the right to silence. The value of maintaining the privilege in the discussion of trial rights is to distinguish privileged information from nonprivileged information incriminating of others.

Assessing Interrogation and Investigation Methods

In February of 1988, Baltimore homicide detectives investigated the brutal rape and murder of an 11-year-old girl named LaTonya Wallace. Suspicion quickly fell on the owner of a fish store where she sometimes did odd jobs, known locally as "the Fish Man." LaTonya's parents had told her to stay away from the store, concerned that the man seemed "too friendly" with her; indeed, there were neighborhood rumors of the man's interest in young girls, and LaTonya's classmates reported being uncomfortable with the way the man looked at them. Detectives learned he had a 30 year old statutory rape charge filed against him. When questioned, the Fish Man was evasive and seemed untroubled by news of the girl's murder. He was unable to provide an alibi for the time of death; failed a polygraph; and was subsequently found to have had contact with another little girl, resembling LaTonya, who'd gone missing ten years before from a local neighborhood. Yet detectives were unable to find any hard evidence linking him to either crime.[50]

Having clarified the relevance of the privilege and right to silence in police custody, we are now in the position to assess interrogation and investigation methods with those rights in mind. This will be done at a fairly general level in this section, before focusing on specific interrogation techniques in chapter 5. Prior to the 1966 *Miranda* ruling, a confession's legal admissibility in American courts depended on its "voluntariness." The "totality of circumstances" of the confession's context was assessed in contested cases to determine if the confessor's will had been wrongly "overborne" by police tactics. The voluntariness standard is still used, but *Miranda* created a new legal reference for it by linking the standard to the Fifth Amendment's privilege against compelled self-incrimination rather than the Fourteenth Amendment's guarantee of due process. The *Miranda* Court decided that the interrogation room was so "coercive" a setting that any failure to warn the suspect of a right to remain silent would amount to a per se violation of his privilege against compulsory self-incrimination. Apart from compelling legally inadmissible confessions, police practices in and outside interrogation room that "shock the conscience" are also unconstitutional on the grounds that they violate due process (the phrase is taken from a case in which police pumped a suspect's stomach in order to retrieve swallowed contraband).

The "totality of circumstances" and "shocking to the conscience" tests are problematic. Before and after *Miranda*, the otherwise vague voluntariness standard[51] with its "totality of circumstances" test has led to finding mental illness sufficient grounds for rendering confessions involuntary in some cases[52] and insufficient grounds in others, including a case where a schizophrenic reported that God told him to confess.[53] According to the voluntariness standard, the confession of a suspect who was hung from a tree and horsewhipped was deemed involuntary,[54] as was a confession procured after thirty-six hours of continuous interrogation,[55] but the confession of a suspect who was kicked and threatened with a blackjack was deemed voluntary, as was one from a suspect who was beaten and held incommunicado for twelve days.[56] The obviously subjective standard of what is "shocking to the conscience" has also been highly criticized for its indeterminacy.[57]

Whether the legal reference is the Fifth or Fourteenth Amendment, the underlying justification for the voluntariness standard, many jurists agree, is the state's respect for citizens' mental freedom. From a philosophical perspective, the standard for assessing investigative and interrogation practices should instead be indicated by the suspicious person's occupying a hybrid status of possibly innocent and possibly guilty.[58] This hybrid profile binds the state by two (immediately) contradictory expectations: broad deference to political autonomy, on one hand, and some order of prudential treatment of persons in the course of crime detection and prevention, on the other.[59] The standard for assessment is not the suspect's voluntariness (i.e., mental freedom), which would be analyzed at the level of moral autonomy, because a person does not have the right to keep criminal secrets. This intuition, perhaps shared by those who hope guilty suspects fail to invoke their right to silence, is correct to the extent that the state need not care about the integrity of a guilty suspect's moral autonomy when trying to procure a confession from him.[60] Yet talk of compulsion is presumptuous, because police are not in a position to know that a suspect has criminal secrets; they are also not in a position to necessarily judge the extent of his volitional commitment. So the voluntariness standard's attention to volition is doubly inappropriate. Rather, the relevant question is whether the suspect's *political* autonomy is being infringed with cause. If it is being infringed with cause, then assessments based on a political right to *privacy* are not apt, again, because it would be irrational for inhabitants enjoying their rights in a basically just state to dissent to proportionate infringements of their privacy consistent with criminal investigation. To judge whether these material infringements are consistent with criminal investigations, and so are at a level of intrusiveness to which inhabitants cannot rationally dissent, we must evaluate whether state actions are consistent with available evidence indicating the person's status in the criminal justice arena.

The following questions are meant to assess whether the state meets this standard, thereby ensuring that its policing methods are politically legitimate. They are oriented to determining (1) the status of inhabitants in the criminal justice arena; (2) the fittingness of various actions for a specific category of inhabitant; and (3) the reliability of various actions.

1) Are police using reliable standards for distinguishing suspicious persons from apparently innocent persons?

2) Are the increasingly prudential measures of interrogation and investigation proportional to the level of a person's suspiciousness?

3) Do interrogation methods pose little risk of inducing false confessions?

The benefits of the evaluative questions over the "totality of circumstances" and "shocking to the conscience" tests are as follows. They are related to the state's actions rather than the mental state of the suspect, which is difficult to assess. The third question is empirical, and as a result, objectively measurable; the first two questions, I think, are answerable to a "reasonable man" standard.[61] As such, in sum, in addition to being properly oriented to the suspect's hybrid status, rather than his mental freedom, these questions are also more determinate and objective means for assessing interrogation and investigative methods than the totality of circumstances or shocking to the conscience tests. Even if these questions invalidate the same police tactics rejected by a particular judge's construal of the two constitutional tests, or other tests meant to assess voluntariness, the rejections will be less ambiguous and less subject to critique if based on the above three questions.

If authorities cannot affirmatively answer these questions, they are acting prudentially toward people who do not deserve prudential treatment; treating them more prudentially than they deserve; or carelessly employing prudential measures. In such cases, authorities muddy the distinctions the liberal state should properly make in the criminal justice arena between different categories of inhabitants. Authorities exceed their authority when they treat a person in a way commensurate with a category without grounds for placing him there.

Asking the first question in regards to the Wallace case—"are police using reliable standards for distinguishing suspicious persons from apparently innocent persons?"—one can conclude that police would have erred if they detained everyone in the neighborhood for interrogation in a dragnet sweep, because such measures make no distinctions between the likelihood of innocence or guilt. Though it was not relevant in this case because of the neighborhood's homogonous population, racial profiling would also fail this standard.

According to the standard of the second question—"are the increasingly prudential measures of interrogation and investigation proportional to the level of a person's suspiciousness?"—police would have also erred if they questioned people unlikely to have any information about the particular crime or if they took people into custody for stationhouse questioning without strong cause. Once there, police would err if they badgered or deceived suspects unlikely to have information. By this standard, police were not wrong to bring the Fish Man in for interrogation since circumstantial evidence implicated him, and his initial responses to the questions detectives asked him in his apartment reasonably aroused further suspicion.

We will now focus in greater detail on the standards associated with the second and third questions as they apply to interrogation. The police interrogator must act toward a suspect in part as he would toward an apparently innocent person and in part as he would toward a guilty person, in deference to the suspect's hybrid political identity. In keeping with the former obligation, the interrogator should inform the suspect that he can remain silent (because apparently innocent people do not have to speak to people they wish to ignore), or that he can answer the interrogator's questions, perhaps explaining away the suspicion (people persuade others paradigmatically through the provision of reasons). On this point, the detectives asked the Fish Man for an alibi; later they would ask him if he could explain why smudge marks on LaTonya's clothes were consistent with soot in his burned-out store. In keeping with an obligation to treat a suspicious person as possibly guilty, the interrogator also properly begins to treat the suspect prudentially, as a quasi-object, or means (to the truth) if the suspect is uncooperative. The interrogator can deceive or emotionally manipulate the suspect into producing the truth, though the interrogator's gambits should be proportional to the likelihood the suspect is withholding criminal knowledge (discussed in detail next chapter).[62] On this point, the lead detective was not wrong to become more antagonistic toward the Fish Man the guiltier his words and actions made him appear, eventually accusing him of the murder and even lying to him about incriminating forensic evidence.

If the Fish Man was the murderer, he did not have a right to his criminal knowledge. However, the detectives did not know for certain he was concealing criminal information. An interrogator's prudential gambits are justified to the extent that they are oriented to the possibly guilty half of the suspect's hybrid identity and are modulated based on the level of the officer's suspicion. This standard is not entirely subjective. The interrogator ought to be able to give reasons for his suspicion—and therefore, the fittingness of the prudential measures he employed—to disinterested parties. In this case, the lead detective was able to convince his superiors that the circumstantial evidence implicating the Fish Man was strong enough to justify hundreds of overtime hours as well as the hiring of an outside specialist to interrogate him.

The different elements of the interrogator's hybrid approach should correlate with the relevant political characteristics of the suspect's hybrid character. Otherwise, authorities are effectively treating a suspect as apparently innocent or apparently guilty alone, ignoring the other half of his hybrid character. Either approach precludes the rationales for investigation and trial.[63] The standard of respecting the hybrid quality of the suspect precludes (at least) nonprovision of a *Miranda*-style warning, interrogatory torture (including deprivation of sleep,[64] food, water,[65] or the use of a toilet), the threat of violence, solitary confinement,[66] and threats to the suspect's loved ones.[67] The *Miranda*-style warning informing the suspect of his (political) right to silence reminds him that the state still considers him possibly innocent even while it departs from the usual deference afforded apparently innocent persons (in order to verify that he is indeed truly innocent). All of the other, above-mentioned methods fail to affirmatively answer questions 2 and 3. They are disproportionate to the suspect's level of suspiciousness, because they are all predicated on the assumption that the suspect *does* have criminal knowledge; with all these techniques, the interrogator presents confession as the price of a respite from pain, discomfort, or solitude, or in exchange for the nonharassment of a relative. These techniques also ignore a suspect's right to silence insofar as they are attempts to force him to speak. Given the cost of noncooperation, these techniques obviously also risk making innocent people confess, and so fail the reliability standard of the third question. Note, this approach excludes less brutal techniques like solitary confinement that more permissive jurists or judges might consider non conscience-shocking or nonprejudicial to the voluntariness of a person's confession.

If a suspect really is guilty and keeps silent, he has not done a disservice to a liberal regime of criminal justice. His silence is not aberrant noise in a system tolerated in exchange for the benefits to the innocent.[68] The state does not yet have cause to know he is truly guilty, so still should afford him a good deal of deference. A liberal regime should not depend on confessions to determine guilt, but should have law enforcement and prosecutory organs professional enough to "shoulder the entire load" in proving its case. This burden in the pretrial phase especially functions against police laziness and ineptitude, making the police more effective at crime prevention and detection.[69] An image of police effectiveness should also serve as a deterrent to crime. In this sense, a guilty suspect's silence does a favor to his community by giving the state a workout, as it were, keeping its judicial and investigative organs in shape. Indeed, at its height, the Wallace case saw over twenty officers working around the clock, necessitating extraordinary coordination and planning. The care with which the lead detective went over the case files also exposed errors in the initial evidence collection that might have provided possible grounds for departmental reforms.

If a guilty suspect waives his right to silence and is tricked into confessing (as most who waive are),[70] he has only behaved like a quasi-object in keeping with the way authorities were in part treating him. He "lets slip" the truth, rather than deciding to confess it. He has no right to conceal criminal information, so there is no cause to lament his overborne will as such.

If an innocent suspect is silent, or agrees to answer the interrogator's questions, he has submitted to the level of material privacy infringements to which it is irrational to dissent (being asked questions by authorities, given cause, and answering, if one wishes). There would be cause to make counsel mandatory during police interrogations if innocent persons' truthful responses to police questions regularly led to wrongful convictions. This would mean that the apparently innocent part of the suspect's status could not really be maintained in police custody.

The strongest case for concern is if police tactics regularly make innocent suspects falsely confess. Again, this means that the apparently innocent status of suspects' hybrid identity cannot be maintained in police custody, possibly because suspicious people are treated as though they were already proven guilty. The confessions in the cases mentioned at the head of this section involving physical mistreatment, extortion, and threats should have all been thrown out on this basis. The reliability standard also should preclude interrogations of vulnerable suspects like minors or the mentally ill (who have been empirically shown to be more likely to falsely confess)[71] without counsel or family members present.

FIVE

Police Interrogation

Joe, was hurting this guy part of your original plan, or did it just happen on the
spur of the moment? If you went in there with the full intention of pulling that
trigger, it tells me you have no regard for human life and that you are capable of
doing anything. If that's the case we might as well end this right now because I
know people like that are not capable of telling the truth. But, Joe, I think the gun
just went off. I think all you wanted was a few bucks; you didn't want to hurt him,
Joe. But because this is out of character for you, you panicked and the darn thing
went off. Gosh, if that's what happened you've got to let me know, because I'm no
mind reader. The guy who plans something like this for months in advance and
walks into a store knowing full well that he's going to shoot and kill any possible
witness looks the same to me as the fellow who acts out of desperation and, on
the spur of the moment, finds himself with a gun in his hand and in the heat of
the moment panics and ends up doing something he really regrets. Joe, this wasn't
part of the plan, was it? It just went off, didn't it, Joe? [A police interrogator's "alternate question," put to an armed robbery suspect.][1]

The literature about police interrogation in the United States suggests that
the interrogation manual by Fred Inbau, John Reid et. al. is so widely used by
American police departments that a description of contemporary American
police interrogations would be remiss without a description of the manual's
"Reid technique."[2] However, since there is little public information about
actual interrogation practices in American police departments, the risk in
focusing on the manual is confusing the map with the territory, that is, assuming the manual's *advocated* practices are the same as interrogators' *actual*
practices. Many detectives learn the Reid technique in training seminars,
but many others learn interrogation techniques from more experienced colleagues instead of by reading manuals.[3] Just the same, civilian commentators

have few alternatives besides looking at manuals if interested in making general comments about police interrogation, given the dearth of publicly available transcripts or empirical studies of interrogations. Indeed, the 1966 *Miranda* Court relied on the Inbau and Reid manual for a description of police interrogation because it had no empirical studies at its disposal (most states' privacy laws preclude access to transcripts, if interrogations are transcribed at all). It should be noted that interrogation transcripts quoted in law review articles do seem to broadly reflect the strategies advocated in the manual. Finally, even though a commentator must hesitate to say that the manual universally describes American police behavior, the fact that it is widely used by American municipalities to *prescribe* interrogation methods is a sufficient basis for normative comment on the acceptability of a state prescribing such methods.

Interviews and Interrogations

Normative comments on interview and interrogation procedures will follow their description in this section. The Inbau and Reid manual encourages investigators to "interview" a potential suspect or witness prior to an "interrogation" in order to gain information about the crime and distinguish witnesses from potential suspects. An interview is nonaccusatory and can take place in any setting. Part of its purpose is to determine if an interrogation of the interviewee is warranted.[4] An interrogation should only occur when the investigator believes that the interrogatee is likely guilty, in part because an interrogation involves an accusation of guilt. Inbau et. al. write that an interrogation's purpose is to determine the truth, rather than necessarily to induce a confession; interrogators' accusations tend to stimulate responses on the part of guilty suspects indicative of guilt and responses on the part of innocent suspects indicative of innocence.[5] Also, even if the suspect does not confess, his suspicious answers may aid detectives by indicating that attention is indeed properly focused on him.

The purpose of interviewing people suspicious from the start of an investigation is for investigators to establish a baseline of the suspect's behavior.[6] As the interview is nonaccusatory and is supposed to be relaxed and congenial, the investigator should be able to develop a sense of the interviewee's demeanor when he is not under the pressure of a criminal accusation and is presumably telling the truth about mundane biographic details.[7] This baseline can be compared with the person's demeanor if and when he is accused of a crime. A third purpose of the interview is to establish trust and rapport between investigator and interviewee.

The manual directs investigators to be friendly and solicitous in an interview, stressing that investigators are merely seeking to get a picture of the crime in question. The investigator should ask broad questions, affording the interviewee the opportunity to give an account of what occurred in his own voice and at his own speed.[8] While the authors do not make this comparison, it strikes me that what investigators are asked to then perform is akin to a literary analysis of a text. Investigators must consider what the tone, level of detail, vocabulary, omissions, redundancies, and idiosyncrasies of the narrative reveal about the interviewee.

People typically give linguistic and nonlinguistic cues when they are lying. Truthful narrators typically recall and describe events out of order and so will sometimes have to backtrack and explain things they forgot to mention. By contrast, deceitful accounts are often *too perfect*, unfolding in temporal order, and including only details that are relevant to the subject of the story.[9] It strikes me that deceitful narratives *would* be good stories, on a formal level, because they are conceived *as* stories—as fictional accounts— by the liar. He has the rational remove to carefully construct the events in a logical order and exclude irrelevant details. Unlike truthful accounts, deceitful accounts are also usually emotionally flat: events supposedly experienced firsthand are described from a curiously neutral and detached perspective.[10] Again, this makes sense since the liar is imagining the event from the perspective of a third party rather than that of a participant.

The interviewer goes on to ask "direct questions" as blunt as "did you shoot the victim?" in order to prompt nonverbal behavior indicative of the person's emotional state—useful since certain emotional states may be associated with deception.[11] The direct questions will also force a deceptive suspect to offer incriminating evidence or lie.[12] Detected lies provide grounds for detectives focusing their attentions on a particular suspect. Lying can potentially be detected because liars typically cannot simultaneously control the content of what they are saying, the manner in which they are saying it (pauses, stammers, tonal shifts, etc.), and associated physical behavior to mimic the behavior of truth-tellers. (It should be noted that the authors' claims about the relation of linguistic and nonlinguistic behavior to deception are supported by current psychological research into lying.)[13] The manual notes that the investigator must also be aware of cultural differences between himself and the interviewee that could assign different meaning to behaviors like eye contact and the differing significance of certain behaviors when the interviewee is medicated, physically or mentally ill, or poorly educated.[14]

Based on the interview, investigators may conclude that the interviewee is innocent and so can be eliminated from the investigation; that he cannot be eliminated (though there is not enough evidence to warrant an interrogation); or that he is likely guilty and an immediate interrogation is appropriate.[15] The authors stress that interrogations are only appropriate for suspects who are likely guilty. (In the context of interrogations, I will refer to "suspects" rather than "interviewees" and to "interrogators" rather than "investigators" for clarity of emphasis. Most, if not all police interrogations in the United States are conducted by the detectives who investigate the case, rather than by full-time interrogators, as is the case in the military.) The authors argue, seemingly on practical grounds, that the accusatory methods used in interrogations are not appropriate to establish the truthfulness of interviewees—the nonaccusatory techniques of the interview sufficing. However, they may also be allowing that the accusatory approach is distressing to suspects and so should not be used cavalierly when they state that rationales for each stage of the Reid technique will be presented "for investigators who have qualms or reservations about utilizing some of the steps." Without giving supporting rationales, the authors assert that the Reid technique will not cause an innocent person to confess and that the Reid technique is legally and morally justifiable. The basis of the former claim would seem to be their "many years of experience" interrogating people.[16] This claim will be addressed in the section regarding efficacy below; the normative claim will be addressed in later sections of this chapter.

The interrogator using the Reid technique constructs a sort of rhetorical maze for the suspect, leading him down certain corridors, closing doors, and blocking routes, as the guilty suspect seeks a way out, testing various stories to see which the interrogator might believe. The interrogator aims to break down the guilty suspect's confidence that he can get away with his crime and creates psychological stress by confronting the suspect both with the facts of the crime and the interrogator's knowledge of the suspect's involvement. The interrogator then provides a release—confession—affirming that the suspect has done the right thing once he has complied.

The authors' instructions for applying the Reid technique in interrogations are minutely detailed, even dictating the number of seconds the interrogator should pause between certain questions. The directions are framed by constitutional concerns: the interrogation may only proceed after the suspect has been given his *Miranda* warning and has waived the rights described therein. Also, based on case law, the interrogator cannot make specific threats or promises contingent on the suspect's confession.

The interrogator needs to assess whether a suspect is an "emotional" or "nonemotional" type based on the information gleaned from the interview. The "emotional" suspect feels guilty over his crime, which the interrogator can exploit with pseudo-sympathy. The "nonemotional" type may be a career criminal or at least someone who does not believe what he did was wrong. A fact-based approach appealing to the suspect's rational self-interest is advocated in such cases. For example, a Boston police superintendent indicates that his homicide detectives usually employ a fact-based approach with local gang members since they rarely feel remorse for their crimes.[17] Similarly, in the Wallace case, detectives confronted their chief suspect with incriminating evidence since he was stoic during his initial interactions with police. Since many suspects are not purely one or the other, a mixed approach by the interrogator may also be warranted.[18]

The interrogator should maintain a polite and professional demeanor, but one that is firmer and more serious than in the interview. He must maintain a calm and confident affect throughout the interrogation. The basic gambit he presents to the suspect is that he, the interrogator, knows the suspect is guilty, so the suspect might as well confess.[19] A Sonoma County, California, detective expressed his confidence to a suspect this way: "I hope that you're not sittin' here tryin' to conspire how can I get out of this, how can I beat this. You know? It's not a matter of if you did it. That's not the issue. You need to understand that no, we're not here asking you if you did it. If we didn't know, we wouldn't have arrested you. . . . We know that you did it. We don't know why you did it, Alan. You understand what I'm tellin' ya?"[20]

The interrogator should enter the interrogation room with a case folder (even if it's filled with blank paper) and occasionally glance into it to give the suspect the sense that the police already have considerable information about him. The interrogator should sit directly across from the suspect, three to four feet away, in civilian clothes, unarmed, without any badges or other indications of his police affiliation. As the interrogator will exploit the basic social expectations and emotional pressures inherent in everyday conversation—the need for logical coherence and the desire to please, to be believed, and to be respected—he does not want official elements of his appearance reminding the suspect of the legal consequences of a confession.

Addressing the suspect by first name, the interrogator opens by stating firmly and calmly that he knows the suspect is guilty. An innocent person will normally object immediately in an outraged tone, making direct eye contact, while a guilty person will often hesitate, before denying the charge while avoiding eye contact and exhibiting other behavioral tics associated with deception.[21] Overall, it seems that guilty people react to interrogators' provocations less stridently than do innocent people. This is likely because, first, they do not *feel* the indignation of the falsely accused person, because (mentally normal, adult) guilty suspects know they are guilty. Second, they may wish to avoid antagonizing the interrogator, assuming that agitation on their part will further his suspicions and extend the interrogation. Part of what provoked the lead detective's suspicion of the Fish Man in the Wallace case was his nonchalant willingness to submit to three lengthy interrogations as well as numerous informal interviews.[22] The innocent person, by contrast, is likely outraged and indignant at being falsely accused and reacts emotionally, without calculation.

After the accusation, the interrogator introduces a "theme" to emotional suspects, a psychologically palatable rationale for why the suspect committed the crime. A common introduction is something like "Look, I don't believe you're a bad guy; but I'm trying to understand why you did this." From there, the interrogator might suggest that anyone else would have done the same thing in the suspect's position; that the crime was not so egregious, morally speaking; that accomplices were more to blame than the suspect; that the victim was to blame; that there were aspects of the crime that were technically impressive (e.g., getting past a building's security system); or that the current moment is an opportunity to make a clean break and avoid a life of crime.[23] The authors write that it is fairly easy to overcome guilty suspects' denials once a theme is introduced, because they have likely justified the crime in their own mind in some way. By contrast, the interrogator's offered rationalization for the crime strikes the innocent suspect as outrageous, and he will usually become more emphatic in his denial.[24]

Nonemotional offenders will attempt to avoid emotional manipulation so the interrogator needs to argue that logic requires that certain incriminatory facts be true. I think it is right to characterize the situation in this way, though logic might seem like a strange source of pressure for a guilty suspect. Suspects who waive their right to remain silent presumably wish to convince police they are innocent. While the narrative the deceptive suspect has constructed is false, it is still purportedly a description of something that happened in the real world and so has to make sense. In order to maintain the coherence of the fictional narrative, the deceptive suspect has to address incoherencies the interrogator discovers. For example, a Kern County, California, interrogator challenged a murder suspect's claim that she didn't see the blood stains in her kitchen this way:

> I know exactly what you're telling us and we find it very hard to believe because there's blood in the kitchen where you went and got a soda, you know, on the floor and there's blood on two paper towels in the kitchen, two tissues . . . sitting right there at the first chair when you were getting in the refrigerator to get your Sprite, the chair that would be against your back there,

right there . . . in full view of the living room. . . . You can see right there. And there was nobody in that house during the time the guy was found and the time you guys were there so where did these mystery tissues come from. . . . You know how they got there.[25]

The guilty suspect's confidence in lying depends on his or her perception that he or she is succeeding in misleading the interrogator; the more true information the interrogator elicits, the less store the suspect may put into maintaining the facade. If the interrogator catches the suspect in a lie, even a trivial one, he can undercut future fabrications by reminding the suspect that he has already been caught in a lie.[26] Piece by piece, the interrogator seeks to get the suspect to admit facts implicating him in the crime. Again, the interrogator seems to appeal to the inherent pressure—if that's the right word—to make sense to our audience when we speak, to weave narrated events together in a logical order, and to match intentions with appropriate actions. When the interrogator says, "now wait, Joe, what you just told me doesn't make sense," he is drawing attention to the pressure the suspect probably feels since he knows his narrative is nonsense.

The interrogator may also seek to communicate to the suspect the futility of lying by telling him (be it truthfully or deceitfully) that there is evidence implicating him or that his captured accomplice has implicated him in the crime. The authors emphasize this gambit should be used as a last resort, since the suspect might call the interrogator's bluff. Recall, the Vallejo detectives lied to Eugene Livingston in this way. In Baltimore, the Fish Man was falsely told that forensic evidence proved Latonya was in his store the day of the murder.

Many guilty suspects still deny involvement in the crime after the accusation and theme introduction. The interrogator will want to head off further denials by interrupting the suspect, because "the more often a guilty suspect denies involvement in a crime, the less likely he will be to tell the truth."[27] The interrogator's tactic seems to take advantage of what some philosophers call the perlocutionary aspect of language. When we speak, it is often in order to achieve some effect on the listener: to persuade, to amuse, to comfort. It is natural to abandon a rhetorical strategy (such as denial) if it is failing to have its desired effect. Whereas the denials of guilty suspects will usually weaken when confronted with this tactic, most innocent suspects will become more emphatic, interrupting the interrogator and seeking to "take over" the interrogation until he is able to restate his innocence. Some innocent suspects, for cultural or particular biographic reasons, will defer to authority figures when those figures are making accusatory statements but will interrupt when they ask incriminating questions. At this point the suspect will appear genuinely offended and sincere in his denial.[28]

At this stage, having failed to derail the interrogator with his denials and objections, most guilty suspects withdraw from the conversation. They fall silent; stop listening; and physically turn their bodies away from the interrogator. Innocent suspects usually will not withdraw (unless they have been physically threatened) but persist in their objections or invoke their right to silence. The interrogator should seek to reacquire the withdrawn suspect's attention and reestablish rapport by slowly moving his chair closer to the suspect's, seeking eye contact, and asking him hypothetical questions.[29] The interrogator then distills his theme to a single rationale he proposes as the one motivating the suspect's crime, speaking in a sincere, sympathetic tone. Confession is presented as a way of expiating the psychological pressure and/or the guilt the suspect is feeling. Having created this pressure, the interrogator now offers a way out with the "alternative question." Rather than simply ask, "did you do it?" the interrogator presents two alternative rationales for having committing the crime. For example, he might ask the suspect, "Did you take that money to go out and party, or did you take it to help your family?" Even if the interrogator suspects that the crime was the product of base motives, the alternative question gives the suspect a face-saving way of confessing.[30] The suspect has effectively confessed to the crime once he has accepted one of the rationales. The interrogator then needs to prompt the suspect into providing all the details of the crime so that the confession is legally admissible. He should seek specific information only the perpetrator would know as well as information that can corroborated by witnesses or crime scene investigation. At this point, the interrogator can also address elements of the theme or alternate question accepted by the suspect that the interrogator doubts are true. Most successful interrogations conclude within a few hours. The authors write that skilled interrogators will obtain confessions in 80 percent of their interrogations.[31]

Moral Assessment of Deceptive Interrogation

The discussion of government coercion over the previous chapters has been a necessary prelude to discussing police interrogation, because interrogation is coercive in the broad sense of the term. The entire interrogation is *manipulative* in the sense that the skilled interrogator plans how to induce a confession, and then structures his every word, intonation, and physical behavior to that end without regard to his true feelings or beliefs, much less the suspect's desires. The Reid technique directs the interrogator to anticipate typical reactions to the suspect's emotional stress; set rhetorical ambushes for the suspect; and manipulate the suspect's emotional or intellectual shortcomings. The suspect is not treated as an end, but as a means, to securing the confession; in a sense, the suspect is just a container for the secrets the interrogator desires. The interrogator may *act deceptively*, playing a role, sometimes acting friendly, sometimes firm, always affecting a confidence that communicates to the suspect that the interrogator knows the truth, even when he has little evidence implicating the suspect. The interrogator may *lie* to the suspect about the existence of physical evidence or eyewitnesses, and he may lie about his true opinions and/or feelings, perhaps expressing sympathy or admiration for someone he loathes. Thus, all interrogations following the Reid technique (or stratagems similar on these points) are *manipulative;* many involve *deception* about the interrogator's actual knowledge or emotions; and some involve telling lies.[32] Below, I will refer to "deception" as the inclusive term including lying, emotional manipulation, and nonverbal deception accomplished by the interrogator's affect; I will use the term "deceptive interrogation" to refer to an interrogation in which some form of deception is used.[33]

The normative foundation for this chapter has been defended in the previous three. In a liberal state, legitimate police actions are those aimed at preventing or detecting crime that inhabitants enjoying their lives and rights cannot rationally criticize. Such actions will be those that are at once maximally efficacious at crime prevention and detection and minimally offensive to inhabitants' political rights. Does interrogation meet this standard of political legitimacy? Some aspects of interrogation have already been justified by this standard, and so will not be further discussed here. I argued in chapters 3 and 4 that (in a basically just state) police questioning of those believed to have information relevant to crimes is a legitimate part of crime detection and prevention, provided certain caveats including respect for inhabitants' right to silence. This argument justifies noncustodial "interviews" if such interviews merely involve straightforward questioning and no deceptive or manipulative elements. Arrest has already been justified as a constitutive part of legitimate police powers, so the custodial element in interrogation is justified. The accusatory element of interrogation does not need to be justified per se, because its role in an interrogation is not really as an accusation—the assertion of knowledge of another's guilt. The interrogator does not necessarily *know* the suspect is guilty, but accuses the suspect in order to elicit an emotional reaction. In other words, the accusation is a ploy, an instance of manipulative behavior. What remains to be justified then are the manipulative and deceptive elements common to both interrogations and interviews.

There will be three foci of judgment in the following discussion: the efficacy of interrogation techniques, suspects' rights in interrogations, and interrogators' prudence. First, to assess whether deceptive interrogations are a legitimate part of a liberal state's coercive portfolio—both maximally efficacious and minimally offensive to inhabitants' rights—we must determine if deception is efficacious in interrogation; if it is reliably efficacious (and does not carry a significant risk of producing false confessions); and if deceptive practices are indispensable in the sense of being without substitutes. Inhabitants could dissent to deceptive techniques if they were not efficacious, reliable, and indispensable means of crime detection and prevention, instead demanding that police use better available methods. Also, from the perspective of theory, we do not have to bother asking if inefficacious, unreliable, or dispensable practices are politically legitimate. Since they do not work, we need not wonder if there are *also* moral reasons for abandoning them.

Second, we have to determine if these practices are consistent with suspects' rights if deceptive techniques are efficacious, reliable, and indispensable. It is possible for reliably efficacious and indispensable practices to violate people's rights since efficacy, reliability, and indispensability are contingent matters. For example, it so happened in the case discussed in chapter 1 that the elderly orchard keeper's only practical way of stopping the apple thief was to shoot him, but this violated the thief's rights.

Finally, if a given set of practices are respectful of suspects' rights, it is still a matter of prudence whether police should employ them. If deceptive interrogation practices do not violate suspects' rights, but carry some risk of negative side effects—including occasional false confessions, the generation of distrust between citizens and police, and the corruption of police personnel—it is a question of prudence whether the balance of bad and good results of deceptive interrogation practices justifies those practices. Inhabitants could dissent to police actions that are in principle justifiable but which have more bad effects than good ones when actually implemented in particular real world contexts. Therefore, in the final sections of this chapter, we will ask if negative effects of deceptive interrogations are probable enough to make their use imprudent.

Efficacy and Other Practical Matters

The sparse data available about police interrogations suggests deceptive interrogation techniques are effective at inducing confessions. Criminals rarely choose to confess to police on their own.[34] Yet the most broad-based empirical survey of American police interrogations, conducted in 1994 by Richard Leo, found that 76 percent of criminal suspects who waived their right to silence confessed.[35] This would suggest that *something* transpiring in the interrogation room compelled suspects to confess. The rapidity with which most of these interrogations concluded (within one hour) suggests that professional skill, rather than blind luck or homeostatic factors affecting the suspect like fatigue or hunger, was responsible for the confessions.[36]

Gaining an empirical view of the reliability of interrogation techniques at inducing *true* confessions is difficult given the lack of publicly available data about police interrogations.[37] A handful of studies have been done in which researchers collected cases of alleged false confessions, the two most cited finding forty-nine alleged cases of false confessions (involved in wrongful convictions) between 1900 and 1985,[38] and sixty cases of alleged false confessions since 1966.[39] Scholars strongly disagree about the quality of these studies and, accordingly, whether they provide adequate grounds to indict certain interrogation practices.[40]

The research on confessions is adequate to sustain the following claims. Most interrogations yield confessions. Most confessions are true—a fact allowed by the false confession researchers—if for no other reason than most of the suspects police interrogate are guilty.[41] It seems clear that police-induced false confessions also occur, but that there is no defensible basis on which to make a reliable estimate for their frequency.[42] Since the verdict regarding reliability is murky, we are not in the position to eliminate interrogation as a legitimate tool of policing on empirical grounds alone and must ask the following conceptual question. Is interrogation an acceptable policing tool if it carries some (indeterminate) risk of inducing false confessions?

Any goal-oriented action risks error, and any action instituted on a systemic level runs the risk of inconsistent execution due to the errors of individual agents. So the fallibility of interrogation and the possibility of unprofessional execution by particular detectives are not necessarily fatal shortcomings to the enterprise. Other inquisitorial aspects of the American criminal justice system, including the use of eyewitnesses and analysis of forensic evidence, are subject to these kinds of error as well. With respect to the adversarial elements of the criminal justice system, there is always the risk at trial that defense counsel will be incompetent or that witnesses will perjure themselves. It is obviously impractical to exclude all fallible actions from a state's portfolio. If we wish to consider the relative risk of different aspects of investigations, the data indicates that slightly more wrongful convictions result from mistaken eyewitness accounts than from false confessions.[43]

It would then be more prudent to disallow eyewitness statements than interrogations if reliability is the only relevant standard. Yet it seems absurd for police and prosecutors to tell eyewitnesses, "thank you, but we don't want to know what you saw." So if the fallibility of eyewitness accounts does not preclude their use, the *more* reliable—but still fallible—practice of interrogation (or particular interrogation tactics) should not be barred on account of reliability concerns alone.

One should also distinguish the reliability of certain techniques when properly implemented from their reliability when unprofessionally implemented. Robust standards for training and evaluating interrogators are necessary to maintain a relatively high level of reliability for police interrogations. The state's failure to do so is a legitimate ground for critique. On this point, it is telling that most of the sixty cases of alleged false confessions described in the post-*Miranda* study involved practices contrary to the instructions of the Inbau and Reid manual, including the use of threats and extra long interrogations. While the reader cannot be certain that unprofessional interrogation practices led to false confessions, the correspondence between the two is striking. So in addition to their training regimen being subject to critique, police officers are also subject to critique when they behave unprofessionally, be it in conducting interrogations or in other aspects of investigation.

The other common component in this study of false confessions is the prevalence of mental retardation among false confessors. Apparently, people with mental retardation, along with young children, tend to defer to authority figures and so will assert whatever they think the interrogator wants them to say.[44] Due to the risks of false confessions among suspects with mental retardation, their confessions should be discounted by investigators and prosecutors without strong corroborating evidence.

Threats and blackmail are also apt to produce false confessions and so should be prohibited.[45] (Threats and blackmail are also violations of suspects' rights, to be discussed below.) Obviously, the truth of a confession is dubious if a suspect is told that failure to confess will result in him being beaten, sodomized in jail, or given a longer sentence. In *Lynumn v. Illinois*, the Supreme Court reversed a conviction of a Chicago woman whose confession to a drug offense was induced by police threats to cut off her welfare payments and seize her children after she was sent to jail.[46] Promises of leniency must be excluded for the same reason.[47] For example, in a 1954 case, a police psychiatrist elicited a confession from a man after promising he would be let off easy if he admitted to murdering his parents.[48] The constitutional reason often cited in the literature for voiding these confessions is that they can be assumed to be involuntary. The philosophical reasons for rejecting the voluntariness standard and instead considering reliability the salient issue for political legitimacy were discussed in the preceding chapter.

One might object that interrogation is different from other admittedly fallible investigative methods because of the weight confessions carry in criminal trials. Several authors note that a confession is one of the most damning pieces of evidence that can be raised against a defendant. Yet the ire directed at deceptive interrogation practices on this account may be misplaced. Certainly, unprofessional police behavior should be criticized. However, given that all investigative methods are fallible—and, again, interrogation may be less error prone than other methods—outrage over wrongful convictions should be also directed at the assessors of evidence. Criticism should be directed at prosecutors who go to grand juries with weak evidence (including confessions obviously produced under duress and/or from suspects with mental retardation or minors), toward legislators who inadequately fund defense counsel for the indigent and who fail to mandate compulsory videotaping of interrogation, and toward judges who are remiss in their jury instructions. Given that there is anecdotal evidence of police-induced false confessions, it may well be appropriate to instruct prosecutors to disregard admissions of guilt uncorroborated with physical evidence or admissions of nonpublicized details about the crime.[49] Further, empirical studies need to be done concerning the reliability of various interrogation methods and false confession rates, and the findings need to be incorporated into police training. Until that is done, police at least need to be trained about the risks of false confession in interrogations, and prosecutors, judges, and juries need to be further educated about the possibility of false confessions. Inbau et al.'s claim that "none of these [techniques] are apt to make an innocent person confess" is rightly criticized for being stated so unequivocally. Instead of considering confessions so damning, it seems that properly educated prosecutors, judges, and juries would instead treat them with greater skepticism.

Finally, it is appropriate to ask if interrogation is an indispensable tool since it carries some indeterminate risk of inducing false confessions. Some crimes occur in the absence of witnesses, or in the absence of witnesses willing to testify, and some leave insufficient physical evidence to indict a suspect. For example, no murder weapon was ever found in the Wallace case, nor were many useful forensic clues discovered because the girl's body was exposed to the rain for a full night before discovery. Despite an unusual level of community cooperation, even from local drug dealers, no eyewitnesses were found. In cases like this one, interrogations will likely be the only avenue for gaining indictable evidence against a suspect.[50] I have not seen, and doubt there exist, data sets for the percentages of cases where interrogation has this importance, but we can anticipate that interrogations provide the only means of garnering evidence in a significant portion of criminal cases.[51] Were we to forgo interrogations because of their risk of producing false confessions, we would be abandoning what is likely the only means to solving a significant number of crimes. Such failures are not only bad for the criminal's current and future victims, but also for the innocent party who might be wrongfully convicted of the crime based on other fallible means of investigation.[52]

Some authors allow for police interrogations but urge the prohibition of particular deceptive practices including lies and deceptive affectations due to concerns over reliability, alienation of the public, and corruption of the system and individual officers.[53] In addition to assuming that interrogation will sometimes be the only way to garner indictable evidence, it also seems appropriate to assume that a significant portion of guilty suspects will not confess barring the use of deceptive practices. If we assume that interrogators in Leo's study of 182 interrogations used deceptive tactics only in cases where they judged truthful tactics would fail, interrogators judged that appeals to the suspect's conscience would fall on deaf ears in as many as 77 percent of the cases; there were no glaring inconsistencies in the suspect's story to be highlighted by interrogators in as many as 58 percent of the cases; and there was no physical evidence implicating the suspect (leading interrogators to lie about its existence) in as many as 12 percent of the cases. Unmeasured is the number of cases in which the opening assertion of guilt, key to the Reid technique and similar methods, was deceitful, because the interrogator did not in fact know the suspect was guilty. Of course, we cannot be certain that interrogators deceived suspects only in cases where they judged the suspects to be unsusceptible to truthful approaches, nor can we assess the soundness of their judgment. However, it does seem plausible to think that there would be a proportion of guilty suspects who would be inclined to remain silent during police interrogation, and plausible to think that if they confessed, it would only be on account of their believing that the police already had indictable evidence. Therefore, if the Leo study is representative, or at least partially representative of the criminal justice environment in the United States, deceptive interrogations appear to be indispensable in certain situations in the sense that guilty suspects would not confess without them.

Rights

It is a God-given truth: Everyone lies. And this most basic of axioms has three corollaries: A. Murderers lie because they have to. B. Witnesses and other participants lie because they think they have to. C. everyone else lies for the sheer joy of it, and to uphold a general principle that under no circumstances do you provide accurate information to a cop. . . . [T]o a homicide detective, the earth spins on an axis of denial in an orbit of deceit.[54]

Interrogation appears to be a good candidate for being a legitimate part of a liberal state's coercive portfolio since interrogation is a generally efficacious part of policing, is indispensable in certain contexts, and appears to be more reliable than other police practices such as the use of eyewitnesses. The discussion cannot rest here though. The indispensability and efficacy of deceptive interrogations in certain contexts are inadequate to determine their political legitimacy, because of the possibility that deceptive interrogations grossly violate suspects' rights or have such onerous effects as to offset the benefit of confessions. Therefore, it must now be asked if the generally efficacious tool of deceptive interrogation is minimally offensive to inhabitants' rights and does not lead to such serious side effects that it could become the object of inhabitants' coherent dissent.

It is within the legitimate powers of police to accost, question, and arrest suspicious persons. Whether police stay in the bounds of their legitimate powers depends on whether they respect suspects' political rights, and this turns on the question of whether police behavior accords with what they have cause to know about the suspects' possible criminal activity. In order to assess whether police can ever deceive suspects in interrogations, we will first consider whether such behavior can be justified when police know the suspect is lying or concealing criminal information. We will then assess whether police can deceive suspects whom they *believe* to be lying and/or withholding criminal information (without being certain). The questions will be addressed in this order because we do not need to ask if police may deceive those they only suspect of lying if deception cannot be justified even with known liars.

For the discussion that follows, I will assume that police know a suspect is guilty because they directly observed the suspect engaging in a criminal act (though perhaps the suspect was unaware he was being watched). The police are nonetheless seeking a full confession, because they wish to bolster their case, learn about the suspect's associates, or discover the location of contraband, etc. I will assume the guilty suspect initially lies to police when asked questions about these matters and so will consider his rights insofar as he is a liar. The following determinations of the liar's rights are the same whether moral or political rights are being discussed. This follows, because when police know a suspect is lying, they effectively occupy the God's eye view in the sense that they know the information about the suspect's subjective state relevant to determining what he deserves absolutely on account of his lying.[55] For these reasons, the liar's political and moral rights overlap precisely in this instance.

Is a liar owed the truth? The legitimate expectation that others defer to one's rights depends on one's recognition of those same rights on the part of others. As Kant famously argued, the liar exempts himself from this web of reciprocal rights recognition, arrogating to himself a privilege of lying that depends parasitically for its success on others telling and expecting the truth. This putative privilege cannot be universalized because lies would not be efficacious if everyone regularly planned to lie—everyone would know better than to trust others. The liar then cannot legitimately expect others to tell him the truth; he cannot expect them to treat him in a way he is failing to treat them, thereby further contributing to the environment of truth telling that will allow his lies to be effective. Also, he cannot legitimately expect others to refrain from trying to interfere with his lying, perhaps in an attempt to trick him into telling the truth. He is not owed the truth, and so is not wronged when deceived by someone attempting to expose his lies or otherwise reveal the truth.

The liar is not owed the truth, and a criminal does not have a right to his criminal secrets. Yet this does not necessarily imply that others have no obligations to plotters and liars.[56] Just coercion is limited by what is necessary to restore the status quo ante so long as the response does not exceed the general value of the right violated, threatened, or abused. Deceiving the liar would not violate a right of his that is of greater value than the one he violated. So deception of liars for the purpose of exposing their lies is not disproportionate in this sense. Deception appears to be reasonably efficacious and reliable in interrogations, so it is also not disproportionate in the sense of being unnecessary to restore the status quo ante (which is presumably dependent on the interrogator learning the truth about a crime so just punishment and restitution can be ordered).

One might object that a lie as such—focusing for now on this form of deception—does not "cancel out" another lie. Nor does the performance of lying undo the lying of another in the direct way physical force can "undo" an unjust assault (i.e., block a punch, physically push the attacker away, etc.). Now merely both parties are lying. Let us examine the suspect's and interrogator's tactical reasons for lying in order to respond to this critique. The guilty suspect lies to the interrogator in order to manipulate the interrogator's understanding of a crime, tailoring his lies on the basis of what the suspect believes is already known to the interrogator. For example, the guilty suspect will try to fabricate an alibi for noon if he believes that the interrogator thinks the crime occurred then. By lying in turn, the interrogator seeks to manipulate the suspect's understanding of the interrogator's beliefs until the suspect trips over his own lies; reacts in a way indicative of guilt; or concludes that lying is pointless, because the interrogator already knows the truth. (In a less precise way, other forms of deception including emotional affectation also seek to manipulate the suspect's understanding of the interrogator's beliefs.) Still, the connection between the suspect's lying and the interrogator's lies may seem too indirect to justify the latter. The interrogator cannot "aim at" the suspect's lies in the way he could reach for the arm of a knife-waving assailant. There is no certainty that lying, say, about eyewitness testimony or about the interrogator's disdain for the victim will have the desired effect on the guilty suspect. On this point, the Baltimore detectives were prepared to tell multiple lies about incriminating evidence (even generating fake documents) for their final interrogation with the Fish Man, because they were unsure which lie would provoke a reaction. Yet as argued in chapter 1, since a defender or good Samaritan cannot be expected to know exactly how much force is necessary to halt an attacker, and disproportionate levels of force might be necessary for certain defenders to halt particular attacks, instances of just coercion can be thought of as ones where persons are loosed from being *too careful* about the rights of rights violators. The interrogator would not wrong the known liar with some imprecision or excess in the lies he, the interrogator, tells. So while lies do not remediate the situation in the same direct way physical force remediates assault, they can be seen in a broader sense as proportionate responses to lies.[57]

So neither the moral nor political rights of a liar or criminal plotter are violated if he is deceived by a truth seeker who knows he is lying or concealing criminal information. However, this justification—based on the suspect's status as a rights violator—is not completely satisfactory to justify authorities' deception in cases where they think, but are not certain, the suspect is concealing criminal information.[58] This in fact describes the context of many interrogations, where police do not have indictable evidence of guilt prior to the interrogation. The question now is whether the political rights of a suspect are violated when police deceive him before having cause to know he is concealing criminal information. In this case, interrogators have an epistemic limitation more typical for state agents—they do not know the elements of the suspect's subjective state relevant to moral desert (such as whether or not he is lying)—and so the following discussion is in reference to the suspect's political rights alone.

An answer to this question of political rights depends on the previous conclusions about legitimate police powers. In a domestic law enforcement context, authorities' proportionate material infringement on citizens' privacy in the form of questioning is justified when there is probable cause for suspecting they have criminal knowledge and the authorities' aim is the prevention or solving of crimes. As suspicious persons, inhabitants do not morally *deserve* material infringements on their rights—appearing suspicious is not their fault—but it is legitimate for police to act *as if* they deserved less than full deference to their political rights, because police must act to prevent and solve crimes as a way of protecting inhabitants' lives and rights. In performing this job, they are unable to always know immediately who is engaged in criminal behavior, and so they must sometimes act on suspicion rather than certainty. Given this imperative and this limitation, police will sometimes have to act in a way toward a particular suspect that fails to perfectly match with what he or she deserves absolutely. So while the police do not necessarily know a suspect is lying or concealing criminal secrets—and the above justification for deception is only strictly applicable to liars and plotters—the justification has traction to the extent that police have cause to consider a person suspicious and therefore possibly guilty. Another way of making this point is that the prudential aspect of their treatment of the suspect is in keeping with the *possibly guilty* part of his hybrid identity.

In chapters 3 and 4, I argued that authorities must have cause to know a person is criminally guilty before they could revoke a political right to silence (and so could legally compel him to confess/testify or punish him for his silence), but now I am arguing that interrogators can deceive suspects they merely suspect of deception. Due to the nature of the right to silence and the summary nature of its revocation, an assessment of the right to silence has to be categorical: all or nothing. A suspect's silence must either be deemed the subject of legal penalty (in which case he does not have a right to silence) or legally privileged (in which case he does have a right to silence). By contrast, police deception can be permitted following *suspicion* that a suspect is lying, because deception lends itself to gradual implementation as well as reversal. For example, the lead detective in the Wallace case believed that the Fish Man was concealing criminal knowledge; in order to see how the Fish Man would react, the detective falsely told the Fish Man that the police knew he was guilty. He did not react in the way innocent people typically react to false accusations, so the detective proceeded with further fabrications. By the same token, the detective could have backed off his earlier fabrications if he began to believe the Fish Man was innocent or could have revealed the whole truth if convinced he was innocent (e.g., "OK, you weren't really identified by a witness; I just had to say that to see your reaction"). By contrast, there can be no modulating of prudential treatment if the interrogator realizes the suspect is innocent after first ignoring the suspect's right to silence and forcing him to reveal his secrets in some way. In this case, the suspect's right to silence has already been violated, and his secrets have already been forced out.

Since their treatment of persons is properly guided by what they have cause to know about them—and this is a variable, rather than categorical, state—authorities should only dial up prudential treatment of suspects or potential material witnesses incrementally and with cause. Low probable cause (merely living in the building where a crime occurred) is probably sufficient to justify questioning in a noncustodial setting (e.g., a witness canvas where investigators might ask: "Did you hear anything strange last night?"). Here, the only cost to the person is a few minutes inconvenience. More probable cause would be necessary for direct questioning in a custodial setting, and still more for deceptive questioning in a custodial setting. The increasingly strict demands of cause are indicated by the increasing unpleasantness of the encounter for the suspect. Given the possibility of wrongful arrest, it is significant to note that these methods of interrogation have reversible effects on the detainee, whereas, by contrast, a suspect cannot re-conceal personal secrets after they have been compelled from him (in one way or another) and the pain of interrogatory torture is felt even if the suspect is eventually cleared of wrongdoing. At worst, proper police interrogation consists of some hours of aggressive questioning during which the interrogator asserts the suspect has done despicable things. It is certainly an unpleasant experience, and would probably leave the individual shaken for a few days, but probably not worse. An apology and explanation (discussed below) to the cleared suspect would also likely do a good deal to get the former suspect "back to normal."

We can draw some fairly obvious limits to justified instances of deceptive interrogation from the above discussion. The purpose of deceiving suspects is only to learn the truth, not to punish suspected liars by "showing them what it feels like." It is also an obvious abuse of power for an interrogator to deceive a suspect for purposes other than learning the truth, for instance, in order to gratuitously humiliate, confuse, or frighten him. Also, it is gratuitous to deceive or manipulate him further once the suspect has confessed and provided details of the crime.

In summary, in situations where generally reliable and efficacious deceptive techniques appear to well-trained interrogators as indispensable for use with particular suspects to solve particular crimes—and where the suspects' rights to silence and counsel are respected—deception is not inappropriate given what authorities have cause to know about the suspects' status in the criminal justice system and therefore does not violate their political rights. In certain cases, deceptive interrogation techniques appear to be those actions that are both maximally effective at crime detection and prevention and minimally offensive to inhabitants' rights. Therefore, such techniques are a legitimate part of the state's coercive portfolio and are in principle permissible.

Prudential Concerns

To say certain interrogation techniques are permissible (because they are not violations of suspects' rights) is not necessarily to say they *should* be used by police interrogators. Permissible actions are not necessarily ones that a person should perform in a particular situation, because the particular setting may lead a generally permissible action to produce more bad consequences than good ones. For example, St. Augustine famously wrote that while it would be legitimate for a state to ban prostitution, Rome should refrain from doing so because a ban would probably lead to an increase in the more serious sin of adultery.

There might also be concerns about the actors tasked with carrying out generally permissible actions in particular settings. For example, if, for the sake of the argument, it was concluded that omnipresent video surveillance was a politically legitimate police tactic, authorities might nonetheless decline to implement the system because of fears some officers would use the system for prurient purposes. This scenario might be judged worse than the crimes that would occur in the cameras' absence. As discussed in chapter 2, inhabitants could coherently dissent to police practices intended to protect people's rights, but which turn out to have the same or similar effects of intentional rights violations. Therefore, in the final sections of this chapter, we need to consider if potential negative consequences stemming from deceptive interrogations are so serious that police should refrain from employing them. Two possible negative consequences will be considered: harm to police-community relations and professional corruption of police interrogators.[59] A third possible negative consequence—false confessions—was discussed above.

Some critics argue that police deception (in all forms) should be prohibited because of the harm it does to police-community relations.[60] Citizens expect and deserve honesty and fairness from their government,[61] so deception alienates the public, making people less willing to cooperate with police.[62] One former defense attorney writes of the "*crushing*" effect police lying has on the first-time offender anxious for direction from authority figures. State agents should rather exemplify "civic virtues" when dealing with the public, the very virtues they hope citizens will adopt.[63]

One can imagine that it would be upsetting for an innocent person like Eugene Livingston to realize that police deceived him during interrogation. The suspect might feel vulnerable and frightened, because if police can lie in an interrogation—say, about the existence of incriminating evidence—perhaps they can just as readily lie to a judge or manufacture evidence to fit the bill. One can also imagine a degree of outrage, because, after all, who pays that lying detective's salary?

An interrogator's deception of an innocent person is comparable to other cases where police act coercively within the bounds of their authority but make an error (we will assume in these cases that the officers are well trained and use their best judgment). For example, police might break down the wrong door searching for a gas leak or for a fugitive, they might act violently to stop two men fighting when the two are just horsing around, or they might draw their weapons on someone who is holding a realistic toy gun, etc. In such cases, the person on the receiving end of the action is rationally committed to endorsing the behavior, upsetting as it might be. One ought to approve of police breaking into an apartment in cases where it seemed there was a gas leak inside and there was no other means of averting the danger, and so, breaking down one's own door if gas seemed to be escaping from one's own apartment. This sort of acceptance should *not* be forthcoming if one believed the police were in the habit of randomly destroying citizens' property or enjoyed harassing members of a particular social group, etc., since such actions would be abuses of police power.

Since deceptive interrogation practices are a legitimate part of the state's coercive portfolio, it seems the same analysis applying mistaken instances of prudential behavior could be applied to deceptive interrogations of innocent persons, assuming police had reason to believe the person had criminal information; behaved professionally in all other respects; and observed all the appropriate limitations in interrogation. Thus, the unpleasantness of deceptive interrogations for innocent persons (discharged after the interrogation) does not appear to be of sufficient weight to delegitimize the practice.

(It should also be noted that there are cases where evidence initially points toward an innocent party and the interrogation has the beneficial result of clearing that suspect.)

That said, it is incumbent on police to offer a kind of exit interview to cleared suspects following interrogation to ameliorate their concerns. The cause for breaking down the door in the gas leak situation is readily understandable, so it seems that a reasonable tenant would be able to accept the police's explanation in that situation without difficulty. By contrast, most people do not know what goes on in interrogation rooms and may not readily understand why an interrogator would employ deceptive techniques. Therefore, in order to minimize community distrust—even more than in the other cases of mistaken coercion—it is imperative that an interrogator carefully explain to a suspect why he deceived him after the interrogator determines the suspect is innocent. The interrogator needs to explain why he thought the suspect was guilty and why he felt deceptive tactics were necessary so that the (former) suspect does not think police deceive people all the time or employ deceptive techniques arbitrarily. In so doing, the interrogator is explaining to the person that he, the interrogator, acted professionally, in keeping with his protective duty, in order to keep people like the cleared suspect safe from criminals.[64] The police officer is effectively explaining to one of his employers—the taxpayer whom he just interrogated—that this unpleasant process was part of the protective and investigative service police provide. The interrogator's postinterrogation brief is akin to a doctor's apology to a patient for having caused her discomfort in the course of the examination and to the doctor's explanation for the role the uncomfortable procedure played in her overall treatment.

Guilty suspects may resent police deception, especially if it leads to their confession and to a subsequent conviction. It is not clear to me how we should assess this resentment. It seems *possible* that some first-time offenders might become more willing to re-offend because of a hardened attitude brought on by a realization that they were deceived by police. However, it seems likely that other environmental factors would be far more likely to influence a first time offender's future. Police deception might deter confessions from more experienced criminals, because of their memories of prior police deception. Yet more experienced criminals also know it is in their interest to remain silent during interrogation, with or without the prospect of police deception. The most compelling reason to see guilty suspects' resentment of police duplicity as salient regards the possible help ex-cons might give police regarding crimes with which they are uninvolved. It is certainly the case, judging from various accounts, that both career criminals and many noncriminal citizens of American inner cities view the police with hostility. It is beyond my competence to judge the likelihood that both groups would refuse to aid police due to occasional police duplicity in interrogations. It seems likely that actions and circumstances more widespread and public than deceptive interrogations are the key contributors toward poor police-community relations, including police harassment, police brutality, frequent (legitimate) arrests of people from the neighborhood, a general alienation from government among marginalized populations, and antiauthority instigations from community activists.[65] While police duplicity in interrogations likely does not help police-community relations, eliminating the practice will also likely not repair these relations. Also, whatever gains in community trust might be gained by forgoing deceptive techniques might be outweighed by the failure to close cases that could have only been solved with deceptive interrogations. It should be born in mind that effective policing is in the interest of those communities where distrust of police may be prevalent. No one wishes to be the victim of a serious crime, whatever his or her attitude toward the police. Tellingly, fear of a murderous pedophile prompted residents of LaTonya Wallace's neighborhood to cooperate with police despite a history of bad police-community relations. Crime also inhibits the expansion of businesses into underserved areas, which reduces the number of jobs as well as the availability of necessary services. Thus, at this level of generality, the possible negative consequences of community distrust do not seem sufficient to delegitimize the use of deceptive interrogations.

Another possible negative consequence to allowing deception in interrogations is personal and professional corruption of police personnel. After all, the interrogation manuals sometimes recommend deceptive practices that in different contexts are considered immoral. Commentators express concern that allowing deception in interrogations—to say nothing of other possible settings like stings and undercover work—may corrupt police officers' professional behavior.[66] One can imagine scenarios where interrogators not only become increasingly cavalier about lying in interrogations, but also committing perjury and lying to superior officers and attorneys. Police may be more willing to fabricate evidence, take bribes, or engage in other corrupt practices, encouraged by the legal acceptance of deception in interrogation. The thinking here is that an official acceptance of deception in interrogations signals to the officer that he is in a quasi-lawless atmosphere, where perhaps other normally illicit activities are also now acceptable. Corrupt behavior might be vaguely justified by individual corrupt officers with the thought that they are among the "good guys" struggling against the "bad guys" who themselves use every possible tactic to achieve their ends.[67]

Analogous concerns are sometimes expressed about police or soldiers becoming increasingly liberal in their use of force. Indeed, concerns over the negative influence of professional imperatives on personal morality face actors in many professional fields. Broader discussion on this topic than can be conducted here is surely needed, because at first blush, there is a striking inconsistency between ordinary moral expectation and the permissiveness society grants certain professionals. With hardly any explicit discussion or recognition, upon entering the workforce, many professionals are expected to leave behind the moral rules and virtues instilled since childhood. Soldiers after all, are asked—ordered—to *kill*; business executives, to pursue profits single-mindedly; lawyers, to sometimes assist loathsome people; doctors, to touch strangers in intimate places; etc. Each is asked to depart from "normal" moral behavior at work, but then expected to return to a conventional moral persona at home. While attention is sometimes paid to the higher than average incidences of domestic abuse and suicide among police and military personnel—and it makes the headlines when professional athletes behave violently in public—the truth is that many professions tend to significantly mark participants in socially undesirable ways. We all know doctors who are cold, business executives who are obsessed with money, lawyers who are argumentative, and professors who are arrogant. Yet at the same time, our society cannot do without these professionals, nor the kind of narrowly focused training necessary to prepare them for the workforce.

I do not have a ready conceptual metric for judging whether the risk of professional corruption for police interrogators is greater than for other professionals, or if the personal and social effects of such corruption are worse than in other fields. If there is less or equal risk for interrogators—and the society seems to tolerate the frequency and degree of corruption in *other* fields—then the risk of professional corruption for interrogators probably would not justify jettisoning deceptive interrogations. Barring some standard for assessing the relative risk of corruption, I do not see how we can use anecdotes or impressions of police corruption alone to justify abandoning generally efficacious and reliable interrogation tactics. There *would* be grounds for dissenting to deceptive interrogations if the effects of police corruption could be shown to offset whatever good police did by way of protecting inhabitants' lives and rights.

In all professions, law enforcement included, one response to the problem of moral temptations is to have better training, oversight, and evaluations, as well as more counseling to help people integrate their professional and moral imperatives. Training can compensate for social habituation when it comes to employing specialized professional skills. (The repetition of training, coupled with reward and punishment by the instructor, mimics the basic mechanism of habit formation.) In the law enforcement context, police officers studying for their detective's exam need to be told about the moral temptations associated with interrogation and need to discuss and model with experienced trainers how to manage that stress. Videotaping interrogations can facilitate better oversight, evaluations, and training of police interrogators. With respect to counseling, by way of comparison, there is now more acceptance within the American military that psychological counseling should be integrated into deployments in a universal and non-stigmatizing way to help war fighters process the traumatic events they have witnessed. Since many police officers have to routinely deal with difficult things, counseling of some sort should probably be a routine part of their professional life. The view that police *vehicles*, for example, need regular maintenance but police officers' minds will remain unaffected by the daily grind of policing is not sustainable.

With respect to interrogators in particular, it may be appropriate to have overseers who function partly like the "handlers" of undercover officers. Presumably, part of the handler's role is to tacitly remind the undercover officer of his or her professional responsibilities and to serve as a counterbalance to whatever socialization is occurring between the officer and his or her new associates. It seems appropriate to have an analogous party interacting with interrogators, acting in part as an overseer and in part as a therapist. This person—perhaps a more experienced officer—would regularly view some of the interrogator's interrogations and informally compare notes with him afterward.

The utility of this kind of review is as follows. If moral corruption is thought of as a person's new or growing indifference to what he once regarded as illicit,[68] it strikes me that this can occur when it seems that all of one's peers are engaging in suspect behavior, on the one hand, or when a person feels alone in the knowledge of what he's done, on the other. In the latter case, the relevant moral taboo perhaps loses some of its sting when the social sanction one was taught to expect fails to occur. For example, even though the detectives in Vallejo or Baltimore know they lied to suspects as part of their jobs, on some level it may *feel* like they just did something bad and got away with it. Guilt might combine with cynicism toward the whole moral order to make the interrogator feel like he is someone apart from the regular order, at once a pariah and an Übermensch entitled to break moral rules at will. Accordingly, the overseer's role would not be to punish the interrogator (unless he behaved unprofessionally), but in a sense, to normalize and rationalize the tactics the interrogator used. The interrogator may feel less morally isolated, less likely to be secretly ashamed of what he's done—and so less prone to corruption—if he has a regular opportunity to discuss his rationales for using particular approaches with an experienced peer. Knowing that he will have to explain his choices of tactics will also likely make the interrogator more thoughtful about what he does in the interrogation room. Following an interrogation, an interrogator might well discuss with his overseer if his lies were necessary rather than covers for laziness or inept investigation. He might take the opportunity to remind himself that the reasons for lying are relatively restricted, and that they should be deployed with a degree of self-awareness that their utterance does not becomes casual. Since on some moral views, lying is always forbidden, I think it is also right to say the state cannot order police to lie, whether in interrogations or in other instances; individual interrogators might well choose to refrain from lying as a personal policy.[69]

In this chapter, I have argued that deceptive interrogations appear to be generally efficacious, reliable, and in certain situations, indispensable. They do not necessarily violate suspects' political rights. They are therefore a legitimate part of a liberal state's police powers. Concerns about the effects of employing deceptive interrogations, including soured police-community relations, possible false confessions, and the personal and professional corruption of police do not seem sufficient to rule out these interrogations on prudential grounds, so they may be used when well-trained interrogators feel they are necessary. The prudential concerns do suggest that interrogators need to be carefully trained, monitored, and supported in order to use deceptive techniques only when necessary. I also argued that police interrogations should be videotaped; that trial rules should be changed so that defendants are not convicted on uncorroborated confessions alone; and that the confessions of defendants with mental retardation be discounted without the provision in the confession of corroborating details.

PART TWO

Interrogation in International Contexts

SIX

Prisoners of War and Other
Martial Detainees

In May of 2007, six foreign-born residents of New Jersey were arrested for plotting to attack soldiers at Ft. Dix with rocket-propelled grenades and automatic weapons. The plotters had allegedly watched al-Qaeda terrorist training videos; conducted weapons training; and attempted to buy automatic weapons from undercover FBI agents. While inspired by Osama bin Laden, they were apparently not given explicit orders from abroad. Are these men simple criminal suspects, prisoners of war (POWs), or members of some other class of detainees? Were they plotting an act of war or simple murder? They were not acting with pecuniary motives, as many criminals do, nor were they planning to kill to settle a score; silence a witness; or otherwise defend a criminal enterprise. They had political motives and allegedly planned to attack military targets—in these respects resembling soldiers—and yet they were operating on their own, rather than as members of an organized military body. They were neither obeying the orders of a superior nor acting at the behest of a nation-state.

Their categorization as criminal suspects, POWs, or other types of detainees is important because this categorization indicates different treatment following their arrest. If they are criminal suspects, they must be informed of rights to remain silent and to have counsel present during interrogation. Interrogations cannot exceed several hours length lest any subsequent confessions be quashed at trial. Criminal defendants must be sentenced according to civilian law and given a finite prison term or capital sentence if convicted. By contrast, POWs have no right to counsel and are not brought to criminal trial. They cannot be abused or threatened in interrogation but may be interrogated as often as the detaining power desires. While their mode of detention is usually more comfortable than that of criminal convicts, it lasts for an indefinite period, until the end of hostilities. Finally, some argue that there is properly a third class of detainees, "unlawful enemy combatants," who do not qualify for any of these protections.

The purpose of this chapter and the two following is to address inter-rogation ethics in an international context. This chapter will categorize various kinds of prisoners apart from domestic criminals who might come under the control of a state during wartime or in the context of international intelligence operations. Such persons will often be foreign nationals. It is necessary to categorize different types of prisoners prior to addressing their interrogation, because the differences in the relationship people have to foreign states may indicate different sets of prisoner rights and interrogation rules than those discussed in the previous chapters. We must also consider if the differences between war and law enforcement indicate different pris-oner rights and interrogation rules.

This chapter will refer to the Western just war tradition in order to eluci-date the rights of prisoners of war as well as other kinds of martial detainees. The Western just war tradition has an ancient lineage, drawing from classical Roman political theory, Christian theology, and medieval codes of chivalry. Authors working in these different milieus arrived at a fairly consistent set of criteria for judging the justice of going to war (*jus ad bellum*) and the justice of particular tactics within war (*jus in bello*). In the seventeenth century, jurists began using these moral principles as the framework for international laws of war, which have developed to include the late nineteenth and twentieth century Hague and Geneva Conventions.

As we will see, the justification for the special treatment of POWs relies on rationales drawn from the three strands of the just war tradition. This tripartite foundation produces some conceptual puzzles when the disparate sources of the tradition do not recommend the same treatment for martial detainees *other* than conventional soldiers, such as guerillas, terrorists, sabo-teurs, and spies. Much of this chapter will therefore be focused on delin-eating what status and treatment these "irregular" combatants deserve. By "irregular combatant," I mean anyone engaging in political violence (i.e., intended to change a government's behavior) who is not in conventional military uniform, and/or not obeying unified military command, and/or not in the employ or under the conscription of an internationally recog-nized nation-state. Examples of different kinds of irregulars are given below in the section called "Irregular Combatants." I will occasionally refer to extant international law in what follows but will be mainly making a moral argument in reference to the just war tradition; unless otherwise specified, references to "morality" will mean the principles of the Western just war tradition. Since the just war tradition is not limited to states with a particular political character, I will address comparative questions about a liberal state's treatment of its own inhabitants versus that of foreigners with the political theory used in the previous chapters. Finally, in addition to the generic "war fighter," I will use the term "soldier" as a general reference to a state's conventional war-fighting personnel, rather than in the restricted sense of "a member of the army."

The Western Just War Tradition

Classical Roman thinkers conceived of war making as a basic right of states. To judge the legitimacy of a particular war, thinkers like Cicero asked whether a given war had a just cause (e.g., defense or redress of past political wrongs); if the person or group declaring the war had the authority to do so; whether the anticipated benefit of the war outweighed its anticipated harms; whether the eventual aim of the war was peace; and whether the war was the state's last resort to address its grievances.[1] Early Christian thinkers were forced to balance Jesus's apparent pacifism with the coercive responsibilities of the state when the Roman Empire became officially Christian in 313 CE.[2] One theological solution was to draw a distinction between outward action and inward intention; this allowed for the possibility that a soldier or political leader could maintain a properly pacific and loving attitude toward others even while physically engaged in the necessarily violent business of the state. This focus on right intention (both in evaluating the justice of the war and the propriety of individual soldiers' actions) introduced a personal element into just war thinking. St. Augustine and others were sensitive to the possibility that right actions can be done for the wrong reasons; for example, a soldier might fight in a justly defensive campaign motivated by greed for booty rather than the desire to protect his fellow citizens. Developing an understanding that would become key to later justifications of POWs' special treatment, Augustine and others saw soldiers as *morally blameless* for killing enemy soldiers and destroying military targets because (and only if) they acted out of obedience to the state instead of personal animus. On this view, moral blame or praise for launching the war is properly directed at the political rulers, rather than the soldiers who are the mere servants of the state.

As Augustine appropriated secular (Roman) concepts for theological use, the chivalric codes purportedly observed by medieval knights were appropriated by contemporary Christian thinkers to establish *jus in bello* criteria. Knights, we are told, tended to see enemy knights as equals who were worthy of respect by virtue of their class and training. Moreover, as experts in many fields feel disdain for challenges or competitors they feel beneath them, the chivalrous notion of killing and dying well entailed the use of a knight's martial expertise only in combat with other able-bodied knights—not civilians. Nor was it fitting for knights to act as mere butchers in executing captured or wounded combatants. Respect for their opponents meant no more enemy combatants should be killed than absolutely necessary. Certain weapons or tactics (e.g., crossbows, camouflage, ambush) that enabled those with little skill or bravery to kill were prohibited during certain periods. These codes were appropriated by late medieval Christian thinkers like Suarez and Vitoria and expressed as the three main components of *jus in bello*. Regardless of the justice or injustice of the campaign in which they find themselves, all war fighters are to discriminate between combatants and noncombatants when using force ("the principle of discrimination"). They should never cause more damage to persons or property than is necessary to achieve legitimate military goals ("the principle of proportionality"), and they should not use weapons that cause their victims more suffering than is necessary.

The Moral Impunity of Soldiers

The moral impunity (and, in recent centuries, legal immunity) of soldiers depends on their doing the business of the state. While soldiers may perform acts that *look* like the acts done by murderers, vandals, and arsonists, their killing of enemy combatants or destroying military targets is not given the moral designation "murder," "vandalism," or "arson," because the actions are a result of obedience, ultimately, to their political leaders, instead of personal volition. Their personal moral faculties of reason and will in a sense are inert: the conscripted infantryman does not choose his vocation, his nation's policies, his general's strategy, or his NCO's tactics. He does not know the enemy soldier he attacks and so cannot have anything *personally* against him. (I will refer to this argument for moral impunity as the "political justification.") This is why the sort of moral analysis done in chapter 1 is not appropriate for explaining why one soldier may justifiably kill another.[3] There is an argument to be made that people are morally responsible for the choice to enter into the military (if they have not been drafted). However, just war theorists typically invoke Vitoria's doctrine of "invincible ignorance" to excuse even volunteer soldiers from culpability over the decision to enter into the military. This, because of the prima facie value of serving one's country; the uncertainty of whether future wars will be just; the limited information a soldier has about a campaign because of military secrecy; and the difficulty of judging the justice of any particular war.

By contrast, the individual soldier *is* morally responsible for *how* he fights. The *jus in bello* restrictions can be understood as giving political form to soldiers' violent behavior, making an individual soldier's actions expressive of state action. A soldier is authorized by his own government to use force only against an enemy government, which in the context of a war, means the enemy's military personnel, materiel, and infrastructure. The *jus in bello* restrictions can be understood as channeling soldiers' violence toward this end in an efficient manner. *Only* the enemies' troops and materiel are to be targeted; no more of it is to be destroyed than is necessary for victory; and no more suffering than is associated with incapacitation should be inflicted on those troops whose incapacitation is vital to victory. A soldier is doing the state's business if restricting his use of force to these parameters. Behavior outside these parameters does not help advance the political aim of victory and so is extraneous to the state's purpose. It therefore goes wide of the purpose for which the state authorizes certain people to use force. The massacre of civilians, the killing of more troops than necessary, mutilation of the dead, rape, pillage, the killing or mistreatment of prisoners, and other war crimes are not legitimate state actions, and so perpetrating soldiers cannot claim to merely be carrying out the will of the state. Here the Christian contribution to the just war tradition is most germane. Soldiers must be acting on their own initiative when doing things that are not in service of the state. They therefore cannot claim moral impunity on account of political obedience. Rather, their own moral faculties are evidently in play, and so they are morally culpable for the things they do.[4] Under these circumstances, it is appropriate to employ the sort of moral analysis used in chapter 1 to analyze their actions and to criminally prosecute them in a court martial.[5]

Prisoners of War

On the evening of January 18, 2005, U.S. soldiers with the 1st Battalion, 5th Infantry Stryker Brigade Combat Team of the 25th Infantry Division were nearing the end of their patrol in Tal Afar, Iraq, when a car appeared in the distance. Civilian vehicles were not supposed to be on the road then as it was past curfew. The troops fired warning shots as the car sped toward them and then fired at the vehicle when it failed to stop. The car held an Iraqi family of seven. Parents Hussein and Camila Hassan were killed instantly, and their son Racan, 11, was seriously wounded in the abdomen.[6]

This section will discuss the development of the laws and customs of war with regard to prisoners of war and then will evaluate the three main justifications for this treatment mentioned in the literature. The purpose of this evaluation is to determine the relative importance of these justifications before using one or more of them to delineate appropriate treatment for captured irregular combatants. I will argue that the aforementioned political justification for soldiers' moral impunity is the most salient justification for POW status, stronger than the two other commonly raised justifications regarding soldiers' honor and prudence.

Battlefield captives were once at the mercy of their captors—to often summarily have their throats cut and armor stripped, if not suffering enslavement instead or public parade as war booty followed by torture for the gratification of the capturing power's citizenry. Happily, recent centuries have witnessed increasingly standardized, humane, and reciprocal treatment of prisoners of war. A basic principle guiding treatment of POWs is that once a combatant is disarmed and taken prisoner, he is no longer a combatant but a "protected person" like a civilian, whose detention is only to prevent him from returning to battle. His detention is neither punitive nor retributive. He is not to be criminally prosecuted for his legitimate wartime actions (i.e., directing violence at the capturing power's military assets).[7] Neutralized as a military threat, and morally and legally innocent (assuming he has not committed war crimes), there is no purpose or justification for his mistreatment in detention.[8] While in detention, he is to be treated on par with the capturing power's own troops.

The long list of POW rights in the Third Geneva Convention (ratified in 1949) exemplifies this parity.[9] According to the Convention, POWs are allowed to wear their own uniforms and insignias of rank; they are to be housed along with their appropriate units or at least with members of their own nation's troops; they are to be housed, fed, and provided medical care in a manner comparable to the capturing power's troops; they may not be discriminated against based on race, nationality, or religion; they can send and receive mail (subject to military censorship); they cannot be mistreated, humiliated, tortured, or put on public display; they may organize recreational activities among themselves and are even due a salary that can be used in a camp canteen. The capturing power must inform the POW's state of his capture within ten days; to this end, the POW is required to provide his name, rank, and serial number. He may be interrogated (without the presence of counsel) but is not obliged to provide anything beyond this basic information. This means he cannot be harmed, threatened, or punished for refusing to provide interrogators with any other piece of information. As mentioned above, POWs cannot be criminally prosecuted for legitimate wartime activities including killing or maiming the military personnel of the capturing power or destroying its military materiel, or killing civilians, or destroying civilian infrastructure in the course of an attack on a military target. POWs *may* be prosecuted for war crimes, though by the same procedures and in the same impartial and independent courts used to try the capturing power's own troops; they are not to be tried in civilian criminal court. War crimes include acts that are considered crimes in peacetime like murder, rape, and theft, as well as breaches of the customs and laws of war such as executing prisoners, faking surrender, using civilian clothes as camouflage, etc.

The *political justification* for soldiers' moral impunity and legal immunity for military action, as discussed above, is that they are merely acting as agents of the state. They are not personally choosing to kill for the reasons murderers choose to kill. On this line of thinking, it is the individual soldier who pulls the trigger, but in a sense, *the state* who kills enemy soldiers. This justification for soldier's moral impunity and legal immunity provides a justification for the special treatment of POWs. Since they have done nothing wrong, their detention should be nonpunitive. Even though the POW may have killed the capturing power's troops and destroyed its equipment and infrastructure, the capturing power must acknowledge that it has authorized its own troops to do the same abroad, so the enemy POWs are no better or worse on this account than the capturing power's own forces. This recognition of the "moral equality" of soldiers justifies parity in treatment between POWs and the capturing power's own troops.

Irregular combatants must actually be acting like state agents when captured in order to hope to qualify for POW status. (Again, the language of the Third Geneva Convention tracks the morally relevant descriptors.) They must be wearing uniforms or some identifying emblem; carrying their arms in the open; acting under the orders of someone responsible for his subordinates; and otherwise obeying the laws and customs of war. (I will refer to these below as the "four criteria.") In short, they must look and act like soldiers from a nation-state's conventional military.[10] The moral relevance of the third and fourth criteria has already been explained. Self-identification is part of the role of the combatant because combatancy is one of the many state roles that require a certain social recognition and reaction on the part of others in order for the state agent to do his or her job with its appropriate moral authority. For example, in a liberal state, were a person to barge into a restaurant's kitchen and rifle through the pantry, the chefs would be justified in demanding the intruder leave, and even physically restraining him if he refused. However, the chefs would know that the person has the authority to inspect the kitchen—and that they would be wrong to stop him—if he was wearing a health department badge. The health inspector depends on this sort of compliance, because not equipped to storm kitchens by force and fight off attacks from furious chefs while looking for tainted mushrooms. The health inspector would be unable to perform his job without this social recognition and deference toward his moral authority; accomplishing his task would instead be contingent on mere force, in which case his role would presuppose a radically illiberal relation between state and inhabitant, likely obviating the very purpose of a public health inspector. Other types of state functions involving nonhierarchical cooperation, like diplomatic negotiation, would also be impossible if relying on force. State agents who deal with foreign counterparts, like diplomats and trade representatives, must be able to recognize their foreign counterparts and recognize their authority to act on behalf of other states in order to do their jobs. Similarly, soldiers must identify themselves to each other in order for both to do the job of soldiering: they need to know where to shoot and where not to shoot. (The nature of combat precludes the proffering of identification badges or identification through protocol, hence the need for uniforms or some emblem identifiable at a distance.)

Soldiering also includes duties that assume civilians' ability to identify soldiers. Police officers of an enemy state are usually considered civilians, and so immune from military attack, but this deference is contingent on the police officers' noninterference with invading troops. Police officers' noninterference presumably depends on their recognizing that these armed men are soldiers and not mere criminals. This mutual recognition of combatancy has beneficial effects for both states' militaries even though war fighting is not a quasi-cooperative endeavor like diplomacy. Soldiers can do their job more efficiently if they know who is an enemy combatant and who is not, potentially ending the war sooner, and soldiers on both sides can relax when in their own barracks, behind their own lines, among prisoners, and when among their own citizenry or those of occupied territory. War is more awful to combatants and civilians alike without these limits. There is likely no way to distinguish soldiers from adult civilians if soldiers don't self-identify; in this event, everyone (over a certain age) becomes a logical target.

In short, in a strictly physical sense, anyone *can* behave violently, but in war, it is primarily the military representatives of the state who *may* behave violently. A uniform identifies the combatant as someone with the moral authority to act in this way, signally to others how they ought to behave in response. Therefore, self-identification as a certain kind of state agent is an essential part of soldiering. It is his acting as a state agent that justifies his moral impunity and legal immunity for combat violence, and so his special status in detention. Therefore, irregular combatants must wear uniforms or some kind of emblem designating them as a state agent or quasi-state agent to hope to qualify for POW status.

A second justification for POW status is that captured soldiers who have obeyed the laws of war *deserve* "benevolent quarantine"—to use lawyers' language—because of the respect soldiers owe one another.[11] Soldiers expose themselves to mortal risk by donning uniforms and carrying their arms in the open during war time. Military professionals owe their opposite numbers respect for engaging in the same dangerous and selfless task.[12] There is an additional element to this argument implied by discussions of the respect irregular combatants *forfeit* by *not* wearing uniforms. Indeed, the argument connecting military honor to POW status is more often implied by positions denying certain irregulars POW status than it is explicitly asserted. Unlike saboteurs, terrorists, and some guerillas, uniformed combatants do not disguise themselves as civilians, striking only when their enemy's guard is down. These irregulars are cowardly or devious for avoiding the normal risks of combat and fighting "dirty," as well as for exposing civilians to needless danger by blurring the distinction between combatant and civilian.[13] So by implication, uniformed combatants are owed respect both for their courage and their adherence to the principle of discrimination (by not needlessly endangering civilians). A third justification for affording POW status to combatants is simply prudential: the capturing power affords enemy prisoners good treatment because it wishes its own captured troops to be treated in the same way.[14]

These latter two justifications for POW status are weaker than the political justification. On the subject of military virtue, it is certainly true that soldiers expose themselves to great risk by donning uniforms and carrying their weapons in the open. Yet risk taking unto itself is not worthy of moral respect, because many risky behaviors are stupid, irresponsible, and dangerous to third parties. Serving the state in a dangerous role—at least a basically just state—is respectable insofar as one aids the state in protecting and bettering the lives of inhabitants. Yet it seems odd for a state to honor enemy troops' bravery and service, if this is the rationale for their benign treatment of POWs. Some soldiers, politicians, and citizens may be able to acknowledge what Michael Walzer calls the moral equality of soldiers: on both sides of the trench young men and women find themselves pitted against one another, legally obliged to risk their lives in attempts to take those of strangers—all on account of decisions made by their elders. Yet it seems above and beyond the normal business of the state to reward the virtue of foreigners, akin to the U.S. National Endowment of the Arts awarding a medal to a French painter. Such things can and do happen in extraordinary circumstances, but they lack the compelling and necessary characteristics of most regular government actions, of which POW policy would seem to be an example. Such behavior is especially discordant in war time, when generally, the bare minimum of humanitarian respect for foreign citizens (at best) guides the behavior of antagonistic states. Also, in most cases, brave enemy actions would be of the sort coming at the expense of the capturing power's own troops—hardly occasions to celebrate—and the enemies' merely dutiful behavior, presumably, would not be of the sort meriting special foreign attention.

Further, irregular combatants' failure to wear uniforms is not necessarily indicative of a lack of courage.[15] Conventional combatants or intelligence officers sometimes slip behind enemy lines in civilian clothes to spy, destroy military targets, or conduct raids. While these so-called secret agents and intelligence officers *are* taking advantage of their enemy's lowered vigilance in his own territory, they are surely not acting cowardly, because taking tremendous risks behind enemy lines.[16] On the other hand, wholesale acknowledgment of soldiers' courage simply by dint of wearing uniforms seems anachronistic given that modern military technology sometimes allows operators to kill without any great danger to themselves.[17] For example, beyond the inherent dangers of submarine operations, American and British sailors firing cruise missiles against Taliban targets from submarines in the Indian Ocean in 2001 had nothing to fear from an enemy lacking a navy.

At any rate, conscription obviates the claim about courage for many POWs, and military discipline, for all others. Conscripted soldiers have not chosen to enter their dangerous profession; for all the capturing power knows, they are cowards and would-be traitors marched to the front at gunpoint. Further, all soldiers in conventional units, whether conscripted or not, are *compelled* by their superiors to wear uniforms. Even the cowardly soldier who wishes to discard his uniform and weapon cannot so long as his command is competent. Viewed this way, the argument that an identifiable combatant is automatically due special honor seems an anachronistic holdover from the chivalric strand of the just war tradition.[18]

Conscription and mandatory dress do not change the duty to discriminate between combatants and civilians. The second half of the justification concerning soldiers' honor argued that uniformed soldiers deserve POW status because they respect civilians' rights by identifying themselves as combatants. By wearing uniforms or some identifiable martial emblem, combatants are in effect saying to the enemy: shoot here, at me (but not over there at the civilians). As already indicated, combatants' wearing of civilian clothing on the battlefield is immoral, in part, because it puts civilians at undue risk. After the disguised soldiers attack, the enemy will no longer assume civilians are unthreatening and so may begin actively attacking civilians, as occurred in the cavalier categorization of villages as "VC-controlled" during the Vietnam War (relegating them to free-fire zones), or be so nervous around them that civilians are often killed in misunderstandings. Reports from Iraq suggest killings of civilians in circumstances like the ones described above in Tal Afar are common, because of legitimate fears about suicide bombers and car bombs. Rather than protect civilians, or at least seek to isolate them from the fighting, some irregular combatants intentionally confuse the combatant and civilian identities, effectively using civilians as human shields. Worse, their intent may be to deliberately provoke indiscriminate government reprisals against the civilian population in order to mobilize public opinion against the government.[19]

The involuntary nature of conventional troops' dress is determinative on this point as well. The just war tradition's *jus in bello* restrictions apply to the individual soldier such that he is, for example, morally responsible for failing to discriminate between enemy combatants and civilians or for failing to distinguish himself from nearby civilians. So the moral terms of *jus in bello* are relevant only in cases where the soldier can exercise volition. He ought to be blamed if he *chooses* to discard his uniform and attack while disguised as a civilian, but cannot be praised for doing in another instance what he was not able to refuse—wearing his uniform while his commander was in the vicinity. So, in sum, while volunteer war fighters often are due respect for their sacrifice, and individual combatants of all stripes may be due respect for their integrity and valor, honor among soldiers appears to be a weak justification for POW status being universally afforded to conventional combatants.

There is a stronger case to be made for the prudential justification of special POW status. The reasoning associated with the justification seems unassailable: both states in an interstate conflict agree to treat POWs humanely and forgo criminal prosecution, because each wishes for the humane treatment and speedy return of its own captured troops after the war. Simple self-interest motivates compliance. A prudential justification can account for benign treatment of POWs even when leaders of warring states distrust or hate one another, and even when they look at foreign citizens as undeserving of treatment on par with domestic citizens. However, difficulties arise in *intra*state conflicts when irregular fighters may lack the means to hold government prisoners or hold them in humane circumstances.[20] The rejoinder to critics of this apparently unfair asymmetry[21] is that a government holds out the promise of POW status to irregulars as an incentive for them to comply with the four criteria, even barring reciprocity in prisoner detention. (Presumably, the government would expect that the irregulars release government prisoners they do not have the ability to detain.)[22] There are several prudential reasons for governmental forces wanting irregulars to comply with the four criteria. First, particularly since they may lack the facilities and resources to hold government soldiers, irregulars lack an incentive to let government prisoners live if not promised benevolent quarantine themselves. Second, government soldiers are endangered when irregulars disguise themselves as civilians or as fellow government soldiers. Irregulars dressed in civilian clothes or government uniforms can literally creep past government soldiers' doorsteps, as was witnessed when a suicide bomber dressed as a cafeteria worker killed twenty-two U.S. service personnel in a mess hall in Mosul in December of 2004.[23] This tactic is different than an ambush with camouflaged conventional troops, because in those circumstances, the ambushed side is at least typically deployed in force: on patrol, in body armor, weapons deployed—generally ready for engagement. Also, whereas the patrol may not have seen the camouflaged enemy, they at least know where to aim once the shooting starts. This brings up a third, and more straightforward, point: the government soldier knows who his enemy is and whom to engage if the irregular identifies himself. By contrast, the irregular masquerading as something other than an enemy combatant may catch the government soldier in his relatively relaxed posture behind the front line, on base, or in barracks. The government side will want to protect these times of relative calm for their soldiers if for no other reason than because constant combat stress quickly degrades soldiers' effectiveness.

Fourth, a soldier's duty of discrimination is made much harder if irregular combatants masquerade as civilians. This tactic courts war crimes and forces the soldier to view his personal safety at odds with his scruples. As in Tal Afar, the soldier may become the victim of a suicide bomber if he waits to determine if the car approaching him is full of innocent civilians, but he may end up killing innocents if he errs on the side of caution and opens fire. Irregulars' tendency to hide weapons or other materiel in civilian locations also forces soldiers to raid homes, schools, and places of worship, at the constant risk of alienating, if not inadvertently harming civilians.

Aside from the benefits accruing to government forces when irregulars comply with the four criteria, there is another potential cost for the government if irregulars are denied POW status. Refusing to extend POW status to irregular combatants may reduce the likelihood of their surrendering when it might otherwise be tactically indicated. Irregulars may choose to fight to the death rather than face criminal prosecution under a capital charge, or suffer worse treatment, if they are judged by the capturing power to fall into a legal gray area, and so are unprotected from torture.[24]

These prudential reasons can answer the question of why a government might want to grant irregulars POW status when the irregulars are not in a position to reciprocate. However, they are not moral reasons, linked, for example, to what combatants deserve by dint of their roles, intentions, or behaviors. The prudential reasons regarding tactical advantages and quarter for captured government troops are ones of simple self-interest from the government's point of view.[25] It cannot be that there are only prudential reasons—but no moral reasons—for affording POW status (with its entailments of parity of treatment and legal immunity) to captured conventional or irregular combatants. If there were only prudential reasons, there would be no nonarbitrary reason for treating POWs according to the principle of parity or for giving them legal immunity for their combat activities. Prudentially, *any* kind of good treatment could serve as incentive for enemy combatants' compliance with the four criteria, particularly for some irregular combatants. It would seem sufficient (and cheaper), for example, for a wealthy country to treat detainees from its much poorer rival state better than their own government does but not as well as the capturing power's own soldiers. Given the miserable state of some contemporary nations' militaries, to say nothing of the lifestyles of cave-dwelling irregulars, the promise of three meals a day, health care, or an environment free from hazing might suffice to encourage compliance with the four criteria—if not also prompting desertions. These incentives could even conceivably be coupled with legal prosecution for irregulars' combat actions. Irregular combatants must know they will be viewed as outlaws, traitors, or terrorists by the government they are fighting. They likely see the chances of their being captured or killed as high, so even a government promise of criminal prosecution (which they expect anyway) coupled with humane treatment might be sufficient motivation for irregulars to observe the four criteria.

It was argued above that the justification appealing to honor is weak on its own and the argument appealing to prudence fails to account for the two main components of POW status. By contrast, the political justification does explain POWs' legal immunity and treatment equal to that of the capturing power's own soldiers. The political justification holds that all combatants meeting the four criteria are moral equals, innocent of the political decisions their leaders make, engaged in a morally upright and legal activity. They have done nothing deserving of punitive detention or criminal prosecution. They should be held in conditions similar to those enjoyed by the capturing power's own troops because they are no better and no worse, as a class, than the capturing power's own troops.

The purpose of this discussion of rationales for special POW status has been to determine which one is salient, or which is the most salient, so we can determine the criteria to use in judging various irregular combatants' qualification for POW status. The degree to which combatants are honorable fighters, or have the capacity to hold enemy prisoners in humane circumstances, is irrelevant to combatants' potential POW status. POW status is justified principally because conventional soldiers are state agents rather than due to warriors' honor or to prudence. So what then of irregular combatants who do not formally represent a state or who lack some of the conventional elements signifying that role? I will argue below that the status of irregular combatants in detention should be determined by how nearly they approach the role of conventional troops in controlling territory and offering basic services to inhabitants of that territory.

Irregular Combatants

In the spring of 2007, a team of American and Dutch soldiers, Afghan policemen, and American military contractors were razing poppy fields in the Uruzgan Province of Afghanistan when they came under fire from a nearby village. After the several-hour battle ended and a captive taken, it was not immediately clear if the attackers were the drug dealers whose assets were being destroyed, the impoverished villagers the drug dealers contract to grow the poppies, the Taliban militants the drug dealers pay for protection (who depend on drug money to subsidize their insurgency), or the local warlord's militia members.[26]

The main purpose of guerilla tactics is to harass and overextend conventional forces rather than to attack them directly en masse in the manner of a conventional armed force. Tactics include raids on supply lines and convoys, sniping on patrols, the use of booby traps, the destruction of non-military government property, the assassination of government figures, and terrorism. As Mao's general Chu Teh famously put it, "The enemy advances, we retreat; the enemy camps, we harass; the enemy tires, we attack; the enemy retreats, we pursue." While conventionally weaker than regular military units, those employing guerilla tactics use their relatively small numbers and lack of materiel to their advantage. They are able to move quickly, unburdened by logistics trains (instead living off the land or depending on civilians for sustenance), able to disappear into the jungle or mountains after an attack, or blend in with the surrounding civilians. The irregular combatant cannot hope to defeat the government through direct military confrontation (at least initially) but can sap its resources and overstretch its military by seeming to be everywhere at once, "a thing intangible, invulnerable, without front and back, drifting about like a gas."[27] A conventional force can often guard against attack from other conventional military units with a fair degree of efficiency, because the size of conventional detachments and weight of their equipment strictly limit conventional forces to certain routes and points of egress. For example, armored columns can only pass across bridges strong enough to bear their weight and cannot proceed through dense jungle or up the sheer sides of cliffs. By contrast, guerillas' random attacks on supply depots, outposts, or convoys require the government to bolster its forces universally, rather than just at traditional strategic points. For example, guerilla attacks led to the relegation of one third of the Union's troops to guard duty during the American Civil War; T. E. Lawrence's three thousand Arab tribesmen tied down fifty thousand Turks in the Arabian peninsula during WWI; and harassment by the "franc-tireurs" led to one third of the 450,000 German troops in France being posted to "station commands" along a railroad only 250 miles long during the Franco-Prussian War.[28] More recently, roadside bombs left by insurgents have been the number one killer of U.S. troops in the Iraq War.

If conventional military tactics are meant to force political action by concrete military gains like control of territory or destruction of military assets, it could be said that guerilla warfare (when unallied to a conventional force) is meant to force political action through a direct effect on the leadership's political will.[29] The hope of many who employ guerilla tactics is that the government will capitulate to their terms rather than see their coffers drained by interminable low-grade warfare in the hinterlands or that the government will collapse because of the political tensions caused by the fighting and expenditures. Apart from tangible economic effects, guerilla tactics are also typically intended to convince leaders and the citizenry that the war is unwinnable or that it is not worth fighting anymore and so it is better to accede to the guerillas' terms. Again, spectacular military successes are not essential; instead, a steady rate of relatively minor engagements—a derailed train here, a roadside bomb there—will exhaust the public's patience. This is particularly effective if the public is already disenchanted with the war or dubious of the justice of the government's policy toward the minority group the irregulars represent.

As exemplified in the ambush in Uruzgan, there are many different possible types of irregular combatant groups. Some sort of categorization of irregulars is necessary prior to assessment of their rights in detention, because the irregulars' profiles vary widely, from the remnant of a conventional army fighting an invader to a doomsday cult intent on wide-scale massacre. Seven different kinds of irregular combatants in intrastate conflicts are categorized below, with the organizing principle being their relation to a state, remnant state, or nascent state, rather than the particular tactics the groups or individuals regularly employ. Examples of some historical irregular combatant groups or individuals have been included in the list below to illustrate the abstract descriptions. The placement of particular historical groups and individuals in one or another category will not be further defended as this would depend on detailed factual and historical analyses of the groups beyond the focus of this book. Nothing vital to my argument is at stake in the placement of one group or other in a particular category, and the reader may well prefer a different assignment for a given irregular group.[30] The claims of different types of irregulars to POW status will be assessed in the next section.

Irregular combatants:

a) The remnant of a conventional army that adopts irregular tactics after being cut off from the main force, or after the defeat of the government by a foreign power, such as the Soviet Red Army units that were isolated in the forests of Western Russia by the rapid German advance or the Baathist groups in U.S.-occupied Iraq composed of former Iraqi Army or Republican Guard troops.

b) An irregular political and military organization that effectively represents a distinct group and/or controls territory within or nearby a state under foreign occupation, like the Spanish guerillas who fought Napoleon, Tito's partisans in Yugoslavia and the French Maquis partisans during WWII, Hezbollah in Israeli-occupied Southern Lebanon, and the Mahdi Army in U.S.-occupied Iraq.

c) An irregular political and military organization that effectively represents a distinct group and/or controls territory within or nearby a state under colonial rule, such as the Boers in South Africa, the IRA in Northern Ireland, the Vietminh in French Indo-China, the Mau Mau in British-controlled Kenya, and the FLN in French Algeria.

d) An irregular political and military organization that effectively controls territory within or nearby a state without an effective government, following a revolution, civil war, decolonization, coup, or other form of state collapse. For example, the NLF (i.e., Vietcong) in Vietnam, Mao's Red Army in China, the Kosovo Liberation Army in Serbia, and the early 1990s-era Taliban in Afghanistan.

e) An irregular political and military organization that effectively controls territory within or nearby a state with a settled form of government, such as Castro's group in Cuba, FARC in Columbia, Shining Path and Tupacamaru in Peru, Abu Sayyaf in the Philippines, and the ANC in apartheid-era South Africa.

f) Stateless agitator for global or regional change (group), such as al-Qaeda or Che Guevara's *foco*.

g) Violent individual agitator for political change, like Timothy McVeigh or Theodore Kaczynski ("the Unabomber").

I have left out from this list five classes of irregulars seen in *inter*state conflicts. These include detached groups of conventional troops operating deep in enemy territory and using unconventional tactics like "Merrill's Marauders" and the "Chindits" in WWII, as well as irregular groups of indigenous people organized by outsiders to serve as auxiliaries to a conventional force like the Arab tribes organized by T. E. Lawrence in WWI or the Hmong armies organized by CIA and U.S. Special Forces officers in Southeast Asia. Both of these types of irregulars can be considered in the same light as regular combatants since they are obeying a unified command and operating as auxiliaries to conventional state actors. They ought to be afforded POW status, provided they wear uniforms or identifying emblems and obey the laws of war. I have also left out so-called secret agents and intelligence officers. Members of a conventional military or civilian intelligence agency conducting violent acts behind enemy lines in civilian dress or enemy uniform should be afforded POW status since they are state agents, yet can be tried for war crimes since they were out of uniform. (It is trivial from the capturing power's perspective whether the person engaged in sabotage, raids, terrorism, or assassination works for the military or a civilian intelligence agency: in either case, they are nonuniformed persons engaging in political violence.) While these operators could not plausibly be charged with cowardice given the risks they are taking, they are not operating fully in accordance with the profile of state agents and so cannot enjoy the impunity and immunity of state agents. I will beg a discussion of the rights of detained intelligence officers engaged in nonviolent activities such as surveillance, recruitment, and incitement—a complicated matter—to remain focused on combatants. I have also left out the *levee en masse* of private citizens spontaneously taking up arms (or using those provided by the government) to defend their homes and neighborhoods from invaders, such as the franc-tireurs who harried the Prussian occupiers in France in the 1870s or the Serbian peasants who attacked Nazis with axes and pitchforks in WWII. The justification for their actions is rooted in arguments about property rights and patriotism rather than the just war tradition per se.[31]

I have not made a distinction in this list between guerillas and terrorists because the terms "guerilla" and "terrorist" are more intelligibly assigned to tactics than persons or groups. "Terrorism," which I define as "intentional attacks on civilian targets meant to create a political effect through the inducement of wide-scale terror," has been employed by states, individuals, transnational groups, secret agents, and various kinds of irregular combatant groups. The definition includes too many types of groups to be a useful term of organization. For its part, "guerillas" is also too broad a categorizing term if it is used to describe detached groups of regular military troops living off the land and using unconventional tactics, indigenous groups of militants organized by outside advisers, volunteer militias, anticolonial rebels, revolutionaries, partisans, and levees en masse.

Irregular Combatants and POW Status

To assess whether POW status is appropriate for various classes of irregular combatants, we need to analyze the bases for the special status of POWs: the relationship between states and conventional combatants. In chapter 2, I argued it is irrational for a person to dissent to the police powers of the basically just state in which she enjoys her life and rights and to particular police tactics that effectively, efficiently, and proportionately maintain a relatively crime-free environment. A government's jurisdiction spans the territory over which it can administer and enforce its laws. The justification for police powers aimed at protecting inhabitants' lives and rights is also adequate to justify proportionate military and intelligence operations aimed at the same goal when the threat to inhabitants' lives and rights comes from abroad.

It is irrational to dissent to whichever stable power effectively and fairly administers rights-protective laws and maintains a relatively crime-free environment in the territory one finds herself. In the contemporary world, the entities able to protect the lives and rights of people within given territories will usually be the central governments of states, but in the absence of such centralized control, the entities in question could be warlords, tribal councils, or foreign occupying armies.

Irregular combatants should get POW status if they serve politically legitimate entities controlling territory in which those entities provide basic governmental services, or at least have plausible claim to better representing inhabitants' rights than a central government hostile or neglectful of them. Another way of expressing this idea—given the definition of political legitimacy developed in chapter 2—is that irregular politico-military groups from whose governance inhabitants cannot rationally dissent are the groups whose members are owed POW status. In short, irregular combatants should enjoy POW status if they are very much like the conventional soldiers representing a state. The claim of these irregulars would be that they represent a nascent state (perhaps developing within the internationally recognized borders of an existing state); represent a reconstituting state (following foreign invasion or a coup); or better represent and protect inhabitants than the oppressive or incompetent government of an existing state. While at first chiefly concerned with fighting the security forces of another government (the colonizer, foreign occupier, or the "illegitimate" domestic government, which the rebels may charge has the parasitic relationship to the people of a foreign occupier), politically legitimate irregular groups will also move to administer the territory under their physical control in a manner respectful of inhabitants' lives and rights. It has been said that victory comes for many irregulars ultimately, by outadministering, rather than outfighting the central government.[32]

It is important to remember that acknowledging an irregular group's qualification for POW status is not necessarily to say that they adhere to a good political program or that people in the relevant territory will necessarily be enthused about their plans for governance. Even soldiers fighting on behalf of the Nazi regime were given POW status. Rather, the POW status of irregular detainees is a recognition that they are members of a belligerent power at war, rather than a criminal gang, and that their violent actions are in service of a state or quasi-state rather than the product of personal volition. To qualify, the group needs to meet the bare criteria of a governmental entity on the political theory I have been defending: administering and enforcing rights-respecting law in a given territory.

According to the just war tradition, detained members of a conventional military get POW status even if they have committed war crimes, in which event they can be tried in a court martial. It is not controversial whether uniformed members of a conventional military represent a state. By contrast, it is an open question whether irregular combatants represent a state or a

nascent state and should thereby get POW status. Part of their claim to being like conventional soldiers and not mere criminals must be their soldier-
like behavior, and so the four criteria are relevant in the case of irregulars
for determining if they get POW status or are tried according to domestic
criminal law. By contrast, the four criteria are not relevant for determining
whether uniformed members of a conventional military ought to get POW
status—since they obviously represent a state—but instead are relevant only
for determining whether they should be tried under military law for war
crimes. As mentioned before, war crimes are on the soldier's own account,
as it were, not covered by the legal immunity he enjoys in his role as a state
agent.

Conventional soldiers enjoy POW status by virtue of their corporate
identity as members of a conventional military. By the same logic, irregular
combatants should get POW status if their group plays a role similar to a
conventional military, and individual crimes should be tried according to
military law.[33] In some cases, such as with Mao's Red Army, which had 1 mil-
lion troops in 1945, it is relatively easy to judge if the irregular group as a
whole observes the four criteria. There may be more ambiguity with respect
to smaller, less organized groups when it comes to determining whether
infractions to the laws and customs of war are endorsed by the group or
are only the product of a few individuals' misbehavior. In some cases, the
distinction between a POW who will be tried under military law for a war
crime and a domestic criminal suspect to be tried in civilian criminal court
does not make much of a practical difference in terms of trial rights or possible punishments. Both the POW and the criminal defendant would be
charged with murder for intentionally killing an innocent civilian. However, the distinction between the detainees does make a difference when it
comes to killing soldiers or destroying military materiel and other types of
government property. Unlike the POW, the irregular without POW status
can be legally charged with murder and vandalism in these cases (and morally blamed for these acts as well).

We will now begin to apply this general standard for irregular POW status
to the aforementioned classes of irregulars. As indicated in chapter 2, space
for a legitimate insurgent movement is created by the consistent failure of
a sitting government to equally protect inhabitants' lives and rights. Rebels
win political legitimacy when they provide basic governmental-type services
in a particular territory, or to a group neglected by the central government
(even barring significant land holdings), and do not otherwise violate the
rights of those living in the territory they control. At a certain point, it may

become irrational for inhabitants of an oppressive or negligent government to prefer central government rule to that of diligent, competent rebels.

The group led by Castro could probably be said to have enjoyed this quasi-government legitimacy in the context of a state administered by the incompetent, corrupt Batista regime, first in the region of Castro's hideout in the Sierra Maestra, and later throughout Cuba. Depending at which point between 1927 and 1949 one views Mao's struggles with the Nationalists and Japanese occupiers, his Chinese Communist Party's rise could be seen as taking place against the chaotic background of a failed state or against a brutal foreign occupier. After the Long March, Mao's Red Army—which at various points approached the size, training, and equipage of a conventional army—had firm control of Jiangxi and, later, even broader swaths of the Chinese countryside. Mao directed that scrupulous respect be paid to the rights of the peasants. Captives from Mao's and Castro's groups would qualify for POW status.

That said, it is irrational to dissent to the government's coercive authority where the government effectively protects the lives and rights of all inhabitants equally. It is therefore irrational to support a rebel movement or foreign invader in a basically just state. Insurgents in such an environment do not qualify for POW status. Regarding foreign invaders, direct, coercive political power exerted domestically by foreign countries is prima facie illegitimate when there is a functioning central government, because legitimate political coercion in the first instance is the province of a territory's sitting government. It is possible that the rebels or invaders promise a political program more to one's taste—burkhas for all or burkhas for none, what have you—but it is irrational to prefer the tumult of violent regime change (even if coupled with the promise of future political benefits) over the stability of the existing regime where the existing government is successful at protecting inhabitants' lives and rights. Recall, the foundation of political legitimacy defended in this book relates to the necessary conditions for autonomy, and therefore, to what can or cannot be coherently endorsed by anyone (conceived as autonomous), rather than what one particular person happens to prefer. Even if in analyzing the concept of autonomy, we consider only that element of positive freedom entailing the ability to plan for the future, it can be seen that the stability of a basically just regime is rationally preferable for this general purpose compared to the certain instability of revolution or invasion. This is not to say that one cannot argue, demand, write, protest, and vote in favor of whatever political program one prefers, just that the title of political legitimacy, abstract as it is, is not easily won or lost.

Assuming one's government is competent and basically just, invaders are politically illegitimate and so may justifiably resisted.[34] Even after the government falls, the remnant army still fighting the occupiers from a remote base enjoys political legitimacy and, as such, qualifies for POW status if captured, provided their compliance with the four criteria. (While soldiers of the former regime have some prima facie legitimacy, their new circumstances may have reduced them to brigandage, so their status has to be measured according to their compliance with the four criteria.) Members of an insurgent movement raised after the occupation has taken hold, be it one composed of ex-soldiers and civilians, or civilians alone would also qualify for POW status, provided again, their compliance with the four criteria.

Presumably, a colonial power rules at the expense of the colonized country's indigenous people, employing the sort of discriminatory laws, grossly unequal land holdings, and brutal repression once seen in the Belgian Congo, South Africa, Indo-China, Rhodesia, etc. It follows then that anti-colonial insurgents able to control and administer land have prima facie political legitimacy and are due POW status if captured, provided their compliance with the four criteria.

There may be a point where it is rational for inhabitants to switch allegiance from the defeated government to the occupying or colonizing power or to dissent to the nascent authority of insurgent groups in favor of the colonizing power. (While resistance to invaders is legitimate, it is not obligatory on the minimal political theory I am defending.) While a defeated government is obviously not able to protect inhabitants' lives and rights on the same scale it once did, the conquering power is not necessarily interested in taking up that role, so political legitimacy does not immediately accrue to whichever power is dominant in the case of occupation or colonization. The prima facie illegitimacy of direct foreign rule endures at least until the point when the occupier has consolidated rule (something that might take years, as current events in Iraq suggest). Until that point, it may be unclear which party has real power and control over the territory, even after the sitting government has fallen. A wider sphere of militant groups could have claim to political legitimacy and potential POW status under these circumstances than would be the case if they were threatening a seated government during peacetime. (I have found the current situation in Iraq too fluid to categorize the dozens of groups under arms there, with different groups' allegiances, tactics, and aims seeming to shift monthly.) Given the prima facie illegitimacy of foreign rule, it may well be appropriate in contexts of occupation or colonization to afford insurgents POW status even if they do not control territory or are not yet able to deliver governmental-style services, so long as they observe the four criteria. That said, an occupying or even colonizing power that has consolidated rule and equally protects inhabitants' lives and rights might be rationally preferable for inhabitants to the ragtag guerilla groups promising to ban kite flying or bring about the dictatorship of the proletariat or whatever (more on this below).

With respect to governmental-type services, standing in for a regular government would require at a minimum, basic crime control, as a means of safeguarding the lives and rights of inhabitants. It may well be that irregular combatants have some kind of ersatz civil service auxiliary to administer criminal justice or provide other services. It is probably correct to see Hezbollah, for instance, maintaining basic law and order, as well as welfare and educational services, for the Shia of Southern Lebanon; perhaps Hamas will prove able to do the same for Palestinians in the Gaza Strip (illustratively referred to as "Hamastan" by Israelis since Hamas's successful June 2007 takeover of the territory).

Some irregulars are voluntarily supported by civilians who actively believe in their cause. Tito had to turn away peasant volunteers in Serbia for lack of arms. On the other hand, irregulars sometimes forcibly levy "taxes" on civilians in their area of control and sometimes fail to even dignify confiscations of civilian property with that label. Reasonable taxation of a sort is acceptable if irregulars really are substituting, or are soon to be substituting, for the central government in the provision of basic governmental services protective of inhabitants' lives and rights. Eventually, for this taxation to be just, civilians need to have some sort of direct input on taxation for less basic services not aimed at the minimal protection of lives and rights. However, irregulars actually providing basic services protective of inhabitants' lives and rights initially do not need explicit consent for tax collection anymore than does the central government. (Presumably, if irregulars have established control over an area, government tax collectors are not able to assess civilians a second time.)

Just as there are rational grounds to dissent to government behavior that fails to protect inhabitants' lives and rights equally, there are also grounds to dissent to governmental-style behavior on the part of irregular combatants failing to serve the interests of the inhabitants in the territory irregulars control. Excessive "taxation," terrorism, heavy-handed law enforcement, etc., override whatever other claims irregulars have to political legitimacy and POW status in detention. (For their part, some insurgent leaders like Mao and the leaders of the NLF were particularly sensitive to the potential of terrorism to alienate the people from the insurgent movement.)[35] So, for example, whatever the value of the political critiques animating South

American insurgencies in the second half of the twentieth century, the random bombings, kidnappings, and murders perpetrated by the ALN, FALN, MLN, Tupacamaru, and Shining Path in an effort to coerce popular support robbed these movements of legitimacy. The Taliban arguably gained political legitimacy (and were owed POW status if captured by the nominal government in Kabul) in the mid-1990s when they began taking territory from Afghanistan's motley warlords and imposed law and order. However, their heavy hand at enforcing Sharia once they consolidated power arguably voided this legitimacy.

If directly attacking civilians voids irregular combatants' claims to political legitimacy, it must be asked if *all* forms of guerilla war delegitimates irregulars on account of the danger guerilla warfare poses to civilians. Irregulars endanger civilians when they live among them and rely on them for support—even in cases where that support is coerced—as counterinsurgency campaigns can often consist of general counterpopulation campaigns highlighted by ethnic cleansing and terrorism. In its least disruptive (and most professional) forms, counterinsurgency in urban areas involves curfews, cordons, checkpoints, and house to house searches for guerillas and weapon caches. In rural areas, counterinsurgency can involve forcible relocation of civilians, destruction of crops and livestock (on which guerillas depend), and the deployment of small "hunter-killer" counterinsurgent teams of government troops and/or indigenous militias. Sweeping responses like these are necessary even when irregulars are few in number, because of the disproportionate effect random, limited guerilla attacks have on a government or conventional military force. Instructively, some of the *less brutal* counterinsurgencies over the last two centuries involved the burning of all homes and farms within five miles of Union railroads in the Shenandoah valley during the Civil War, the detention of seventy-eight thousand people in "re-education" camps accompanied by the liberal use of torture in Kenya, and the massive relocation of tens of thousands Boer civilians to squalid camps followed by universal burning of farmland in South Africa.

As severe as these responses, state terrorism and the imposition of collective punishments on the people are more typical government responses to insurgencies. Since the government cannot find the insurgents, it aims at their visible civilian means of support. The history books describe graveyards: Nazi reprisals of fifty to a hundred executions of civilians for every German soldier killed by Yugoslav partisans, widespread preventive detention and systemic torture in Algeria, fifteen thousand "disappearances" in Argentina, the Anfal campaign against the Kurds in Iraq, and the systematic depopulating of young men in Chechnya through abduction and murder. Worse, state terrorism tends to provoke reciprocal insurgent terrorism in a grim test of who can monopolize civilians' fear (and, therefore, allegiance) through massacre, torture, disappearance, and mutilation.

Some insurgent groups purposely court these kinds of government responses. Particularly where the local population seems quiescent to government control, some revolutionaries like Guevara (in Bolivia),[36] Grivas (Cyprus), and Marighela (Brazil),[37] among others, admitted to relying on anticipated government overreactions in order to radicalize the population and goad them into supporting the resistance. Guevara seemed to feel that small *focos* of ideologically committed militants could spark popular uprisings even without widespread political education of the people (contra Mao and Giap), precisely because government retaliation against guerilla attacks would alienate *any* group of peasants from the governing regime.[38] Particularly as media coverage of global events has expanded, groups from the Kosovar Liberation Army to Fatah have seemed to try to provoke war crimes in order to rally support and cow the government into retreat or negotiation.[39] This tactic is a gross violation of the principle of discrimination. The irregulars attack the government in the hope that the government terrorizes the people, and the people then rise up against the government. Irregular groups embracing this tactic are using civilians as a means to an end, as human shields of a sort.[40] In fact, resorting to this tactic is prima facie indication that insurgents lack legitimacy.

I argued above that there is a prima facie case for the political legitimacy of irregulars who are fighting occupying or colonial powers. Given the onerous nature of many, if not all counterinsurgent campaigns, insurgencies against *settled, indigenous* forms of government are only politically legitimate when government misrule is so complete or unjust as to make the potentially brutal government response, along with the general tumult of a government collapse, rationally preferable to the current state of affairs. Only irregulars rebelling against seated, indigenous governments of this sort qualify for POW status, assuming adherence to the four criteria.[41] The ANC in apartheid-era South Africa perhaps qualifies (if the three-century Afrikaner political structure was considered a de facto seated, indigenous government). It is a more complicated position than can be addressed here—as it would require developing a fuller political theory able to address questions of patriotism, national culture, and ethnic self-determination— but it may be that even long-term, relatively benign occupiers should be considered in the same light as seated, competent indigenous governments, and insurgents fighting them, accordingly denied POW status.

It is worth bearing in mind that there are many ways to express political grievances without resorting to violence, even apart from participation in democratic systems. Recent peaceful revolutions in Lebanon and Ukraine, the ouster of Milosevic in Belgrade in 2000, the Velvet Revolution in Czechoslovakia, the civil rights movement in the American South and the decolonization of India provide peaceful models for political action in less than free environments. Historically, resorting to violence, particularly terrorism, robs irregular groups of popular support. For example, given the support their causes once enjoyed from portions of the colonial powers' majority populations as well as the wider world, it is likely that the violent paths taken by the IRA, PLO, and other irregular groups, delayed the political gains the groups or their associated political wings eventually made by decades. Similarly, I have often wondered what would have happened had bin Laden poured his millions into satellite TV stations publicizing the injustices he perceives afflicting Muslims worldwide instead of building a paramilitary franchise to kill perceived colonizers and apostates.

Also, against the romantic image of the rebel, a brief survey of the last two centuries' insurgencies reveals few popular insurgencies against indigenous governments carried out in a disciplined and discriminate manner (and vanishingly few successes), but far more insurgencies led by small numbers of naive intellectuals whose frustrations at the obduracy of the masses quickly degenerate into nihilistic spasms of terrorism—if not first self-sabotaged by their own bungling—and whose ranks are often swelled by simple gangsters as well as those benighted young men always available who need little encouragement to create mayhem.

A few comments about responsible irregular tactics is warranted given these critical comments about some irregular tactics. First, irregulars must separate themselves from civilians as much as possible, ideally living apart from villages or cities.[42] The modern just war tradition expects occupation forces to act as a stand-in for the defeated government, preserving basic law and order and avoiding mistreatment of civilians in occupied territory. Yet this duty assumes that civilians are not threats to occupying forces; as Walzer puts it, "soldiers must feel safe among civilians if civilians are ever to be safe from soldiers."[43] Occupation will be increasingly onerous to civilians to the extent that irregulars do not wear some kind of marker; carry weapons in the open; separate themselves from civilians; or avoid attacking government forces when civilians are nearby. On this point, one of the many sad footnotes to the Israeli-Palestinian conflict is the frequency with which news reports mention that family members of Palestinian militants were among the casualties when Israeli forces attack militants in their homes or cars.

Physical separation from civilians may be impossible in some environ-ments, and, in such cases, guerillas at least need to carry their arms in the open and wear some identifying emblem like an armband or headband when engaged in attacks or sabotage. (Whether or not it is meant for this purpose, some photos of Mahdi Army militants in Iraq have shown them with Moqtād al-Sadr pictures pinned to their shirts; I think this would suf-fice for identification.) As government troops may wear articles of civilian clothes while "off duty" in their bases—pictures from Iraq sometimes show U.S. troops relaxing in baseball caps and college sweatshirts—it seems rea-sonable to allow irregular combatants who cannot live apart from their regular dwellings to wear civilian clothes when similarly "off duty" in their homes.

Regarding the carrying of arms, it is argued that carrying weapons in the open would be suicidal for urban guerillas.[44] This is not necessarily the case, and it *is* incumbent on irregulars to carry their weapons in the open when on a mission, because civilians will be in peril if soldiers suspect every civilian of secreting a gun under his coat or a bomb in his car. This moral necessity may rule out certain attacks, just as the duty of discrimination rules out certain operations for conventional combatants. For example, if insurgents want to attack a forward operating base soldiers have set up in an abandoned store, the insurgents ought to advance under cover of night, wearing their armbands and carrying their rifles; such an attack is no more dangerous for them than it would be for conventional troops. If army pa-trols make it impossible to sneak up to the base unless the insurgents mas-querade as civilians, the insurgents will have to pick a new target, perhaps one of the patrols.

Irregulars Ineligible for POW Status

On April 19th, 1995, American Army veteran Timothy McVeigh exploded a truck bomb in front of the Murrah Federal Building in Oklahoma City, OK, killing 168 people. Active in anti-government, gun-rights circles, he claimed the bombing was in retaliation for the killings of Branch Davidian cult members in Waco, TX and members of the Weaver family in Ruby Ridge, ID by Federal agents.

Stateless agitators for global/regional political change and individuals vio-lently agitating for political change within their own nations fail to meet the criteria for POW status. The outside agitators do not necessarily have a natural constituency by virtue of residency or even ethnic or religious solidarity. They are essentially persons with radical political ideas looking for national laboratories. They may sincerely care about the people in the country in which they hope to operate; they may share an ethnic or religious affiliation with the indigenous people; and they may well have ideas which would improve their lives. However, they cannot claim to represent a people or a state simply by fiat—much less take it upon themselves to goad a government into visiting its wrath upon the people as a shortcut to radicalizing/enlightening them. There are possible grounds for assigning POW status to members of a stateless agitator group *if* they take up residency in a state under foreign occupation, colonization, or unjust indigenous rule, and the group begins to seize territory and provide governmental-type services, provided their compliance with the four criteria.

Al-Qaeda is a paradigmatic stateless agitator. Its transnational aim is ultimately to reclaim and unite the lands held by the seventh-century Muslim caliphate, and it runs training camps in various locales as well as provides instructions and exhortation in various media to jihadists around the world to both engage in actions directed by the central al-Qaeda leadership and instigate homegrown Islamist insurgencies in their respective countries.[45] The group has decided for itself that the various territories conquered by Arab horsemen in the seventh century need to be once again united into a single political unit, governed according to the group's version of Salafist Islam. Given these features, a member of the group like Dhiren Barot (who supplied tactical information to insurgents in multiple countries), or alleged fellow travelers like the Ft. Dix plotters, do not meet the criteria for POW status.[46] However, some of the people al-Qaeda has trained could potentially qualify if and when they successfully began insurgencies meeting the above criteria. To be clear, I am not aware of any al-Qaeda affiliates or "franchises," from Jemaah Islamiyah to al-Qaeda in Mesopotamia to the Moroccan Islamic Combatant Group, which has not forfeited potential political legitimacy through terrorist tactics.

Similarly, the lone revolutionary, like Timothy McVeigh is not in a position to control territory or provide governmental services, and so cannot claim to be representing more than his own views when attacking government assets. Granted, both the lone revolutionary and outside agitator may share the views of many within a state, but the moral impunity and legal immunity of POWs depends on concrete connections between combatants and communities of people that make the combatants' actions those of the community, rather than personal ones. Acknowledging moral impunity and legal immunity for violent acts in the absence of such concrete linkage (the provision of governmental services) potentially widens the scope of nonpunishable acts past any limit.[47] One would only need invoke the interests of some underprivileged group or cite some perceived political injustice to escape punishment for assaulting one's irksome neighbor or robbing a local convenience store. Rather, such persons' violent acts can be evaluated by the sort of moral analysis conducted in chapter 1 and tried and punished according to states' domestic criminal justice system.

To draw together the points made above about failure to observe the four criteria, in addition to stateless agitators and lone revolutionaries, irregular groups from any of the aforementioned classes who do not as a rule self-identify, or who commit other types of war crimes, fail to qualify for POW status. Also, rebels committing or conspiring to commit political violence against a basically just, seated indigenous government fail to qualify for POW status, regardless of the tactics they use. (This applies to the Ft. Dix plotters as well.) All these irregulars could be prosecuted as common criminals according to a state's internal law. The rights of criminal suspects during police interrogation were discussed in chapter 5. Interrogation rules for POWs will be discussed in the next chapter. While irregulars failing to qualify for POW status *may* be tried as common criminals, the next chapter will take up the question of whether a third mode of detention, interrogation, and trial is better suited for such detainees.

Objective Determinations

The foregoing argument has involved determinations about irregular groups made from the all-encompassing view of theory where the totality of a group's behavior and motivation is known. In the real world, one can perhaps envision states making determinations about the legitimacy of an insurgent group acting within the borders of another state, but it seems strange to expect a government to officially acknowledge a nascent state growing embryonically within its borders, as such recognition would suggest that the sitting government was incompetent or unjust. Moreover, acknowledging the political legitimacy of the rebel movement would seem to ennoble those "bandits" or "terrorists" who have been attacking military convoys and garroting policemen. From the perspective of the government at least, it seems absurd that people who hijack government vehicles, steal government supplies, kill government employees, and perhaps steal from and terrorize civilians can escape criminal prosecution by merely declaring themselves at war with the state. Since POWs are to be held until the end of hostilities, could a group of thieves captured at an armory demand POW status by declaring themselves at war with the state and then declare the war over and demand immediate release?

Some objective criteria are clearly necessary, given the possibility of bad governments spuriously refusing POW status to insurgents and bad people spuriously demanding it. A number of the above distinctions turn on circumstances like occupation and colonization that are fairly straightforward descriptive states of affair, with perhaps only some ambiguity where a weak or only nominally independent government "invites" a foreign army to occupy its land for the sake of security, as the government of Lebanon did Syria in the 1980s. A foreign occupier might term their occupation a benevolent one, a liberation perhaps, but the presence of foreign troops and administrators in the capital should be determinative for assigning insurgents POW status. Government oppression of its own people is potentially less readily identified; standards were given in chapter 2 for judging when government coercion becomes more onerous than the depredations that might follow in the absence of basic government services. Outsiders looking for objective standards might look to the existence of legislation discriminating against minority groups such as South Africa's apartheid laws or America's Jim Crow laws; violent campaigns led against particular groups such as Sudan's persecutions of Southern non-Muslims; or patterns of systematic discrimination in measurable arenas like state offices, public housing, or land ownership, as was seen in Northern Ireland to the detriment of Catholics.

Regardless of the political context for their activity, it is harder to judge the political legitimacy of irregular groups claiming POW status at the beginning of their struggle, prior to the point when they have control over territory. In both cases, violence directed at government, and especially military targets prima facie suggests political rather than criminal motivation. Why else would someone blow up a military outpost or snipe on an army patrol? Granted, a criminal gang might desire to intimidate local police or judges and engage military patrols if the military is being used in law enforcement roles. Drug cartels have assassinated police chiefs in Nuevo Leon, Mexico, with such rapidity of late that a local newspaper quipped that the life expectancy of a Nuevo Leon police chief could be measured in hours. Also hijackers or thieves of military materiel might have pecuniary motives. Some kind of impartial trial at the level of a grand jury (discussed next chapter) could assess evidence that points toward political or pecuniary motives for detainees' actions and determine whether the detainee is appropriately treated as a POW or should be entered into the criminal justice system. Though there may well be difficult cases in counterinsurgency contexts, such as with the attack in the poppy fields of Uruzgan Province, normal investigative methods as well as interrogation should be able to determine if attackers are drug dealers, farmers, or insurgents. For example, criminals are likely going to sell weapons they have stolen from a government armory, where insurgents will use them in their own operations.

The motivation behind attacks or other rights violations against civilians (at least those who are not in government employ) need not be evaluated as such attacks void claims to political legitimacy and POW status. This standard could be used to distinguish a legitimate insurgent movement from a criminal gang successful at eliminating local government officials and establishing a monopoly on violence in a particular region.

SEVEN

Noncoercive Interrogation

The typically opaque title of the U.S. Army's newest interrogation manual, *Human Intelligence Collector Operations* (FM 2-22.3), belies the "ripped from the headlines" specificity of some of its prohibitions. The manual forbids waterboarding, hooding, "putting duct tape across the eyes," inducing hypothermia, and "forcing the detainee to be naked, perform sexual acts, or pose in a sexual manner" (5-75). Military police may not be ordered to "soften up" detainees and—we are glad to learn—military working dogs may not be used for the purposes of interrogation (5-59). Compared to previous incarnations of U.S. Army and CIA manuals, the 2005 Army manual is striking for its focus on preventing abuse of detainees. In addition to the very specific prohibitions and frequent invocation of the Geneva Conventions and 2005 Detainee Treatment Act, the manual stresses oversight, both by requiring interrogators to get approval for their interrogation plans from a supervisor and frequently admonishing supervisors to carefully monitor certain interrogation approaches or restrict certain approaches to their most experienced and responsible interrogators. Two techniques that run the risk of implying threats to detainees—the Mutt and Jeff (i.e., good cop/bad cop) approach and the false flag approach, where the interrogator poses as a foreign military officer—need special permission from a colonel. The manual directs interrogators uncertain about the permissibility of certain ploys to consult with a JAG (a military lawyer); it also includes a bullet-pointed list of steps to take if a soldier feels he has been given an unlawful order. The context in which the manual was written is also apparent in its reference to the War on Terror, the Taliban, and al-Qaeda and its frequent qualification that interrogators need to be cognizant of how cultural differences may assign different meanings to certain behavioral tics and speaking patterns.

This chapter will discuss moral and legal implications of interrogations and detention of national security threats in military and intelligence contexts; FM 2-22.3 will be used as an example of a training text used by military interrogators in liberal states. As with the Inbau and Reid police manual, we must proceed with the awareness that interrogation manuals are something like fine arts manuals: certain techniques can be described, but the real expression of the "art" is an idiosyncratic, improvisational, and creative process that will differ from practitioner to practitioner. As a former CIA interrogator puts it, there is no "one size fits all" to interrogation since what is necessary to convince or trick an interrogatee into cooperating—and what ploys an interrogator judges himself capable of pulling off—will vary from person to person.[1] It should also be pointed out that the efficacy of these approaches has never been systematically tested nor have they necessarily been endorsed by successive generations of interrogators.[2] The approaches were designed during World War II and have been passed down in successive field manuals; given the nature of American military deployments, most interrogators would have had an opportunity to use the techniques in a combat setting in only one campaign. Undoubtedly, a great deal of real world knowledge has been lost as officers retire or are rotated to other postings.

In this chapter, I will delineate the rights POWs enjoy in interrogations and defend the use of deceptive interrogation techniques with POWs. I will discuss the differences between POW-style and law enforcement–style interrogations in an effort to determine which is appropriate for use with unprivileged irregulars, irregular combatants who do not qualify for POW status; I will reject the creation of a third style of interrogation especially for unprivileged irregulars. I will argue that *positively identified* unprivileged irregulars can be given POW-style interrogation in a domestic context, though such treatment precludes criminal prosecution following interrogation. By contrast, *suspected* domestic unprivileged irregulars must be afforded the same rights as domestic criminal suspects. Both positively identified and suspected unprivileged irregulars *captured abroad* can be interrogated according to POW standards. Positively identified unprivileged irregulars given POW-style interrogations should be held as POWs following interrogation instead of being criminally prosecuted, despite their failing to qualify for POW status.

FM 2-22.3 concerns the collection of human intelligence (HUMINT)—information garnered from persons' testimony encompassing debriefing of fellow soldiers, refugees, and émigrés; liaising with allies; and interrogating enemy POWs or other detainees. In this chapter, I will focus on interrogations of enemy detainees and so will refer to "interrogators" instead the manual's broader "HUMINT collectors." I will also continue to use the term

"POW," instead of the manual's "Enemy Prisoners of War (EPWs)": the terms have the same meaning.

As described in the manual, military interrogators will sometimes operate in the field with the infantry where their responsibility is to conduct "tactical screening" of potential detainees in an effort to aid the ongoing operation or determine which potential detainees might be of intelligence value. More frequently, interrogators are stationed at a facility that receives detainees captured by troops who have conducted tactical screening themselves. After observing the initial screening process, where detainees are photographed, fingerprinted, and examined by medical staff, interrogators will garner any available information about the detainees from the troops who captured them or the military police (MPs) who transported them. Then, during the initial "approach phase" of the interrogation, the interrogator will seek to establish a level of rapport with the detainee such that the detainee is willing to divulge the information the interrogator wants. Interrogators are instructed to adopt a persona best able to establish this rapport, based on the dominant personality traits observed in the detainee. Interrogations usually begin with the "direct approach," where the interrogator simply asks the detainee for the desired information. Surprisingly, nearly all detainees in recent U.S conflicts cooperated with interrogators employing this approach: U.S. interrogators in Vietnam, Grenada, Panama, and Desert Storm saw 95 percent cooperation rates. (However, the manual notes that preliminary evidence from Operations Enduring Freedom and Iraqi Freedom indicates that the direct approach has been much less effective in Afghanistan and Iraq.)[3]

As with interrogations in domestic law enforcement contexts, interrogations in military and intelligence contexts exploit interrogatees' basic social and psychological tendencies. Detainees are typically anxious and frightened due to the circumstances of their capture; a natural human reaction to stress is to want to communicate with another person. Ideally, MPs have not allowed detainees to speak during transportation and screening so the interrogator is the first person with whom they have the opportunity to interact. Many people are also conditioned to respond to authority figures; others are prone to boasting about their accomplishments or complaining about their frustrations.[4]

If the direct approach fails, interrogators are trained to exploit these human frailties with one or more of eighteen approaches approved for use with all detainees, most involving emotional manipulation. The manual points out that the detainee will not always realize he is divulging security-sensitive information to the interrogator. The interrogator might offer an incentive for cooperation, something as simple as a cigarette or cup of coffee. Even a small gesture supposedly may be sufficient to ingratiate a psychologically vulnerable detainee to the interrogator. Indeed, one approach called "emotional fear down" counsels interrogators to calm frightened detainees with soothing words; the grateful detainee typically wants to cooperate with whoever is offering him relief from stress. Interrogators might also exploit detainees' love for their comrades, families, or country by saying cooperation will end the war sooner, allow them a quicker return to their families, or enable capturing forces to treat wounded comrades. Conversely, detainees' negative feelings toward others can be exploited by interrogators who promise that cooperation will mean the downfall of some hated officer, political leader, or oppressive ethnic majority. An interrogator might flatter a detainee he perceives to have low self-esteem or, alternately, might profess admiration of an arrogant one; the former may cooperate in order to hear more compliments, and the latter may begin to boast about his technical prowess or his unit's tactical accomplishments. The same arrogant types can also be provoked through insults into defensively telling the interrogator what he seeks. An example given in the manual has the interrogator asking, "Why did you surrender so easily when you could have escaped by crossing the nearby ford in the river?" Feeling that he is being accused of cowardice, the detainee replies, "No one could have crossed the ford because it's mined." The interrogator also might lie and say that other captured persons are cooperating or that the detainee's unit is out of ammunition and so nothing will be lost in telling the interrogator information that will end the battle sooner. The "emotional fear up" approach is designed to subtly play on the detainee's apprehension; it is better in this case to be vague, for example, asking the detainee "I wonder how your family is doing without you?" The manual frequently cautions the interrogator not to cross the line and explicitly threaten or humiliate detainees. All forms of mental or physical torture, degrading treatment, and humiliation are prohibited for all detainees. POWs may not have their legal privileges (enumerated in the Geneva Conventions) restricted as a penalty for noncooperation in interrogation.

Moral Issues Associated with POW Interrogation

This section will consider the moral implications of using the "direct approach" and deceptive or manipulative tactics in POW interrogation. Direct questioning unto itself raises few moral concerns. The detainee can ostensibly remain silent and can attempt to derail the interrogator. True, his detention is psychologically stressful.[5] The detainee is likely anxious as a direct result of his capture. He is alone with the interrogator in an unfamiliar place and has no support in concealing the information the interrogator desires. Even if the detainee knows the rights afforded him as a POW, he may be uncertain about what will happen if he refuses to cooperate. Nonetheless, the actual asking of straightforward questions is not itself abusive or punitive.

Looking at the issue now in a broader context, a POW who is questioned in the direct manner has no rights violated, though he is under no obligation to answer the interrogator's questions, and the interrogator is prohibited by international law and the tenets of just war theory from causing the POW any mental or physical duress to get him to answer. A war fighter who meets POW criteria has a right to his secrets regarding lawful military maneuvers; they are professional secrets akin to a businessperson's trade secrets. Even if the POW has killed troops belonging to the detaining power, the POW is not morally culpable for murder. He may no more be intentionally harmed now than may a civilian, because once he is disarmed, he is no longer playing the political role that made him vulnerable to the enemy's attack.

We will now address the deceptive elements of POW interrogation. In chapter 1, I argued that Locke's and Aquinas's summary devaluation of a miscreant's rights—designating him as a beast to be dealt with by "the rule of force"—was not justified from the "God's eye" point of view where the actors' intentions are known. However, this summary and relatively superficial moral view *is* adequate for considering combat violence since war fighters' personal intentions are irrelevant when they are acting in their political roles. They *are* operating by the "rule of force," but on behalf of their states rather than due to private motives. Their behavior is therefore not morally problematic in the first instance in the way it would be for a private citizen. That said, their status as agents of political coercion makes them vulnerable to prudential behavior from enemy soldiers once hostilities are under way. (Recall, I have argued deception and emotional manipulation are part of a spectrum of prudential activities that includes physical force as well.) In a war, the militaries of an antagonistic pair of nations justly operate by the rule of force—each justified in dealing prudentially with the other side. When we are focusing on the fighting of war—rather than the decision to go to war—neither nation's military wrongs the other by fighting. This non- culpability contrasts with the domestic arena where one is not necessarily justified in forcefully resisting other's prudential behavior. For example, a thief may not shoot police serving an arrest warrant.

The purpose of an interrogator's manipulation of a POW is not punitive, since a war fighter meeting POW criteria is not criminally culpable for his combat actions. He does not deserve disrespectful treatment because he is an enemy. Rather, the interrogator's prudential tactics are justified to nullify the threat posed by the POW's unit by collecting security-sensitive information the POW might know. The POW need not be afforded complete deference to his preferences (e.g., to conceal his military secrets), because he is engaged in a prudential enterprise in an arena where other state agents may legitimately counter him. The interrogator's questions and ruses should only be aimed at eliciting the POW's security-sensitive secrets, which in a sense, are not his own, personal secrets, but "state property" that he is guarding. Since the interrogator is not acting of personal volition but as a state agent, deception and manipulation can be justified in the same manner as other instances of state coercion of foreign enemies, as detailed in the last chapter.[6]

The interrogator's actions have to be proportionate to the end of neutralizing the enemy's threat to be permissible. Deceptive ruses that are not aimed at the detainee's security-sensitive secrets are not justified by the interrogator's political role, and therefore, must be a result of his personal motives or incompetence. In such cases, he is personally, morally culpable for these actions. From this purpose, we can derive limitations on interrogation: do not lie or manipulate if the direct approach will do, nor lie or manipulate more than necessary to reveal security-sensitive information. While it will not always be clear which actions are strictly necessary to elicit information, questions and ruses not aimed at eliciting security-sensitive information (but instead motivated by the interrogator's prurient interests, for example) would be clearly beyond the scope of the interrogator's authority.[7]

Even if they have engaged in violence against the detaining power's forces, assuming they have not committed war crimes, enemy POWs are legally and morally innocent (on this account), and so should not be punished in detention; the purpose of detention is merely to keep them from returning to the battlefield. Again, interrogation tactics should not have any sort of punitive character. Physical force in particular should not be used against them since POWs are not a physical threat. Interrogators should not impose sanctions on the detainee for failing to divulge military secrets because POWs have a right to them. The interrogator is entitled to try to trick or cajole the POW into revealing his secrets, but the POW is not wronging the interrogator by keeping mum or lying in turn. By way of comparison, infantrymen are permitted to attack the enemy, and the enemy is permitted to use force in response; neither can be punished afterward since neither wrongs the other.

POWs do not need to be afforded the same rights afforded domestic criminal suspects in interrogation. The justification for the rights to silence and counsel in *police* interrogation is based on the baseline rights of an inhabitant of a liberal state as well as the subjective nature of suspicion. Interrogators do not face the relevant epistemic limitations when questioning POWs, because the POWs' uniforms identify them as possible intelligence sources. By contrast, in a domestic law enforcement context, the liberal state does not have cause to know that a suspect has criminal knowledge; the police interrogator must therefore advise the suspect that the state still officially considers him innocent even while it begins to treat him in a prudential fashion. All POWs have moral and political rights to silence in the sense of having a right to their professional (i.e., military) secrets. Concealing this information is part of a war fighter's job. Yet interrogators do not have to formally advise POWs of a *political* right to remain silent, as police do domestic criminal suspects, because the political right to silence mitigates a state's power toward its own inhabitants rather than toward foreigners abroad. The detaining power does not need to observe a hybrid attitude toward the uniformed enemy combatant since there is none of the ambiguity about his identity as there is with a domestic criminal suspect. Nor is there ambiguity in regards to his relation with the detaining power. It is openly and officially antagonistic. Unlike a domestic criminal suspect, the uniformed POW cannot claim that the detaining power has no cause to consider him a possible source of security-sensitive information and so he should be left alone. Further due process protections such as a right to counsel are not relevant since POWs enjoy legal immunity for their combat actions. (The arguments about the rights to silence and counsel *do* apply if POWs are suspected of war crimes, in which case they should be given the relevant admonitions and privileges; more on this below.)[8] Finally, since POWs are detained until the end of the war, their being released is not related to the interrogator's securing of certain kinds of information. Therefore, their interrogations are not subject to the time limits facing police interrogators who must either secure indictable evidence or release suspects in short order. POWs may be interrogated as often as their interrogators wish, so long as the duration of the interrogation sessions is not to the point where they become punitive unto themselves.

Different Interrogation Styles

In the summer of 1967, young Catholic protestors in Northern Ireland demonstrated against discriminatory treatment by the Protestant establishment. Protestant militants and the Protestant-dominated Royal Ulster Constabulary regularly met demonstrators with violence. The annual Orange parade in August—commemorating a 1694 Protestant victory over Catholics in the Battle of Boyne—provoked rioting in Ulster and Belfast. Six people were killed on the fourteenth of August, and a day later, British troops were ordered into the cities.

Designing appropriate interrogation and detention rules for irregular combatants who do not qualify for POW status is harder than it is for POWs. The following discussion will refer to the three main categories of irregular combatants who do not meet POW criteria: stateless agitators, indigenous insurgents attacking a basically just central government, and all other irregulars who routinely flout the rules and customs of war. I will refer to these types of irregulars as "unprivileged irregulars" since they do not enjoy moral impunity or legal immunity for political violence. For example, their killing of soldiers and civilians can be called "murder" in legal and moral senses of the term. By "positively identified" unprivileged irregulars, I mean people who self-identify as members of unprivileged irregular groups by wearing unique emblems or claiming membership in such groups when they are captured or those who expose their affiliation by attacking out of uniform or committing other war crimes. Since the territorial context of their capture is relevant to the rights of irregular detainees, I will address domestic capture and capture abroad, be it on a foreign battlefield, in occupied territory, or in foreign territory where the detaining power is not engaged in wide-scale combat.

The difficulty in crafting appropriate interrogation rules for unprivileged irregulars is due to the fact that they share traits with both war fighters and criminals. They are perpetuating political violence, like war fighters, and yet they are not observing all the features of legitimate martial activity such as representing a determinate people, controlling territory, self-identifying as combatants, and avoiding civilian targets. To the detaining power, their violent actions therefore have more of a criminal than a military profile. Their operational secrets are essentially criminal ones to which they do not have a right. Nevertheless, the detaining power may wish to interrogate these detainees as part of ongoing military operations rather than through law enforcement modes, because of the scope and severity of the threat as well as the nature of the detaining power's own security apparatus. For example, as sectarian violence in Northern Ireland grew out of control in August of 1967, London deployed the army to bolster overwhelmed police. In the event that military or paramilitary troops are actively engaged in counterinsurgency or counterterror operations, be it at home or abroad, the interrogators' initial purpose will often be to extract security-sensitive information useful to troops in the field rather than indictable evidence in service of criminal prosecution. The threat of imminent terrorist attacks may also spur the detaining power to be chiefly concerned with gaining action-able intelligence from terrorist suspects. These motives indicate a POW-style interrogation rather than a law enforcement–style interrogation, because the interrogator does not want to risk an early termination of questioning due to the intervention of counsel, the detainee's formal invocation of a right to silence, or the passage of some set amount of time.[9] Granted, police interrogators may dread the same things—indeed the *Miranda* ruling was widely criticized by those who anticipated its protections hampering inves-tigations—but in most cases, there is probably less urgency in law enforce-ment contexts because police are more likely interested in gaining indictable information about past crimes rather than in interrupting ongoing crimi-nal enterprises. In cases where investigators are seeking to disrupt ongoing criminal conspiracies, or to catch offenders still at large, there is still less urgency than in military contexts because most forms of crime do not pose an existential danger to the state. (Whereas ordinary crime is parasitic on a functioning society with a sitting government, the aim of most insurgencies or terror campaigns is to bring down the sitting state or occupying power.[10]) Law enforcement–style interrogations are also far more difficult for typical military units to perform because lacking the investigative resources to un-cover the evidence that detectives typically use as leverage in interrogations. Whether the convenience of the detaining power should determine the style of interrogation depends in part on the rights of detainees and will be addressed below.

The differences between POW-style and law enforcement–style inter-rogations need to be further clarified before the fit of one or the other is defended for use with unprivileged irregulars. As already mentioned, an interrogator has more liberty in a POW-style interrogation than in an inter-rogation run according to law enforcement standards. The domestic crimi-nal suspect's formal invocation of his right to silence or right to counsel formally ends the interrogation; it is a way of the suspect making good on the "apparently innocent" element of his hybrid profile, and (in his capacity of an apparently innocent person) demanding to be left alone by the state. By contrast, there is no ambiguity over the POW's relation to the state. Captured in uniform, and possibly in the midst of martial activity, the POW cannot credibly claim to be other than an enemy of the detaining power. He is not obliged to do anything other than identify himself and his unit, yet there is nothing about his relation with the detaining power comparable to the baseline deference the state owes its apparently innocent inhabitants.

The detaining power does not need to observe a hybrid attitude toward the uniformed enemy combatant since there is no ambiguity about his identity or his relation with the detaining power. In the context of war, the relation is *always* antagonistic: the state is always going to try and discern its enemies' secrets and its enemy is always going to try and conceal them. Nor does the POW have a right that, when invoked, summarily halts the detaining power's efforts to learn his secrets (through permissible means).[11]

Given the similarities between interrogation techniques in police and military contexts, one might wonder if the distinctions between the two styles of interrogation make a difference when considering which is appropriate for unprivileged irregulars. There is no right to counsel, admonition about the right to silence, or overall time limit in POW-style interrogation, but otherwise, military and police interrogators use similar deceptive ploys. Physical force and threats about specific consequences for noncooperation are impermissible in both types of interrogation. Both types of interrogation have high success rates (though POW-style interrogation traditionally has a higher rate—this may be ascribable to the fact that POWs know, or should know, that they do not face criminal prosecution for their legitimate military actions).[12]

The main significance of the admonition about rights to silence and counsel, and the time limit on interrogations in this instance, is their relation to the reliability of information the interrogatee provides and, therefore, its fittingness for use as evidence in a criminal trial. As discussed in chapter 5, there is some degree of unreliability with any confession procured in interrogation given the psychological pressure to comply with the interrogator's wishes. There is no open source information regarding reliability in military interrogations, but one suspects that there is more psychological pressure in a military or intelligence setting than in a police station given the circumstances of the detainee's capture and the fear of what could occur if the enemy interrogator is not satisfied. These fears and pressures are not mitigated in POW-style interrogations by an admonition that the detainee can remain silent if he wishes (suffering no adverse consequences); by the offer or presence of counsel; or by the detainee's knowledge that the authorities will have to release him after a few hours, barring arrest. One can readily imagine a detainee—who has perhaps been wounded or escaped near death in combat—telling an imposing foreign interrogator whatever he wanted to hear following days of interrogations, especially if the interrogator is the detainee's sole human contact.

To this point, only POW- and law enforcement–style interrogations have been discussed for use with unprivileged irregulars. There is not a strong case to be made for a *third* style of interrogation designed specifically for unprivileged irregulars. Addressing this possibility is indicated because one might wonder if unprivileged irregulars' lack of combatant immunity justifies using certain interrogation techniques with them prohibited for POWs and domestic criminal suspects. Readers will recall that Bush administration officials repeatedly made this argument in the years following 9/11 for those they termed "unlawful enemy combatants." Unlike POWs, positively identified unprivileged irregulars do not have a right to their professional secrets and do not necessarily have to be treated according to the principle of parity. Unlike domestic criminal suspects, there is no ambiguity over their criminal culpability, and the detaining power is not obliged to officially defer to that ambiguity.

History offers a few grim suggestions for interrogations where detainees are seen as lacking fundamental rights: torture, the threat of torture, blackmail, and harm done to the detainee's relatives. Recent anecdotes of threats and blackmail have the following dimensions. A version of the "false flag" technique has the interrogator threaten to send the detainee to a country infamous for torture, as a way of overcoming the detainee's confidence that he will not be mistreated by the detaining power. Blackmail, including sexual blackmail, is a tried and true tool of intelligence agencies and has been reportedly been in used in the War on Terror. Persons of intelligence value are told that rumors of their collaboration will be published unless they actually collaborate, or they are photographed in compromising positions with mistresses, prostitutes, or undercover officers and blackmailed accordingly.

The tactic of harming or threatening the detainee's relatives can readily be rejected. The detainee's relatives cannot be harmed, because the detainee's behavior and plans do nothing to make his relatives' rights violable. Regarding his rights, the unprivileged irregular does not have a right to his professional secrets so his possible preference to conceal them is not a preference others must respect. Interrogators can therefore act in a proportionately prudential way to elicit them. It would be disproportionate for the interrogator to be violent or otherwise attempt to incapacitate the detainee since he is no longer a direct physical threat. This presumptively rules out torture. The standard for proportional coercive responses I detailed in chapter 1 limits coercive responses to those affecting rights of roughly equal value to the rights abused by the offender or the rights threatened or violated by the offender. Given that the irregular's plans may include murder, one might think that coercive responses up to and including lethal ones *would* be legitimate means of eliciting the detainee's criminal knowledge. Yet the exact nature of his plans are unknown, and even if they include murder, he is not directly threatening to murder someone, but at best, facilitate murder by refusing to give information that might enable operators to capture his colleagues. As will be discussed at greater length in the next chapter, there might be many other ways to disrupt the group's plans, and torture is of such dubious efficacy that it cannot be seen as a direct, efficient means of learning the truth. Lethal force would be legitimate if the detainee was actively, physically threatening lethal violence (e.g., if he stole an MP's pistol), but it is disproportionate to his current state if he is unarmed and shackled. Since he is not an immediate physical threat, prudential responses should not include those actions directly affecting his physical state beyond what is necessary to keep him secure (e.g., handcuffs).

Blackmail and threats do not themselves risk the detainee's life or affect his bodily integrity. While they may cause fear, the purpose of threats and blackmail (which distinguishes them from other fear-producing actions like yelling at the detainee) is to present the detainee with a rational incentive to comply with the interrogator's demands; as such, they actually depend on the detainee's decision-making processes remaining intact. By way of comparison, POWs have a right to their professional secrets so should not be threatened with harm for noncooperation nor be blackmailed into cooperating if the blackmail involves threats for noncooperation ("tell us what you know or else . . ."). Domestic criminal suspects should not be threatened or blackmailed, because both actions presumptuously assume that the suspect has criminal knowledge. By contrast, the positively identified unprivileged irregular can in theory be compelled to divulge what he knows through threats or blackmail, because he is a member of a class that can be presumed to have criminal knowledge, and threats and blackmail do not go too far in causing him physical harm.

Despite their potential permissibility, practical concerns counsel against frequent use of threats or blackmail. The interrogation manuals advise against all forms of threats because the interrogator will lose his psychological advantage if the detainee calls his bluff and the interrogator does not follow through on his threat. Also, if it used frequently, word of the tactic's use will eventually leak out among a given facility's detainees, and past the facility's walls, reducing its efficacy. Publicity regarding blackmail will also reduce its efficacy (e.g., the targeted irregular movement may become savvy to the government's tactic of sowing disinformation about collaborators) as well as create scandal, particularly in the case of sexual blackmail. Also, when considering blackmail, it is worth considering the applicability of the following practical critique of torture: that it sometimes transforms marginal players in a militant movement into dedicated, implacable foes of the government. For example, a depressingly common element in the pedigree of high-ranking Muslim Brotherhood and al-Qaeda figures is torture suffered in Egyptian jails. The same dynamic can be expected to occur for victims of blackmail, particularly sexual blackmail, if they are ever released. Finally, both threats and blackmail carry a high risk of producing false information, defeating the purpose of interrogation.

Rights of Unprivileged Irregulars Detained Domestically

On May 8, 2002, José Padilla, a U.S. citizen, was detained by federal agents at Chicago's O'Hare airport and held as a material witness in connection with the 9/11 attacks. He was later designated an "unlawful enemy combatant" by President Bush and publicly accused of planning terrorist attacks on U.S. soil. The administration asserted this designation stripped him of due process rights; Padilla was held largely incommunicado in a naval brig until January 3, 2006, when he was transferred to a Miami jail and charged with criminal conspiracy. A jury found him guilty of all charges on August 16, 2007.

Creating a special style of interrogation for unprivileged irregulars different from POW- or law enforcement–style interrogation is not warranted. In reference to only two interrogation styles then, the following discussion will first assign interrogation, detention, and trial rules for positively identified and suspected unprivileged irregulars detained in the territory of the detaining power and, then, positively identified and suspected unprivileged irregulars detained abroad. Comment on modes of detention and prosecution is relevant here, because the style of interrogation affects what the detaining power may do with the detainee after interrogation. Interrogation procedures will need to be tailored in a certain way, for instance, if the detaining power wants to criminally prosecute detainees instead of holding them as POWs.

The context for domestic capture of unprivileged irregulars could be an insurgency or infiltration by stateless agitators—the proverbial sleeper cell. (Padilla was described by the attorney general as an al-Qaeda sleeper agent at the time of his arrest.) Depending on the stage of the insurgency or terrorist threat, the state might view the irregulars' actions more as a criminal nuisance or more as a full-blown internal war. As mentioned before, whether the law enforcement or military and intelligence apparatuses of the state are deployed to meet the threat will also have to do with contingent factors regarding the government's structure and laws, as well as its perception of the security threat. Accordingly, it may be tactically preferable for the government to conduct POW-style instead of law enforcement–style interrogations even if unprivileged irregulars do not qualify for POW status. Unprivileged irregulars presumably *want* to be treated as POWs rather than criminal suspects if they *self*-identify as members of a politico-military organization. In chapter 2, emigration was mentioned as a means of opting out of the moral obligation to obey the just laws of one's state. Openly rebelling against the state and attempting to overthrow it militarily would also suffice to put one in the same *enemy of the state* category as a foreigner who attacks the state from abroad. Therefore, a government may have interrogators belonging to military or intelligence agencies conduct POW-style interrogations domestically with *positively identified* unprivileged irregulars if it feels the security environment is inappropriate for law enforcement officers. That said, the style of interrogation will indicate how the detainee is to be treated after the interrogation.

If the detainees are *not* self-identifying themselves as members of an unprivileged irregular group, their lack of self-identification presents epistemological problems for the government at odds with its possible desire to use the military to meet internal disturbances. People like José Padilla, or those suspected of plotting to attack soldiers at Fort Dix, mentioned in the last chapter, are suspected of plotting unprivileged political violence instead of run of the mill criminality, but the same arguments about the state's epistemic limits and baseline deference to inhabitants' rights in a domestic law enforcement context made in part 1 apply to those suspects if they are not self-identifying as part of an irregular militant group. The state cannot initially be sure such a detainee is an unprivileged irregular any more than he is a common thief. Even if he is captured in the midst of an attack on government property or personnel, the suspect could have pecuniary motives and be innocent of perpetrating unprivileged political violence. For example, those who attacked the Afghan policemen in the poppy fields of Uruzgan, mentioned in the preceding chapter, may simply have been opium traffickers. By contrast, the uniforms of conventional combatants or privileged irregulars identify them as members of a class of security threats of interest to military or intelligence interrogators, and relieves the interrogators of the need to investigate whether such detainees are security threats in the first place.[13]

Therefore, nonuniformed persons detained domestically on suspicion that they are unprivileged irregulars (regardless of their citizenship) ought to be given normal due process rights, including the rights afforded domestic criminal suspects in police interrogation if the detaining power wants to prosecute them either as criminals under its internal criminal law or as war criminals under its military law. (Under some construals, military law is applicable to civilians who commit crimes against military personnel or property.)[14] Confessions procured without the appropriate deference paid to the suspect's rights during interrogation would and should be quashed in court. This point about due process is moot for American military or CIA interrogators since they are legally prohibited from operating in the United States. No matter which organization the interrogator represents, the same interrogation rights afforded a domestic criminal suspect should be afforded suspected unprivileged irregulars in liberal states where comparable laws are not in place, and the military is actively fighting internal rebellions (as in e.g., Mexico, Columbia, and the Philippines), or domestic intelligence services are involved in counterinsurgency or anti-terror operations (as in, e.g., the U.K. or Israel).

Since suspected unprivileged irregulars detained domestically should be afforded the same rights as domestic criminal suspects, internal security threats should be met by law enforcement agencies trained in due process procedures whenever possible. Conventional militaries are poorly suited to observe all the relevant rights and conduct the investigations normally associated with law enforcement–style interrogations and criminal prosecutions. While providing legal counsel to domestic detainees would not necessarily be much more difficult than in normal criminal justice settings (particularly in urban environments), evidence gathering will often be at odds with the tactical requirements of military operations (discussed below). There are at least three real-world examples of how agencies with robust investigative powers can be structured to meet quasi-military domestic threats. There are regular police departments with paramilitary (e.g., SWAT) elements; agencies apart from the police that comprehensively marry paramilitary and law enforcement investigative capabilities, such as the Italian Carbinari or British Special Branch; and domestic intelligence agencies that have protocols for cooperation with the military such as MI-5 and Shin Bet (the military is used primarily to capture or kill irregulars). Ideally, joint operations would see investigators immediately move into areas secured by military or paramilitary operators and then act in the same manner as police investigating a crime scene or executing a search warrant, including advising suspects of their rights.

These arrangements are not just to the benefit of suspected unprivileged irregulars (who, we must recall, may be innocent people) since interrogations are more successful if interrogators have the sort of information about the suspect that military actors are usually ill equipped and ill trained to gather. Also, law enforcement–style investigations and surveillance will be necessary anyway to identify and locate suspected unprivileged irregulars, particularly in urban environments. It is telling that many of the al-Qaeda fighters seized by U.S. authorities abroad have been arrested by combined FBI and military teams.

Finally, we should consider if the above argument justifying deceptive interrogations of POWs applies to suspected domestic unprivileged irregulars. This justification, based on the detainee's status as an enemy of the detaining power, is *not* completely satisfactory to justify authorities' use of deception in cases where they suspect but are not sure the detainee is an unprivileged irregular. Also, the above argument applies to foreign enemies, not inhabitants of the detaining power's home territory (be they citizens or aliens) who are owed a particular set of rights by their own government.[15] Finally, unprivileged irregulars differ from conventional troops and privileged irregulars in lacking a right to their security-threatening secrets. For these reasons then, the justification of deception based on the hybrid nature of criminal suspects, mitigated by the rights afforded the suspects—detailed in chapters 4 and 5—applies instead.

Positively Identified Unprivileged Irregulars Captured Abroad

The paramilitary organization Sadaam Fedayeen was founded in 1995 by Saddam Hussein's son, Uday, and tasked with special security-related tasks including political assassinations. Its fighters conducted guerilla-style attacks against invading Coalition troops in 2003. There are numerous accounts of Sadaam Fedayeen attacking troops while dressed in civilian clothes; using human shields; and feigning surrender as a prelude to attacks.

An occupying army is responsible for basic policing duties in occupied territory since it is standing in for the defeated government. Agents of the occupying power face the same epistemic limitations when arresting suspected unprivileged irregulars ordinary police face when arresting criminal suspects. Therefore, the occupying power owes inhabitants of occupied territory the same baseline deference due to them by local police during peacetime, including the standard interrogation rights. Since these obligations are based on human rights, they are not affected by the differing nationalities of the occupiers and the inhabitants of the occupied territory. *Positively identified* unprivileged irregulars may be interrogated as POWs if the occupying power is more interested in engaging irregular groups militarily than through its law enforcement organs, though this treatment will also indicate POW-style detention following interrogation.

Prior to occupation, in the midst of ongoing hostilities, the detaining power will likely want to conduct POW-style rather than law enforcement–style interrogations with all those detainees captured in the midst of martial activity. The detaining power will want to proceed in this manner for the same tactical and security-related reasons it might prefer POW-style interrogations for unprivileged irregulars detained domestically. While positively identified unprivileged irregulars do not meet the criteria for POW status, and *do* have a quasi-criminal profile to the detaining power, POW-style interrogation is further recommended for them because providing law enforcement–style interrogations abroad is neither practical nor politically legitimate for the detaining power.

It is impractical to conduct law enforcement–style interrogations in the context of an invasion or other foreign campaign. It would probably be impossible to guarantee detainees a right to choose their own *local* counsel, and it would be burdensome to bring along public defenders for all the potential detainees—particularly in the context of ongoing hostilities where security for support staff is a significant drain on manpower. While American forces (and presumably others) do deploy abroad with judicial apparatuses, including JAG corps, to conduct any necessary courts-martial, I suspect unrealistically large numbers of lawyers would be necessary to represent the often large numbers of foreign detainees. Also, judicial independence in prosecutions of foreign nationals could be questioned if the defense attorneys and judges were members of the invading army.[16]

Law enforcement–style interrogation is of a piece with other investigative methods meant to secure indictable evidence, which would also likely be impractical on a foreign battlefield.[17] Deposing the soldiers who captured detainees might prove difficult if they are immersed in ongoing operations, much less gravely wounded in a field hospital. While U.S. soldiers, at least, are currently instructed to bag and label items of possible intelligence value like documents and computers they find on raids, it is probably unrealistic to expect them to conduct thorough police-style investigations of an unprivileged irregular's home, including forensic analyses. In theory, soldiers *could* be provided with this sort of training (at considerable expense and commitment of time), but soldiers would be in an unenviable role if doubly tasked with war fighting and criminal investigations since the roles would often work at cross purposes.[18] For example, a journalist related to me a (probably common) incident that occurred during the 2003 invasion of Baghdad where the battalion he was accompanying took fire from a warehouse; after exchanging fires for some time, the commander called in an airstrike that leveled the building. Obviously, such tactics would defeat the unit's purpose if it wished to collect evidence from the building for a criminal prosecution. Even regarding the material collected for intelligence purposes during raids—which could potentially be used later as evidence—one can imagine that defense counsel could easily challenge the integrity of the evidence on chain of custody grounds.[19]

Therefore, from the perspective of the detaining power, conducting law enforcement–style interrogation and investigation with positively identified unprivileged irregulars is both undesirable and impractical. Further, such behavior is not politically legitimate for the detaining power and so would serve no moral purpose. While unprivileged irregulars like the Sadaam Fedayeen do not have a right to their "professional" secrets—and in this way more closely resemble criminals than conventional combatants—they do not have the relationship with the detaining power justifying the various interrogation and trial rights afforded domestic criminal suspects. Until the invading army has settled into an occupying role, it is not assuming policing duties in enemy territory, and so cannot claim to be detaining and questioning criminal suspects in service of the overall enterprise of protecting those persons' lives and rights. Rather, the purpose of interrogation is strictly for the benefit of the invading army, the interests of which are at odds with those of the unprivileged irregular. Therefore, for both practical and moral reasons, prior to occupation, law enforcement–style interrogation is not indicated for *positively identified* unprivileged irregulars captured abroad, but rather, its alternate, POW-style interrogation.

Postinterrogation Treatment of Unprivileged Irregulars Captured Abroad

POW- rather than law enforcement–style interrogation is indicated for *positively identified* unprivileged irregulars captured on a foreign battlefield. However, such irregulars do not meet the criteria for POWs' moral impunity and legal immunity. While the detaining power may wish to criminally try and punish such detainees following interrogation, the absence of due process protections in POW-style interrogations is at odds with the requirements of fair trials. As argued above, POW-style interrogations likely run too high a risk of producing false confessions for these confessions to be used as evidence in criminal trials.

There are three possible options for postinterrogation treatment if unprivileged irregulars are given POW-style interrogations. First, the detaining power could attempt to prosecute detainees without using information gained in interrogations. In this scenario, the detaining power could conduct a POW-style interrogation and then hand the positively identified, or sus-pected, unprivileged irregulars over to a law enforcement agency or interna-tional tribunal for criminal investigation and prosecution as war criminals. Law enforcement investigators (in an American context, either civilian agen-cies like the FBI or civilian agencies attached to the military like the Army's Criminal Investigation Division) would start from scratch, interrogating the detainees without benefit of information from the military interrogation; advising the detainees of their rights to silence and counsel; and eventu-ally releasing them if unable to secure enough evidence to warrant their continued detention and prosecution. Second, the detaining power could use the information garnered in POW-style interrogations to prosecute the detainees in a military tribunal without traditional due process standards. In this scenario, the detaining power might use statements elicited from the detainees during interrogations against them at a tribunal. Third, the detain-ing power could refrain from using information elicited in interrogation to prosecute detainees and continue to hold them without formal sentencing. That is, the detaining power could treat positively identified unprivileged irregulars as POWs even though they do not qualify for POW status, con-ducting POW-style interrogations and holding them as POWs until the end of hostilities. There are serious problems with the first two options. I will advocate the third option, which despite imperfections, meets many of the detaining power's needs and does not violate detainees' rights.

The first option is to conduct a POW-style interrogation and, then, when the interrogator is satisfied that he has extracted all militarily useful infor-mation from the detainee, hand the detainee over to an investigative entity that will reinterrogate the detainee according to law enforcement standards. The first interrogator could also switch to "law enforcement mode" himself; advise the detainee of his rights; and then conduct the interrogation for a second time. On this model, self-incriminating statements made during the initial POW-style interrogation would be discounted, though the same sort of questions could be repeated after a *Miranda*-style warning (under U.S. military law, persons being interrogated for war crimes are advised of their Article 31B rights, analogous to the *Miranda* rights). The purpose of the admonition about rights to silence and counsel would not play the role they do in a domestic law enforcement context of deferring to the suspect's hybrid identity, because his clear identification as an unprivileged irregular obviates the need to defer to ambiguity over his status. Rather, the main purpose of the admonition would be to foster an atmosphere in which subsequent confessions could reasonably be judged to be reliable. In chap-ter 4, I argued that a suspect's rights during interrogation were not merely based on the needs of a fair trial but were appropriate elements of the state-inhabitant relationship given what the state had cause to know about the suspect's status. By contrast, this model for dealing with unprivileged irregulars *would* extend interrogation rights to them for the purpose of conducting fair trials. If mere membership in an unprivileged irregular group is criminal according to the internal law of the detaining power, the detainee would be in a similar situation to that of a domestic criminal suspect caught red-handed; the substantive purpose of the trial would be more to assign the level of culpability and appropriate punishment than to determine guilt or innocence.

There are difficulties with this proposal. Military interrogators are often under pressure to quickly process a large number of detainees since interrogation is most effective when detainees are still disconcerted from their capture. Since operations can bring in large numbers of detainees to an interrogation facility all at once, it is likely unrealistic in most cases for interrogators to initially continue interrogations after extracting tactically relevant information or after it is determined that the detainee is not of intelligence value. In some situations it might be possible for interrogators to return to conduct law enforcement–style interrogations with criminally culpable detainees in a lull after the initial flurry of interrogations. However, it is fairly dubious in this event that subsequent confessions would be admissible in court since defense counsel could plausibly argue that the admonition about the detainee's right to silence would come across as nominal since the detainee knows he's already confessed.[20] The same critique could be made if the detainee is handed over to a law enforcement agency that begins a criminal investigation from scratch. One suspects that a detainee from a country where the *Miranda* warning is not part of the popular culture would be confused as to why the new interrogator was saying he does not have to admit what the first interrogator demanded to know. Moreover, counsel could argue that the initial confession was coerced since the detainee was stressed and frightened after the likely traumatic experience of being captured and was additionally frightened of what his captors would do to him if he did not tell them what they wanted to hear.[21] All the difficulties of collecting evidence and interviewing witnesses in the context of ongoing hostilities, mentioned above, would also apply.

The second option is to conduct a POW-style interrogation and then move directly to prosecution in some kind of military tribunal, be it a court-martial (held according to the existing statutes of military law) or a military commission (an ad hoc body functioning according to rules set by the political leader or military commander, rooted in the common law of war). There may be difficulty meeting a court-martial's due process standards (similar to those required in domestic criminal trials) for the reasons just cited, so proponents of the second option might prefer an ad hoc military commission, where rules of evidence are generally looser.[22] Given the circumstances surrounding typical battlefield captures, a looser standard for indictment than the use of a grand jury would be desirable on this view, as would the use of confessions and witness statements produced in potentially coercive environments (defined as the nonadmonition of a right to silence, multi-day interrogations, and an absence of defense counsel—also taking into account the frightening and stressful circumstances of the detainee's capture and detention). If trial rules could be further tailored to protect secret intelligence-gathering methods and sources, then it would also be desirable to close the proceedings to the public; to refuse a suspect access to evidence against him; and deny him the opportunity to confront his accusers.[23] Concerns over secrecy as well as security might suggest using military officers or military judges instead of civilian judges.[24] Moreover, there might be some limit made on habeas corpus type appeals and postconviction appeals, since the detaining power does not want to risk losing custody of a security-threatening alien in a foreign environment where continued surveillance would presumably be difficult.

President George W. Bush's military order of November 13, 2001, creating the establishment of military commissions to hear cases against "unlawful enemy combatants" contained all of these elements and also denied the defendant the right to know the charges against him and required only a two-thirds vote among the military officers presiding for the death penalty. The subsequent global outcry led to reformulations and, most recently, the 2006 Military Commissions Act, passed by Congress, which still allows the use of some secret evidence; denies the right of habeas corpus to foreigners held by the United States; allows the president to summarily designate persons as "unlawful enemy combatants"; and may, given the ambiguity of some passages, permit the use of testimony produced through torture.

The second option and its American incarnation wrongly distort judicial procedures to accommodate the lack of due process inherent in wartime detentions and interrogations.[25] In typical wartime scenarios, the equivalent of an indictment is performed at a tribunal held within days of capture to determine if a detainee is a civilian or a POW. Typically, representatives from the unit that captured the detainee communicate the circumstances of the capture to the tribunal. The uniforms of the conventional POW presumably correct for many errors in initial identification of detainees as well as errors in communication between persons with custody of the detainees or between troops and the tribunal. Presumably, the man in the Republican Guard uniform is a member of the Republican Guard. Yet there is far more ambiguity regarding the identity of unprivileged irregulars, who may not be wearing any identifying emblem and who may not have been captured in military barracks or on military equipment. Indeed, given the nature of counterinsurgency and counterterror operations, people out of military dress will be seized by troops acting on less information than would be required for a domestic arrest warrant. If one can imagine easy and frequent cases of mistaken identity when relatively well-trained American soldiers are honestly trying to distinguish innocent civilians from insurgents in a foreign culture, one should consider the fact that a number of the detainees held incommunicado by the United States in Guantanamo Bay for over five years were not even seized by U.S. personnel but by Northern Alliance militiamen or Pakistani intelligence officers who received $5,000 for every purported al-Qaeda fighter they produced. Also, while the inadequate investigative and recording capacities of frontline soldiers are usually not a problem since the particular actions of the average (noncriminal) POW prior to capture are irrelevant to his treatment in detention—since he is immune from prosecution—investigative shortcomings would be relevant in cases where the particular actions of an unprivileged irregular are relevant for war crimes prosecutions.[26]

Similarly, there should be no negative consequence for the average POW who divulges what the interrogator wants to know, so the lower degree of reliability for information garnered in POW-style interrogations is not a problem for the POW. By contrast, an admission of war crimes or of membership in an outlawed terrorist organization might be sufficient to earn an unprivileged irregular a life sentence or capital punishment in a military tribunal with relaxed standards of evidence and nonprofessional judges selected from the detaining power's own general staff.[27] It would be inimical to a trial's mandate to determine the truth if prosecutors introduced confessions elicited in fairly harrowing interrogation environments—which also lack the safeguards of law enforcement interrogations—much less incriminating third party testimony perhaps produced in foreign torture chambers. To close trials to public view and deny defendants a chance to confront their accusers; view the evidence against them; demand a writ of habeas corpus; or enjoy a right to meaningful judicial appeal is to insulate possible error against their normal remedies.

Classification of a conventional combatant as a POW is a summary and categorical classification, based on superficial criteria like the presence of uniforms, rather than an assessment of the specific actions of the detainee. When POWs are suspected of war crimes, the detaining power launches investigations and courts-martial with due process protections; in part, the purpose of these due process standards is to ensure that the truth of the matter is revealed and a punishment fitting the crime is assigned. So even if unprivileged irregulars self-identify, the second option for postinterrogation treatment inappropriately mixes the outcomes of criminal prosecutions with procedures that have the summary, wholesale nature of POW classification.

Proponents of the second option are right to note the difficulty if not the absurdity of holding soldiers on a foreign battlefield to the same due process standards as police but wrongly propose that trials be deformed to meet the input available from battlefield conditions, rather than changing the nature of punishment to be assigned unprivileged irregulars. By contrast, the third option is guided by the detaining power's interrogation needs, but then accepts the consequences this mode of interrogation indicates for the detainee. Information collected in a POW-style interrogation should not be used as trial evidence since it is collected in an environment lacking in due process protections. An absence of a fair court proceeding precludes punishment consequent to trial, because it would be unjust to arbitrarily levy punishment without any kind of due process–mediated procedure for determining the level of the defendant's culpability. Presumably, the detaining power would not want to summarily release the detainee when his organization is still fighting the state, so the end of hostilities stands as a nonarbitrary and practical termination point for the unprivileged irregular's detention. If there is no court procedure to determine punishments, the mode of detention cannot be punitive without those punitive elements being arbitrarily assigned. Therefore, unprivileged irregulars should be nonpunitively detained, which is to say, according to the principle of parity, in the manner of POWs, until the end of hostilities. That said, since the detaining power is extending POW status to the detainee in deference to the consequences of its chosen mode of interrogation rather than in deference to the rights the detainee enjoys as a state actor, the detaining power may withhold certain aspects of typical POW treatment so long as detainees are not legally tried or treated punitively in detention (discussed below).

This solution meets the detaining power's desire to conduct POW-style interrogations and perhaps gain militarily useful information but might be considered morally dissatisfying, since it means people with essentially criminal profiles are ineligible for punitive fines, capital punishment, or detention past the end of hostilities. There is also a practical problem of there possibly being no nation-state to receive the detainees at the end of hostilities if the irregulars are stateless agitators.

Regarding the issue of punishment, apart from the prospect of fines and the death penalty, there should not be a great difference between the conditions of detention for POWs and domestic criminals since both group should be treated humanely.[28] POWs are to be released at the end of hostilities, but the duration of detention for unprivileged irregulars might be quite long as insurgencies and terror campaigns typically last decades. To this point, no al-Qaeda figures prosecuted in the U.S. under its internal criminal law have been given the death penalty, so apart from the privilege of being housed in secure, barracks-style conditions with fellow jihadis instead of solitary cells in "Super-Max" prisons, there do not seem to be too many advantages future al-Qaeda detainees might enjoy if treated as POWs. Granted, at least under the Geneva Conventions, POWs are due some fairly trivial amenities like a small stipend, athletic equipment, and the liberty to organize recreational activities among themselves. These amenities are not out of line with those enjoyed by the majority of domestic prisoners. These types of liberties and other types of fraternization between unprivileged irregular detainees could be circumscribed out of safety concerns since violent POWs may be punished with solitary confinement and/or reduction of privileges. Even if this is not the case, the admittedly unpalatable idea of imprisoned jihadis holding volleyball tournaments perhaps can be suffered in exchange for the possible intelligence garnered from them through POW-style interrogations.

The Geneva Conventions mandate that the detaining power inform its POWs' home nation of their capture within ten days of capture. The home nation can be expected to know in most cases that the POWs in question were either casualties or taken captive given that units are typically obliged to keep in regular contact with their chain of command. By contrast, the cell-like and secretive nature of many irregular groups means that operatives may well be out of contact with one another for days or weeks. The detaining power will be anxious to take advantage of those factors to extract what the detainee knows before his comrades conclude that he has been captured and roll up the networks or operations with which he was involved. It is therefore tactically desirable for the detaining power to hold and interrogate an unprivileged irregular without informing anyone of his capture, be it the International Committee of the Red Cross, local law enforcement, or the detainee's family for at least a few weeks. Since he does not qualify for POW status and its attendant rights—and the detaining power is merely affording him that status for convenience—it can derogate privileges as it requires so long as the derogation does not affect his basic human rights and does not unfairly use information garnered in interrogation against him. After that time period has elapsed, there is no reason to refuse the detainee communication with his family via censored correspondence.[29] In addition to not informing an outside party of the irregular's capture for a period of a few weeks (the length ought to vary based on what the detaining power knows about his group's standard communication protocols), it may also be indicated that the detainee should be separated from other detainees lest he be coached or encouraged by them. The Soviet Union and China once used isolation for four- to six-week periods as a form of torture and prelude to brainwashing. Separating a detainee from others does not rise to this level, because he will have contact with his interrogator. Separating him from others *is* likely to make him more susceptible to the interrogator's attempt to establish rapport and ultimately, to extract his secrets, but again, the unprivileged irregular does not have a right to his secrets.

Regarding the issue of release, concern is often expressed that some unprivileged irregulars will simply return to political violence once free. In the case of insurgencies, an end to hostilities justifying prisoners' release may mean a complete routing of the rebels, as occurred in the 1990s in Peru and in the 1960s in Bolivia; in such cases, there may be little likelihood of the released irregular starting a new movement from scratch. Insurgencies also end when the political situation provoking the insurgency changes, or when rebels' demands are largely met, as in Northern Ireland and 1970s Sudan. In any event, it seems reasonable to have something akin to probation for released irregulars. If arrangements for monitoring cannot be made between the detaining power and the government of the irregular's country of origin, perhaps the detainee can be released to the custody of a third country that will agree to monitor him or even be integrated into a community in the detaining power's own country. Bearing in mind that many participants in radical movements have minimal education and have been "programmed" by radical mullahs or manipulative cadres, some kind of noncoercive, rehabilitative "re-education" of detainees is probably appropriate prior to their release. For example, Saudi Arabia has a fairly robust program for "deprogramming" Islamist militants, involving their meeting with clerics who refute the theological errors of the militants' recruiters.

While imperfect, the third option has fewer problems than its alternatives. If fair, open trials cannot be held for unprivileged irregulars because of the need to protect secret intelligence-gathering methods; the difficulty in securing witness statements; the inherent ambiguity of initial identification due to the "fog of war"; and the likely inadmissibility of statements elicited in POW-style interrogations, it is better to forgo trials altogether than hold what would effectively be show trials. Just the same, states may not simply seize people and hold them without charge and eventual conviction of a criminal offense or classification as a POW. Once the type of detention is determined, a right to challenge one's detention and appeal one's conviction is a basic human right, given the possibility of wrongful detention, and so accrues to both conventional POWs and unprivileged irregulars treated as POWs.

Suspected Unprivileged Irregulars Captured Abroad

Khalid al-Masri, a German citizen of Lebanese descent, was arrested by police in Macedonia in December 2003 because he had the same name as a suspected terrorist. He was handed over to a CIA team which flew him to a secret installation in Afghanistan. According to al-Masri's deposition in a Federal lawsuit, he was kept there in squalid conditions for five months, beaten, and repeatedly questioned about terrorist ties before his captors determined he was innocent and released him in Albania.

Unprivileged irregulars do not always self-identify and are not only captured while engaged in attacks. Standard counterinsurgency operations involve cordons and searches in civilian areas where insurgent activity is suspected. Troops then conduct field interviews; detain people suspected of being insurgents or insurgent supporters; and transport them to a secure location for interrogation. Away from active conflict zones, intelligence officers also sometimes seize suspected security threats and transport them to secret locations for interrogations.

The following argument applies to *suspected* unprivileged irregulars detained by foreign military or intelligence officers on the battlefield or in nonoccupied territory in peacetime. By way of comparison, police officers' prudential behavior in keeping with the level of incriminating information they have about a domestic criminal suspect does not violate the suspect's political rights, because such behavior is a part of a general enterprise necessary to protect inhabitants' lives and rights. The rights police properly afford to suspects during the interrogation phases of a criminal inquiry and prosecution balance the prudential behaviors police undertake (accosting, arresting, interrogating) to ensure that both elements of the suspect's civic identity—possibly innocent but possibly guilty—are observed. However, be it during war (prior to enemy occupation) or during peacetime, a person in civilian dress has his political rights violated if he is detained and interrogated by an agent of a foreign state, regardless of how benignly he is treated during interrogation and in detention. It does not matter which style of interrogation is used. While it would be irrational for him to dissent to reasonable policing actions taken by his *own* country's police (assuming he lives in a basically just state), it is not irrational for him to dissent to the prudential behavior of a *foreign agent* acting solely in the service of the agent's own nation. For example, American officers were not (allegedly) interrogating the German citizen Khalid al-Masri as part of the general enterprise of protecting his life and rights in *Germany* but, rather, to protect American interests. The justification for deceptive interrogations of domestic criminal suspects does not transfer to international contexts, because the implicit social contracts granting state authorities police powers are limited to the territory where they effectively protect inhabitants' lives and rights. Any direct prudential action perpetrated domestically by a foreign power, including arrest, detention, and interrogation, violates civilians' political rights, because such forms of political coercion are only legitimate when exercised by these persons' own government and when performed in the service of protecting their lives and rights.

One might wonder if nonuniformed foreigners' are really greatly harmed when interrogated by professional foreign agents, even if allowing that their political rights are violated on an abstract level. The practical scope of rights violations in counterinsurgency operations can indeed be broad since conventional military units are usually ill trained and ill prepared to do the sort of investigative work necessary to distinguish unprivileged irregulars from civilians. For example, at times in 2004, American military units in Iraq took a wholesale approach to tactical screening, sweeping up huge numbers of innocent Iraqis whom poorly prepared, and in many cases, culturally obtuse soldiers mistook for being insurgents. An Army interrogator stationed in northern Iraq describes a typical day:

> At a routine checkpoint stop, a search revealed that Mahdi had a cell phone and a shovel. The sworn statement said that the arresting infantry suspected the shovel would be used to bury a roadside bomb, and the cell phone would be used to detonate it. This was so far-fetched that even Mahdi had to laugh about it. . . . As we worked our way through this group, we found it was a good day for arbitrary arrests. The old man, Akram, owned a small roadside restaurant. He was arrested because someone, somewhere, asserted that insurgents ate lunch there. The fifteen year old kid [who had been beaten by the arresting marines], Taslim, was arrested in a cordon search. When the infantry tossed his father's house, they found $3,000 cash. The kid explained that . . .

the money was their savings for a new truck. No adults were home, so they arrested the kid. . . . Isam had been arrested at a checkpoint. His car had no backseats, so the arresting infantry decided he was building a car bomb. No other evidence supported this. Abbas . . . was another checkpoint arrest. His tribal name was the same as that of a man on the blacklist. I'd seen this many times before. [Tens of thousands of people can have the same tribal name.] Finally, we had Hanbal. . . . As we went through the standard questions, he seethed both fear and contempt. On this guy, we had some actual intelli- gence—a source that I trusted—but no physical evidence. So if Hanbal turned out to be an actual insurgent and/or could provide some intelligence, then the ratio of "good" prisoners to worthless (probably innocent) in this micro- cosm was one to six. As bad as that was, it was far better than usual. If this was acceptable, I had to wonder, why bother with coming up with ridiculous reasons—cell phones, shovels, lack of backseats, or possession of money—to detain someone? Why not just do mass arrests and see what we get?

The Army interrogator notes with disgust in his memoir that people he quickly determined to be innocent often arrived in the interrogation facility bruised from beatings they received in the field; endured torture his incom- petent commanding officer authorized when poorly trained interrogators were unable to procure intelligence from the (largely innocent) detainees; and then, in the best case scenario, still had to wait two weeks for release because of the pace of Army bureaucracy. This while being held incom- municado and without any avenue for appeal or redress.[30] Aptly expressing a military mindset geared toward confronting enemies, rather than a law enforcement mindset that views suspects as innocent until proven guilty, the commanding officer of the facility in North Babel where these detainees were held, said, "Anyone who comes into this prison is guilty, and if I let them out it's because of overwhelming evidence of innocence."[31] In fact, the treatment of Iraqi civilians can be viewed as a lesson in what domestic police investigations might look like in the absence of due process rights.

There *is* a strong case to be made that a civilian should aid foreign inves- tigators in criminal inquiries, at least regarding third parties, when foreign investigators are accompanied by domestic law enforcement agents—for example, if FBI special agents facilitate the questioning of an American by Canadian authorities in regards to a Canadian fugitive. This is because, on a moral level, all persons ought to do what they can easily do to help oth- ers (at least), and no one has a right to abet criminals. The presence of domestic authorities ought to ensure that the American's rights in this case are respected; if they are violated, she has a readily accessible target, and familiar procedure, to pursue a lawsuit. (By contrast, al-Masri's lawsuit was thrown out by an American judge on the grounds that it would require exposing secret government programs vital to national security.) However, during a war, a military or intelligence officer of a foreign power is not interrogating battlefield detainees in the service of local or transnational crime prevention, but as part of an effort to overthrow the detainee's government or at least damage its national security. In the case of suspected stateless agitators captured abroad like al-Masri, the detaining power is not seeking to coerce or overthrow a government, but is also not acting in the name of *local* crime prevention and is not working with local law enforcement. Rather, the detaining power is interacting with such detainees as enemies of the state, more in the way it would with conventional combatants than domestic criminals.

Therefore, if unaccompanied by local law enforcement, foreign agents cannot act prudentially toward nonuniformed people (presumptive civilians) without violating their political rights. In pursuing unprivileged irregulars, foreign agents will not violate nonuniformed persons' rights if they limit themselves to modes of interaction that are ordinarily permissible between private citizens, including pollsters and salespeople. This means they may politely question nonuniformed people on their doorsteps during cordons and searches, but more aggressive actions—demanding answers, searching homes without permission, or applying punishments for noncooperation—will violate these people's rights. Householders are not obliged to respond to foreign agents' questions and are not obliged to give them permission to search their homes.

Despite their lack of entitlement for prudential behavior comparable to that of local police, a foreign military or intelligence officer *is* justified in detaining and interrogating a nonuniformed person (or searching his house) given strong reasonable indications that he is an unprivileged irregular. The justifiability of the state agents' behavior does not detract from the rights-violating character of the actions.[32] This disjuncture is surprising since we expect that people will not be wronged when others act in a justifiable way toward them. People are not wronged when another has perfect knowledge of the context for his actions; acts within his rights; and executes the action he intended without incurring any unintended side effects. The reason it is possible for civilians to be wronged even when military actors do nothing morally wrong is that the military actors are obliged to take steps to protect their nation but are sometimes unable to perform the state's business in a way that completely avoids harm to foreign civilians because of available technology, intelligence, terrain, and the like. If unprivileged irregulars all flew flags outside their homes, or if the government had perfect intelligence on insurgents' identities, government troops would be able to behave prudentially toward unprivileged irregulars alone without inconveniencing uninvolved neighbors. However, the irregulars' tactic of hiding among civilians makes "clean" operations like this nearly impossible.

Just war theorists typically address such matters by utilizing a moral calculation known as the doctrine of double effect, advanced by St. Thomas Aquinas in the thirteenth century. Militarily necessary actions anticipated to have simultaneous and inseparable good and bad effects—for example, bombing a radar site might also injure some nearby civilians—are justifiable if only the good effect (the destruction of a radar site) is desired by the actor; the actor has no less damaging option available to him; and the bad effect incurred (civilians casualties) is judged proportional to the good desired. Civilians harmed in such an attack are wronged since they have done nothing to void their rights even if the perpetrator of the action is not wrong in acting. He is understood to be innocent of willing their harm if he did not desire the harm to occur but was nonetheless compelled to act to bring about a good end in a situation where preventing negative secondary effects was impossible. However, he *is* culpable if forgoing an option that would minimize secondary harm and instead choosing an action causing more secondary harm than necessary, be it through deliberate intent or negligence.

The doctrine of double effect can also be used to justify detention and interrogation of nonuniformed foreigners who are suspected of being unprivileged irregulars. It is unlikely that interrogators will only be able to interrogate actual unprivileged irregulars without ever inconveniencing innocent people because of the very ambiguity that serves as unprivileged irregulars' camouflage. Limiting interrogators' actions to situations where they are certain of their targets' status is likely not prudent and proactive enough for them to meet their legitimate obligations to their home nations; they will sometimes have no other means of determining whether someone suspected of being an unprivileged irregular truly is an unprivileged irregular without detaining and interrogating him. Unprivileged irregulars who do not self-identify deserve the blame in this situation for placing their civilian neighbors in the cross hairs of foreign troops. With the force of the collateral damage analogy in mind though, state agents should use maximum discretion and caution before taking any actions against unarmed, nonuniformed foreigners beyond simple in situ questioning, and procedures should be implemented for expediting the release of innocent people. As in law enforcement contexts, the ambiguity over suspects' identity is another reason to avoid any sort of harsh treatment of suspects. Finally, since they have been wronged, albeit nonculpably, it would also be appropriate to compensate innocent persons who suffered detention, interrogation, or searches of their homes.

We can use the doctrine of double effect to assess the above-mentioned cases. The doctrine cannot justify the kidnapping and detention of Khalid al-Masri, because merely having the same name as a wanted man is not an adequate reason for long-term detention, much less abuse. The above-mentioned cases from Iraq similarly cannot be excused with the doctrine on account of the Americans' incompetence and lack of professionalism. In both cases, the actors had less harmful alternatives to the methods they chose, and so their actions are not justified on the basis of necessity.

Investigative Tactics in Unconventional Warfare

A few practical comments about interrogation in unconventional warfare are indicated here since the doctrine of double effect does not excuse actors using bad tactics. While abusive treatment of detainees is unacceptable for any type of detainee—evidence of failures in discipline, training, and leadership—the excesses seen in at least a portion of the Iraq War also appear to be a result of the inadequacies of some conventional military intelligence approaches to counterinsurgency and anti-terror operations. (In several instances, the failure of ineffective noncoercive techniques seems to have motivated frustrated interrogators to embrace physically abusive methods.)[33] The post–World War II American military approach to interrogation seemed to conceive of interrogators as fairly low-skilled information processors whose main task would be recording mundane "order of battle" information elicited from POWs (e.g., unit affiliation, unit size, number of artillery pieces, etc.). Interrogators would then send the information up the chain of command for analysts to piece together into a fuller picture of the enemy. Up until 2004 at least, very little time was spent teaching actual interrogation techniques at Ft. Huachuca, the Army's military intelligence school. This was apparently because trainers assumed most POWs would gamely volunteer security-sensitive information to interrogators using the direct approach.[34] While experienced police and intelligence interrogators state that successful interrogation approaches will have to vary with the interrogatee, a "one size fits all" approach may in fact be acceptable in conventional military contexts when the type of information sought is of a kind that is technical and easily quantifiable. However, in unconventional warfare, law enforcement–style investigative tactics including skillful interrogations can be expected to be useful in gathering intelligence to the extent that terrorist campaigns and some insurgencies have the conspiratorial nature of criminal enterprises and involves combatants living incognito among civilians. Regardless of whether the information is eventually meant to be used as evidence in a courtroom, many of the techniques associated with domestic criminal investigations must be used to find irregulars. Physical materials must be gathered and analyzed; informants cultivated; witnesses interviewed and reinterviewed; and suspects interrogated by skilled interrogators using information gained from other investigative avenues as leverage in the interrogation booth. None of these individual actions are necessarily beyond the portfolio of military intelligence operations. However, what appears to be necessary in unconventional warfare is the integration of these actions at a tactical, rather than higher-echelon operational or strategic levels, with interrogators acting more in the role of police detectives or assistant district attorneys in directing the overall effort of which interrogation is a part, or at least closely advising a commanding officer with that portfolio. This, as opposed to viewing interrogators as specialists performing a stand-alone function in a compartmentalized process integrated only far afield. Interrogation needs to be seen as part of an overall investigative approach with interrogation as the capstone activity, drawing intelligence from informants, analysts' research, and searches in the field. Interrogation should have claim to these intelligence streams in unconventional warfare because it is potentially a much more potent weapon in these contexts than in conventional warfare—on account of the relative wealth of security-sensitive information an irregular combatant might possess. In a conventional conflict, the high-ranking officers with the most security-sensitive information can be expected to be the farthest from the frontline and the hardest to capture; by contrast, high-ranking irregulars may be comparatively easy to capture (once their whereabouts are known) since they conduct their planning from apartments or rural hideouts with rudimentary defenses.

These comments are motivated by the distance between what the literature suggests is necessary for successful interrogations and some of the practices of the American military in the years following 9/11. In a number of cases, inadequate interrogation training and improper interrogation protocols undoubtedly led to abuse of detainees. Some commentators have advocated coercive techniques on Islamist terrorists because of their alleged nonsusceptibility to noncoercive techniques—wrongly inferring from cases of unsuccessful interrogations in which the interrogators were poorly trained in noncoercive techniques.[35] Interrogation manuals emphasize that interrogators need as much information as possible about the incident in question so they can affect confidence and frame effective questions, yet

Army interrogators in Iraq and Afghanistan consistently complained about troops depositing detainees in interrogation facilities with little to no information about the circumstances of their capture.[36] Further, as of 2004 at least, interrogators in Iraq and Afghanistan had no authority to request or order field operations to verify information detainees provided, and so had few objective means of determining whether a particular interrogation approach was promising. Interrogators were in fact discouraged from trying to verify information elicited from detainees, instead entering all information (no matter how dubious) into a computer server relaying information to analysts and "consumers" at various commands. Not only does this appear to be counterproductive for the larger intelligence effort, it inhibits effective interrogations since key interrogation techniques include catching the interrogatee in a lie or convincing him that resistance is futile since the interrogator "knows all." Indeed, interrogators found they did not have much success with al-Qaeda and Taliban prisoners in Afghanistan until they acted *against* regulations and pooled information about detainees in order to build up profiles and time lines that were then used to catch interrogatees in lies.[37]

For interrogators to be successful in unconventional warfare, they need to either accompany troops in the field—where they can direct, or act closely in concert with the ranking officer to direct, the investigative aspects of the mission including tactical screening, document recovery, and searches after a site has been secured—or work from hardened sites where they stay in real-time contact with troops in the field in order to request additional information or direct new searches for people or materiel based on interrogations. At the very least, troops in the field need to be instructed that there is little point in detaining suspected irregulars if operators do not also relay information about the suspects and the circumstances of their capture to interrogators. Troops in the field as well as interrogators need to be better trained in the investigative aspects of unconventional warfare, which in particular theaters will involve intensive cultural training so that they are better able to distinguish genuinely suspicious behavior from behavior that is normal in the local culture. Critics will object that extra training costs money, but ineffective operations born of inadequate training are costlier.

In this chapter, I argued that positively identified unprivileged irregulars can be met with military force, interrogated, and held as POWs when captured domestically. Where domestic unprivileged irregulars are operating incognito, law enforcement–style investigation and interrogation are tactically and morally indicated instead. Suspected unprivileged irregulars are to be given the same due process protections as ordinary criminal suspects, and for the same reasons. When fighting unprivileged irregulars abroad, positively identified militants can be interrogated and held as POWs, though troops engaged in counterinsurgency will often have to utilize law enforcement style investigative techniques to garner intelligence about irregulars and to conduct successful interrogations. Foreign agents have no special privilege to detain and interrogate unarmed, nonuniformed people on suspicion of involvement with militant groups, yet often have no other means of determining who is secretly involved in the irregular movement. Since such prudential actions violate the political rights of unarmed, nonuniformed people, foreign troops must take steps to be as deferential as possible when interacting with the civilian population.

EIGHT

Coercive Interrogation

Everyone reading this book will be familiar with the "ticking bomb" thought experiment, used as a kind of trump card against those who would prohibit interrogatory torture. Most will also probably appreciate the implausibility of a scenario in which interrogators *know* they have a terrorist in custody and *know* he has knowledge of an imminent terrorist operation. Even if one has in mind a fairly pedestrian interdiction of a low level operative, the literature suggests that the number of cases where security officials interrogate someone they know is culpable pales compared to the number of cases where the interrogatee is only suspected of involvement in terrorist activity. Consideration of the disparity between the contrived details of most ticking bomb thought experiments and the circumstances of real-life interrogations can lead one to conclude that such thought experiments are not experiments at all, but "intellectual frauds," justifications tailored to arrive at an assumed premise that interrogatory torture is justifiable (as well as efficacious).[1]

I know from conversations with other scholars that the ticking bomb argument tends to lurk in one's mind, despite its dubious nature. Some of its tenacity no doubt stems from the images of interrogatory torture one sees in films and on TV, where torture is often portrayed as quickly yielding results. It would likely be wrong to underestimate the emotional weight these images have in comparison to abstract arguments about detainees' rights. Following more deliberate reflection, one can perceive that the implausibility of the ticking bomb thought experiment can also paradoxically account for its tenacity. Since some of the arguments against the use of torture are based on torture's plausibly anticipated outcomes, a rare, *im*plausible event such as the ticking bomb scenario can be seen as an exception to those arguments. Of course torture will not be routine policy, the proponent implies, but just an extreme measure in a rare case when all other methods have failed. Still, it is unlikely that many would support other actions, identified with torture's onerous effects, which depended on such implausible circumstances for justification. Indeed, while many public debates are animated by wrongheaded assumptions, torture has come to have a set of values associated with it in contemporary American discourse putting it in a slim category of policy issues like abortion or welfare where the debate seems to be about more about the proponents' self-regard than the policy ostensibly in question. Interrogatory torture either works or does not work, and it can either be justified or not be justified according to a given moral standard. While these questions will be addressed in this chapter, something too will need to be said about the psychological allure of the ticking bomb argument and what it says about those thinking and writing about national security in an age of terrorism.

There is a good deal of redundancy in the many pro- and anti-torture pieces written after 9/11.[2] Therefore, I will not be addressing the subject with the same strategy I used to discuss police interrogation,[3] but will instead try to draw some conclusions about the types of arguments that can be made about interrogatory torture, or "coercive interrogation" as it is sometimes called.[4] I will advance three arguments against interrogatory torture in this chapter. The first argument, the restricted deontological argument briefly mentioned in the last chapter—physical force is disproportionate to use against a detainee because the detainee is not a physical threat to the interrogator—is coherent, so far as I can see. The deontological limits related to the detainee's rights would have to be removed to permit coercive interrogation. Removing these limits yields the *unrestricted* deontological argument that protecting innocent people from terrorism justifies any interrogatory technique. This argument courts grotesque consequences most torture advocates would probably not endorse. Since torture does not admit of a moderate stance between restricted and unrestricted deontological arguments, a persistent proponent of coercive interrogation would have to abandon the deontological route altogether and make an argument appealing to consequences of interrogation alone. It seems important to address a *consequentialist* argument here even though it assumes different methodological bases than those used in this book because such arguments are often made in reference to torture. Indeed, consequentialist reasoning is central to the ticking bomb argument, the desperate circumstances described in its usual articulations suggesting its proponents' impatience with the neat abstraction of deontological prohibitions. I will argue that the consequentialist approach is ill suited to this subject because the data on which it depends is chronically ambiguous.

Each of the three anti-torture arguments could be seen as sufficient on its own, depending on one's presuppositions. Nonetheless, I have arranged them in series, showing the increasingly absurd consequences entailed by a rejection of each one. This structure is indicated by a dynamic present in some of the contemporary literature on torture. There, one can see an odd set of rational tics exemplified by the more florid ticking bomb arguments: an ignoring of countervailing data, a looking for exceptions, and an impatience with abstract argument in favor of vivid thought experiment. Frankly, decades from now, these tendencies may appear as flagrant a capitulation to unexamined conventional views as modern readers perceive in late nineteenth-century scholarship about gender and race.

History of Interrogatory Torture

Historically, noncoercive interrogation methods like deceit and trickery were not intuitive techniques for security and juridical officers striving to elicit the truth from behind a person's tightly sealed lips. In ancient Greece, a freeman's juridical testimony was taken as true on its face, but a slave's testimony could only be entered if the slave had confirmed the account under torture.[5] The assumption was that freemen were smart enough to prefer torture to self-incrimination, whereas slaves would just incriminate the guilty party in exchange for an immediate respite from pain. The Romans enlisted specially trained torturers in policing, military, and judicial contexts and, as the Empire grew, steadily expanded the categories of peoples who could be tortured. Interrogatory torture was largely replaced by trial by ordeal or combat between legal contestants in the period between the fall of the Roman Empire and the twelfth century. In both cases, it was thought that God would allow the innocent party to endure.[6] Torture was condoned by Pope Innocent IV in 1252 for use in the first Inquisition; its purpose was seen as partly therapeutic in that confessing one's heretical views was a necessary part of penance. Ironically, it was an expanding confidence in human reason, including the power to rationally determine guilt through investigative procedures that led to the return of interrogatory torture in juridical contexts in the early modern period.[7] Courts now needed proof—the word of a gentleman or the strength of a brute no longer sufficed—and confession was considered "queen of proofs."[8] Enlightenment ideas largely led to the disappearance of torture in Europe in the eighteenth and nineteenth centuries, but wide-scale use of interrogatory torture returned under the Nazi and Soviet regimes and in the French antiguerilla campaigns in Algeria and Indo-China.

In the 1950s–1970s, accounts of Soviet and Chinese brainwashing techniques used against political prisoners as well as American POWs spurred intense research on sensory deprivation and sensory bombardment in the United States, Canada, and Great Britain.[9] This research was put to both offensive and defensive uses by Western militaries and intelligence agencies through the creation of psychologically oriented models of coercive interrogation and counterinterrogation training regimens, respectively. Apparently having forgotten its own institutional "discoveries" in this field, the CIA returned to the sensory deprivation research after 9/11 by asking the psychologists who had used that research to design the military's counterinterrogation training regimen (SERE) to reverse-engineer the process and delineate the interrogation techniques SERE training was meant to counteract.[10] Many of these techniques have become familiar through leaks about practices at Abu Ghraib, Guantanamo, Bagram, and various "black sites" created after 9/11 before their use was confirmed by disclosure of U.S. Department of Justice memos to the CIA and Defense Department explicitly authorizing them.

It is not yet fully clear from open-source documents the extent to which the use of isolation, sensory deprivation, sensory bombardment, sleep deprivation, stress positions, and humiliation in all of these locales was the product of systematic instruction and implementation by "experts," or rather the result of permissive environments born of inadequate training, vague orders, and rumors of efficacy. At any rate, these techniques were consciously designed by the CIA and other agencies to avoid the inherent shortcomings of more "traditional" forms of torture. The Vietnam-era CIA "KUBARK" interrogation manual notes that causing interrogatees intense pain risks producing unreliable intelligence or no intelligence at all since some interrogatees will say anything to placate the torturer; others will go into shock or a quasi-catatonic state; and others will be hardened in their resolve to outlast the torturer.[11] The KUBARK manual provides the operational rationales for some of the techniques authorized by the Department of Justice memos, recently used by American forces, and used by other Western governments over the last three decades. The manual is also helpful in dispelling illusions one might have about the intended effects of coercive interrogations using less brutal methods of coercion.

The manual does not present pain as the immediate goal of coercive interrogation, but instead disorientation, anxiety, dread, and physical discomfort pursuant to the pliable and child-like state of "regression."[12]

> Relatively small degrees of homeostatic derangement, fatigue, pain, sleep loss, or anxiety may impair . . . [those defenses most recently acquired by

civilized man . . . the capacity to carry out the highest creative activities, to meet new, challenging, and complex situations, to deal with trying interpersonal relations, and to cope with repeated frustrations.] The interrogatee's mature defenses crumble as he becomes more childlike. . . . [13]

As the interrogatee slips back from maturity toward a more infantile state, his learned or structured personality traits fall away in a reversed chronological order, so that the characteristics most recently acquired—which are also the characteristics drawn upon by the interrogatee in his own defense—are the first to go.[14]

The interrogator attempts to peel away the rational overlays immediately standing in his way of a confession, the part of the interrogatee that seeks to maintain his cover story, and links his silence or deceptive claims to his group identity and loyalty to his cause. The interrogator wants the core of the suspect's faculties to remain intact, such that the man still knows who he (truly) is and what he has done. The aim does not seem to be to make a person gasp out information in a moment of pain, but to get him to a pliable enough state where he answers questions honestly, too disoriented and drained to maintain a deceitful or recalcitrant facade. What is assaulted is not bodily integrity as much as psychological or moral integrity. As the manual puts it, "regression is basically a loss of autonomy."[15]

Regression is the objective of all forms of coercive interrogation. By whatever means, the goal is to sunder the interrogatee's will so that he is unable to offer mental resistance to the interrogator's questions, but instead answers them automatically, with a childlike honesty. Therefore, the relevant basis for identifying a certain technique as "torture" is whether it is intended to cause regression and not whether it causes a certain level of pain. When war fighters resist calling waterboarding torture, on account of their having been waterboarded during SERE training,[16] or when a secretary of defense scoffs at the inclusion of forced standing as a form of torture, since *he* stands all day in his office, they unwittingly express this idea that the intent and context of an action help determine its moral character.[17] They are correct in refusing to call a freely chosen action producing discomfort in a training or professional environment "torture" but are wrong in failing to recognize that the same action *is* torture when it is forced upon a person as a means of breaking his will. One can probably make objective determinations regarding torture, despite the reference to the torturer's intention, since it is hard to imagine that a motive other than the inducement of regression is behind an interrogators' manipulation of the temperature or light in an interrogatee's cell; their subjecting him to strobes and blasting white noise;

or their depriving him of sleep for days.[18] The implication of this definition
of torture is that practices some do not consider torture including sensory
deprivation, sensory bombardment, sleep deprivation, stress positions, and
prolonged exposure to uncomfortable temperatures in the context of interrogation or punishment should indeed be recognized as torture.[19]

A Deontological Objection to Torture

Given the justification for defensive coercion developed in this book—
which I used in the last chapter to reject the use of physical force against
detainees under the physical control of interrogators—a proponent of coercive interrogation would have to address the fact that the detainee is neither being violent nor posing a direct threat to the interrogator. Failing that
route, the proponent would have to reject the underlying justification for
defensive coercion.

It is true that a soldier may justly kill an enemy soldier who does not
pose a *direct* threat to him—for example, in a situation where a camouflaged
soldier waits in ambush or kills his enemy with long-range weapons from
miles away—because the enemy soldier is a general threat to the attacking
soldier's unit and, by extension, his home nation. The enemy soldier is a
general threat in the sense of being part of an enterprise threatening the attacking soldier's unit, by way of threatening his home nation or its interests.
Yet the shackled detainee does not pose even a prospective threat in the
manner of the patrolling soldier since the detainee is unarmed and under
the physical control of the interrogator and guards. Further, the patrolling
soldier's uniform identifies him (morally speaking) as a member of a class
that can be dealt with summarily by others—the ambushing soldier can
shoot first and ask questions later—without the more careful evaluation of
culpability required when acting prudentially toward private citizens suspected of wrongdoing. By contrast, the *suspected* unprivileged irregular captured abroad does not belong to a class whose members can be dealt with
summarily. Rather, as argued in the last chapter, one must proceed more
carefully and in a way consistent with a suspect's possible innocence if his
class identification is unclear.

If a shackled detainee could be said to pose any kind of general threat
to the interrogator's forces and home nation, the threat is obviously not related to his physical powers or arms, but to his *possible* criminal knowledge.
If *any* kind of physical coercion can be justified deontologically against the
detainee (in reference to his rights and the interrogator's proportionate response to rights violations), it seems coercion could only be justified with

positively identified unprivileged irregulars, and then, via an analogy made between the detainee's presumed plot and a general threat such as the one posed by enemy soldiers when they are not actively engaged in an attack. The argument would contend that both types of people are general threats because engaged in enterprises prejudicial to national security. The detained irregular is not engaged in a threatening enterprise in the sense that he could join in fighting if he is not immediately stopped, but in potentially facilitating his comrades' successful actions by concealing their plans from interrogators. Captured soldiers might harbor tactical information as well, but the average infantryman likely has less relevant information than an unprivileged irregular, given the small size and minimal hierarchy of most irregular groups. In fact, one might argue that the threat posed by the average irregular is less connected with his being physically armed than the average soldier since many irregulars, disguised as civilians, spend considerable time unarmed, and many do not participate in direct military-style assaults anyway. So, the argument concludes, while the threat posed by most conventional combatants is neutralized once the combatants are disarmed, the threat posed by irregulars is not necessarily neutralized when they fall under the physical control of the detaining power.

This analogy between the general threats posed by patrolling soldiers and the detained irregulars' operational knowledge is a weak one, obviously. The detainee is not a prospective threat like a patrolling soldier, because he is not at liberty to join the fight while under the interrogator's control. At best, his silence passively facilitates his group's actions by not giving others the information to potentially disrupt those actions—and he may not even have that much relevant information. Further, whereas violence used against enemy soldiers is the most efficient and direct way to incapacitate them (and in some tactical situations, it is the only means), causing pain or disorientation to a detainee has no direct relation to him telling interrogators the truth.

The use of force against any person who is not presently being violent or threatening direct, imminent violence exceeds the limits on force described in chapter 1. Even if the interrogator has strong evidence that the detainee is in fact an unprivileged irregular (and so lacks a right to his operational secrets), prudential responses cannot exceed the general value of the right the detainee is abusing or the right(s) he is directly threatening. In the case of criminal plotting, the rights being abused include the rights to privacy and silence.[20] The detained unprivileged irregular is not wronging others by committing assault or theft, nor by directly threatening harm in the sense one threatens harm when pointing a weapon, but rather by having plotted and now refusing to reveal the plot or related information (if he is in fact harboring such information). While the information may regard operations that will harm others if brought to fruition, the exact nature and scope of the prospective rights violations will be unclear to the interrogator; using force against a detainee will not necessarily reveal the information; and even if torture was reliable, there are innumerable other ways of potentially learning the information and interfering with the irregular group's plans. This idea can be exemplified if we conceive of criminal information like contraband. Storing explosives in one's apartment does not directly, materially harm others, but instead, threatens harm to others. Since the danger is not imminent, police have many other ways of securing the explosives besides shooting the owner on the street. Therefore, by the lights of a restricted deontological argument, coercive interrogation cannot be justified with unprivileged irregulars.

Proponents of interrogatory torture often employ arguments with different bases than those used in this book. Since I have stipulated certain conceptual starting points for this project rather than defended them at length, I will now consider justifications of coercive interrogations assuming different foundations than the ones I used for the sake of argument. In order to justify coercive interrogation with a positively identified unprivileged irregular, one would have to remove the limits on just coercion and make an *unrestricted* deontological argument that justifies *any* action toward him necessary to extract the desired information thereby defending innocent people's lives and rights. Removing limits has this extreme implication, because removing limits pegged to the detainee's rights removes the principled reasons to limit types of prudential responses. If the justice of a defensive action depends on the symmetry between the defender's action and the degree to which the offender has ceded the legitimate expectation that others will respect his freedom, then a defender has a limitless array of prudential options in the event that the offender has made himself *completely* vulnerable to defenders' responses by voiding his rights. *Nothing* the defender does will wrong the offender who has completely voided his rights. Since there are no limits the defender must observe, the only criterion he has in view is success in defending the rights of those threatened or those wronged; in this case, the interrogator may therefore do whatever he sees as necessary to extract the criminal information. There would be no rational purpose in using more force than is necessary, but the interrogator does not know how much force is necessary.

The consequences of such unrestricted deontological arguments were discussed in chapter 1 in response to Locke's and Aquinas's summary devaluation of miscreants' rights (and the orchard keeper's shooting of the apple thief). Similarly extreme consequences are entailed in the context of interrogation. I will engage the unrestricted deontological argument—and further explain the difficulty associated with its conceptual bases—after the following section since a response to the unrestricted deontological argument also serves as a response to efficacy-based objections.

Efficacy-Based Objections to Torture

CIA agents kidnapped an Egyptian cleric known as Abu Omar in Milan on Feb. 17, 2003. He was suspected by the CIA and Italian anti-terror police of aiding al-Qaeda in recruitment and transport of Islamist radicals. The CIA had watched him for a year and tapped his phones; the lead officer in charge believed they were a few months away from having the evidence necessary to indict Omar. Superiors in Langley nonetheless ordered the kidnapping, and did so without informing Italian law enforcement. Omar was transported to Egypt, where Egyptian interrogators compelled Omar to reveal his contacts and financial operations by threatening to harm his son.[21]

There are no open-source scientific studies regarding the efficacy of coercive interrogations. Scientific studies have been conducted on the cognitive and behavioral effects of certain coercive techniques such as isolation or sleep deprivation (in clinical settings), but their findings are more suggestive than definitive.[22] Therefore, scholars and pundits making claims about coercion's efficacy must use real-life anecdotes to supplement nonempirical reasoning and intuition. This practice of anecdote collection does not fill one with confidence since anecdotes can be opportunistically selected to bolster an author's preconceived ideas. In order to illustrate this point, I have selected reports on the next page that effectively nullify one another when paired together. Yet given the secrecy surrounding coercive interrogation, there is likely no alternative to collecting anecdotes and doing one's best to verify them, and I will also marshal anecdotes to illustrate certain points below. The force of this caveat is to urge the reader to accept any argument supported by anecdotes with a degree of caution.

(This anecdote-based form of argument is employed by interrogators as well, who trade stories of perceived success as would practitioners of any sort of practical art. Piecing together diverse accounts of coercive interrogations after 9/11 reveal astonishingly banal methods of transmissions for the techniques involved. Coercive techniques were advocated by interrogators who heard from friends that they worked "in some other theater;" by academics without interrogation experience who wished to be seen as useful by special operation troops; and by interrogators and administrators who desperately wanted to be "tough" with terror suspects, as much it seems, to punish them as to prove their own mettle.)

For a practice meant to reveal truth, interrogatory torture generates ambiguity in series. It will usually be unclear to interrogators if a given detainee has security-sensitive information; unclear if torture has compelled the truth from him; unclear whether he would have spoken without torture (interrogators who claim to have exhausted noncoercive means may simply be unskilled in those methods); and unclear if further torture would reveal more information. Since torture almost always takes place in secret, the true number of people who have been tortured will be unclear to researchers. It will be unclear who is lying about having been tortured as well as who is lying about having never tortured. Indeed, if one believes firsthand accounts by interrogators and torture victims, few interrogators have ever tortured innocent people, and yet, somehow, all torture victims are innocent. One also notices how interrogators tend to defend the utility of the methods they have been taught and which they have used, usually without proffering corroborating evidence for the veracity of the information they have procured. On this point, a Shin Bet officer admitted to a journalist that he once defended the necessity of coercive interrogations, but had not seen a change in the quality of information elicited from Palestinian suspects when his agency largely abandoned coercive measures and instead turned to the use of informants and jail cell listening devices.[23] To a man with a hammer, the world is full of nails.

Real-world anecdotes do not indicate that there is any less ambiguity associated with coercive interrogations than is suggested by a theoretical discussion of the practice. The Shin Bet has said in the past that its coercive interrogations of Palestinian suspects (including beatings, shakings, sensory deprivation, and sexual humiliation) had thwarted hundreds of planned terrorist plots.[24] Yet when pressed by a journalist, Shin Bet officials could name only *one* specific instance in which coercion produced information that stopped an imminent attack.[25] (I have come across only one other case of torture being successfully used in a real ticking bomb situation.) Britain defended the Royal Ulster Constabulary's use of the "five techniques of interrogation in depth" (simultaneous hooding, wall-standing, subjection to deafening noise, temperature manipulation, and sleep deprivation) in the European Court of Human Rights with claims that the six-day interrogation of fourteen IRA suspects in the fall of 1971 elicited identifications of seven hundred IRA members and confessions to eighty-five terrorist incidents.[26]

Yet hardly any of those supposed seven hundred terrorists were ever arrested, and none of the fourteen suspects who were tortured were charged with a crime.[27] One of the suspects, Jim Auld—who was innocent of terrorist ties—said he desperately tried to please his tormenters with false accusations and false admissions: "I would have told anybody anything. The interrogations were nothing for me because I wasn't in the position to tell them what they wanted to know. I admitted to being in everything but the crib [with the baby Jesus in Bethlehem], and if they asked me I would have said, 'Yes, the crib as well, I'm in the background of it there,' because I was just so frightened." [28] A 1995 al-Qaeda plot to bomb eleven planes over the Pacific was thwarted with information allegedly tortured out of Abdul Hakim Murad by Philippine authorities.[29] Yet other evidence suggests that the key information was actually recovered from the hard drive of his computer.[30] The whereabouts of Ramzi bin al-Shibh were allegedly elicited from al-Qaeda leader Abu Zubaydah by withholding pain medication (he had been shot during arrest);[31] locking him in a small box; forcing him to stand for long periods; smashing him repeatedly into a wall; waterboarding him; and exposing him to cold temperatures and cold water until his skin turned blue (over months of relentless abuse). Yet FBI agents had already elicited vital information from him about the 9/11 ringleaders with noncoercive, rapport-building techniques when the CIA took over and implemented a coercive regime; indeed, it appears that the Agency took credit for the FBI's work.[32] (The questions of which techniques produced what information from Zubaydah and when are highly contested by the various officials who claim knowledge of his interrogations.[33] Coercive methods appear to have forced Zubaydah to make at least some false claims leading to errant warnings the Bush administration made to the public about possible attacks aimed at shopping malls, apartments, and nuclear plants in the spring and summer of 2002.[34]) Bin al-Shibh and Zubaydah led authorities to alleged 9/11 mastermind Khalid Sheikh Muhammed who in turned revealed the identities of other al-Qaeda figures after being beaten, deprived of sleep, doused in cold water, and mock-drowned by his CIA interrogators.[35] Yet other sources indicate that Muhammed's location was revealed by an informant motivated by the U.S. Government's $25 million reward,[36] and that Muhammed was a braggart who claimed responsibility for plots prior to any coercive techniques being used.[37]

Contemporary questions about torture's efficacy are nothing new. Indeed, parallel to the history of interrogatory torture in the West is one questioning its efficacy. Ulpian quotes Augustus as warning "confidence should not be unreservedly placed in torture . . . the evidence obtained is weak and dangerous and inimical to truth."[38] In many medieval settings, torture was only indicated when there was already proof, or probable cause, of a suspect's guilt, in which case a confession was sought to "fill out the proof"—which would seem to recognize torture's blindly punitive and unreliable character.[39] In fact, part of a judge's skill was thought to be his ability to formulate questions that could winnow true from false coerced testimony.

The problem, obviously, is that there is no necessary connection between pain and truth. As many commentators point out—and as the manuals concede—a person put to torture will often say whatever he believes will make the torture stop.[40] Famously, the threat of torture forced Galileo to recant his claim that the earth revolves. Tortured Jews falsely implicated coreligionists in anti-Christian plots during the Spanish Inquisition. During Stalin's purges, the NKVD's brutality produced daisy chains of false accusations; departments that had to meet monthly quotas of "captured subversives" found they could tailor the number of accusations in a nearly algebraic manner by arresting a certain number of random people and subjecting them to a given level of abuse. Their methods produced a nearly 100 percent confession rate.[41] More recently, waterboarding and other techniques resulted in Khalid Sheikh Muhammed's confessing to a murder he almost certainly did not commit: the killing of *Wall Street Journal* reporter Daniel Pearl.[42] Most damning, the false claim that Saddam Hussein was training al-Qaeda agents in the use of chemical weapons, one of the key justifications for the Iraq War, was based on accounts given by the al-Qaeda member Ibn Shaykh al-Libi under torture.[43]

It is telling that a number of twentieth-century and contemporary regimes infamous for their use of torture did not and do not use torture for interrogation purposes, but instead to punish, intimidate, or produce false confessions *after* they have elicited security-sensitive information through noncoercive means.[44] A journalist told me that Egyptian authorities tortured Abu Omar, the cleric the CIA kidnapped in Milan, only after they had extracted information about al-Qaeda through noncoercive means, and at that point used torture "for fun, basically—because he pissed them off."[45] On this point, the "scientific" CIA programs designed for the War on Terror by psychologists (who were themselves untrained in interrogation or behavioral profiling) were based on techniques used by socialist regimes to brainwash political prisoners and produce *false* confessions for show trials. Perhaps as a result, one CIA official estimates that 90 percent of the intelligence garnered from high-value detainees the Agency interrogated in its post-9/11 program is unreliable.[46]

Without corroborating evidence, coerced testimony is nearly useless, and practically undesirable in that it would presumably waste investigators' time pursuing errant leads.[47] Time is particularly relevant in cases where tactical exigencies encouraged interrogators to use violence in the first place. (It should be pointed out that contrary to popular belief, torture is not a faster alternative to noncoercive methods; interrogators who routinely use torture concede that torture often takes weeks or months to produce confessions, with no telling of their veracity.)[48] Statements produced through coercion cannot be used in normal trials and so either necessitates deformed legal standards or extrajudicial detention and/or extrajudicial execution.[49]

Further, the inherent ambiguity of all interrogations—the interrogator can never be certain the suspect has disclosed all relevant information—belies suggestions that coercive interrogations can be applied in a clinical manner.[50] Innocent people will be caught up in security sweeps, and with a given suspect, there will be a constant temptation for the interrogator to use more force than is (retrospectively) required to elicit additional information the suspect might be withholding.[51] Also, as Rejali points out, intelligence officers usually do not have determinate parameters for their questions—unlike police who usually interrogate a suspect in regards to a particular crime—but are instead seeking information about networks and operations that they do not currently know anything about. Therefore, they will not necessarily recognize the truth when/if it is revealed. Irregulars with knowledge of imminent plots will realize that they just need to string interrogators along with false information until the actual plot is fulfilled.[52] It should be pointed out that al-Qaeda instructs its members to provide interrogators with misinformation, falsely casting responsibility for an operation on a figure already familiar to the detaining power.[53]

Further, not everyone succumbs to physical pressure. Religiously or ideologically motivated suspects in particular can be expected to be less likely to succumb; for some, their torture plays into a persecutory and martyriological narrative steeling their resolve.[54] It follows, then, that those high-ranking members of terrorist organizations who presumably have the best information about terror plots will also likely be the least apt to break under pressure.[55] Also, it is often said that fear of torture is more effective in interrogations than torture itself. Once a detainee has endured torture, he will be emboldened, and so will gain an edge over the interrogator, since he knows he has withstood the worst the interrogator can dish out.[56] Finally, under extreme stress, some people mentally disassociate from reality and cognitively withdraw. The very violence creating duress for the suspect—meant to break down their conscious ability to dissemble—also saps their ability to coherently answer the interrogator's questions.[57]

Torture appears to be so profoundly unreliable an interrogation tool it is probably misleading to even call it a interrogation tool. Consider a proposed weapon characterized by torture's ambiguities. The weapon has a weak telescopic sight unable to distinguish armed soldiers from farmers with shovels, and unable to discern if a target has been hit once the weapon is fired. The weapon is so inaccurate it misses its target 90 percent of the time and often fails to destroy targets it does hit. The weapon rarely kills its victims, but leaves them horribly maimed for the rest of their lives. The use of the weapon often maims the user. One would hardly consider such a weapon a useful one. One might use the weapon if one was occupying a strategically vital position and had no alternative, but the negligible utility of the weapon makes this point nearly trivial. Obviously, a far more relevant lesson to draw would be that one should make all efforts to find alternate weapons and to avoid situations where this unreliable weapon was one's only option.[58]

Here it is useful to reiterate some points about the efficacy of *non*coercive interrogation. Experienced interrogators—including those legally allowed to torture—argue that noncoercive interrogations are far more likely than coercive interrogations to reveal detailed, accurate information.[59] First, torture may well degrade the detainee's ability to express coherent thoughts. Second, the detainee who is forced, instead of convinced to cooperate with the interrogator will only answer specific questions; he will not provide a broad narrative.[60] This dynamic significantly compromises the interrogator's ability to extract useful intelligence, because he may lack the background information necessary to pose the relevant questions. Again, one is confronted with the difficulty of assessing anecdotes, but one is struck by patterns of apparent success and failure at the hands of two different kinds of interrogators. On the one hand, there are anecdotes of success in interrogations conducted by patient, knowledgeable interrogators who develop rapports with detainees through respectful attitudes; by inquiring about the detainees' religion and background; and by leveraging information garnered from the interrogation and outside sources.[61] (On that last point, it is important to remember that interrogation should not be used as a stand-alone intelligence collection activity, and that significant information can be garnered from informants, signal interception, document recovery, etc.) On the other hand, there are the anecdotes of failed interrogations conducted by poorly trained and poorly supported interrogators who begin interrogations with the demeaning Fear Up Harsh approach and quickly proceed to equally unsuccessful and counterproductive coercive methods.[62]

The Unrestricted Deontological Argument

Given the restricted deontological argument against torture, the only way to justify the practice would be to jettison the sort of deontological limits on just coercion introduced in chapter 1, and to assert that the threat posed by unprivileged irregulars is so great—and the rights of their potential victims so important—that *any* action to extract irregulars' secrets is justified. This argument can withstand an efficacy-based critique since it allows for long shots; without any kind of proportionality restriction related to detainees' rights, the interrogator can use any means which *might* work, even when noncoercive interrogation methods could have been more effective.[63] The detainees' rights are no longer items that the interrogator needs to take into account.

If one were employing the restricted deontological justification for just coercion, one could reject a proposed interrogation technique if it were disproportionate to the right the detainee is abusing or directly threatening, or if the technique was ineffective. By contrast, the *unrestricted* deontological argument cannot be refuted internally, because of the absolute element allowing for *any* action the interrogator deems necessary. Instead, a critique must either show the absurdity of the argument's entailments or attack the argument's presuppositions about autonomy and rights. I will engage in both types of critique now.

The unrestricted detontological argument for just coercion entails the excesses related to Aquinas's and Locke's summary devaluation of miscreants' rights, discussed in chapter 1. Employing this justification, orchard keepers could shoot fleeing apple thieves in the back; for that matter, there would be no moral reason to refrain from *torturing* apple thieves for information about their plans. On this view, their crimes have completely voided the criminals' rights and so there is nothing about the criminals to serve as a check on aggrieved parties' efforts to protect their rights. While a proponent of this position might object that it should only be applied to the interrogation of positively identified unprivileged irregulars, or only of *foreign* irregulars,[64] there would be no principled reason to refrain from applying this ruthless treatment to common criminals as well. This follows because unprivileged irregulars fall into the same general category of rights violators inclusive of common criminals, due to their lack of combatant immunity.

The irregulars' citizenship is irrelevant, because both citizens and noncitizens are owed due process rights during criminal investigations, as discussed in the preceding chapter.[65] The presumed seriousness of unprivileged irregulars' plots does not offer a salient distinction from common criminals either, because the interrogator will usually have no idea if the interrogatee is actually harboring security-sensitive information, nor if the nature of that information is particularly grave.

It is important to consider the entailments of the unrestricted deontological argument because it can be difficult to have a lucid discussion regarding torture amidst fear of terrorism. If one's mercy is not severely strained when it comes to the prospect of torturing straggly bearded zealots, it is important to recognize that abandoning proportional limits on interrogation also commits one to endorsing obvious grotesqueries like torturing petty thieves.

The difficulty with the unrestricted deontological argument is that disproportionate responses to unjust actions create new imbalances of rights between offender and defender. The orchard keeper recovers his apples, but at the cost of the thief's life. This is an unacceptable outcome if it is assumed that all persons have equal rights prior to their interactions. This baseline equality serves as a standard to measure the gravity of the offender's rights violation(s) as well as the proportionality of the defender's response. For example, the status quo prior to the thief and the orchard keeper's interaction saw both men enjoying their lives and bodily integrity and neither possessing stolen property. The thief disturbs this status quo by stealing apples, and while the orchard keeper's response sees the return of his property, it radically upsets the original state of affairs by leaving the thief dead or dying. Slight imbalances consequent to efficient restoration of the status quo (the thief's being bruised after having been tackled, say) would be acceptable, but not gross imbalances.

An interpretation of Lockean autonomy that justifies killing petty thieves sees rights as so important that any action is justified to protect them from unjust violation.[66] A view of national sovereignty similar to Locke's view of personal autonomy seems to be behind a view that sees the threat of terrorism as so grave that any action necessary to reveal the plans of unprivileged irregulars is justified. On this view, it is unprivileged irregulars' very act of attacking the nation that is unacceptable, even if fairly insignificant in terms of lives, money, or other measurable consequences. It is an *outrage* against national sovereignty.

The idea that attacks from irregulars *simply cannot be tolerated,* no matter what, may have some intuitive appeal, but one does not hear comparable arguments justifying any and all actions to avoid *conventional* attacks from other nations—which might be far more disruptive than a single terrorist attack. Such an argument is foreign to just war theory, which for example, rules out "preventative wars" fought against peaceful nations to prevent them from becoming threats in the future.

A view of nations as equally sovereign is part of the foundation for this prohibition on preventative war. The grotesque justifications produced by the Lockean view of autonomy—which can be thought of as *personal* sovereignty—are a reflection of an incoherently atomistic view of autonomy incompatible with a view of society in which all have equal rights. No violation of rights that all have to equal degrees is so extreme that it justifies *any* reaction to restore the status quo ante—for example, the orchard keeper's shooting the apple thief—because disproportionate reactions against offenders would create new moral imbalances between rights-holders. If one contends that disproportionate responses *are* permissible, it must be because one does not see all rights-holders as equal, but rather sees the offended party as morally special: as having more rights than his offender prior to their interaction. In this respect, Locke's view of autonomy seems to owe something to pre-Enlightenment understandings of personal honor. In some pre-liberal cultures, where offenses were measured by the rank of the offended party rather than the culpability of the offender, an assault on a nobleman or cleric was seen as more serious than a comparable assault on a peasant, if the latter was deemed important at all. On this line of thinking, I wonder if the retributive fury of America's response to 9/11—which has included the launching of two wars, the establishment of clandestine detention and torture programs, extraordinary renditions, new collusion with repressive regimes, and the erosion of civil liberties—can be understood in part as a response to the *audacity* of a handful of cave-dwelling zealots attacking the world's remaining superpower.

The absolute view of sovereignty fails to withstand critiques at both the personal and national levels. The absolute view of *personal* sovereignty displays its incoherence when defenders' overreactions to unjust attacks create new imbalances in people's rights. A comparable discussion about nations' rights is unnecessary here, because the argument conferring absolute sovereignty to states would justify actions that are prima facie absurd. For example, if the Canadian navy seized a tiny, uninhabited island on the American side of the Juan de Fuca Straits, the absolute sovereignty argument would justify all U.S. actions against Canada necessary to restore the island, including trade sanctions and the full spectrum of military actions. On the subject of coercive interrogation, the absolute sovereignty argument would justify implementing a regime of coercive interrogation—with all its systemic ills—in order to stop even one minor irregular attack, say a single suicide bomber targeting a DMV office.

Thus far, we have seen how the *restricted* deontological argument prohibits torture on grounds of disproportionality. The *unrestricted* deontological argument does not prohibit torture, but entails absurdities. There is no middle ground between these two positions, because there is no logical reason to omit any interrogatory technique that might yield results if the rights threatened by irregulars' presumed plots are very important and the detained irregulars' rights are voided. A proponent still wishing to defend coercive interrogation would have to change the terms of debate now, abstracting from the rights involved, to focus exclusively on the anticipated consequences of interrogation. The *consequentialist* would argue that the good done in extracting information about a serious plot justifies even the very terrible effects of torture. Perhaps this is what is implied in versions of the ticking bomb argument emphasizing the massive casualties that could result from an unrevealed terrorist plot. If a *nuclear* bomb is secreted somewhere in *Manhattan,* the consequentialist all but states, would not the torture of a few terrorists be proportionally justified in the course of uncovering the plot? Also, the thought experiment gains some of its superficial appeal by implying that torture is going to be used in this case alone. In order to engage in an analysis of the balance of evils, and consider whether restricting coercive interrogation to a certain class of security threats is plausible, we must now bring the discussion out of the realm of fantasy and draw insights from actual torture programs governments have developed in the course of counterinsurgency and counterterror campaigns.

Systemic Drawbacks of Institutionalized Torture

The argument has been made by some that it is better to professionalize and legalize torture so that courts could specify acceptable methods and circumstances for its application.[67] There are modern precedents for this argument in addition to those from the late medieval and Renaissance periods. French counterinsurgency forces sought approval from French courts for coercive interrogations in Algeria;[68] in 1984, an Israeli commission headed by a high court justice allowed "moderate physical pressure" to be used in the interrogation of Palestinian terror suspects;[69] and infamously, U.S. Department of Justice lawyers issued a memorandum in 2002 outlining an understanding of acceptable interrogation techniques to include anything up to those creating pain corresponding to organ failure or death.[70]

With or without the imprimatur of legal approval, some governments have responded to security threats by pushing for the regularization of what is often initially haphazard "competence" in coercive interrogation among security forces. Practices that had hitherto been conducted ad hoc by a handful of intelligence officers come to be taught in special branches of service academies; foreign experts are flown in; whole corps specializing in coercive interrogation are trained. This systematization of interrogatory torture then creates negative effects for the detaining power apart from producing unreliable intelligence, including the corruption of governmental and social institutions.[71] Once operational, the new intelligence wing must, like all parts of government, justify its budget by producing successes in the field and by identifying new threats.[72] What begins as an operation targeting actual terrorists or guerillas then sometimes expands to pursue political dissenters, intellectuals, etc., or devolves to broad dragnets where all males of age are hauled in for interrogation. Particularly when the terrorist or guerilla threat comes from a disenfranchised minority, legitimate security operations can turn into broad, repressive campaigns, as regime leaders conflate military opposition with political opposition and then political affiliation with mere ethnic, religious or class identity.

The experience of U.S. Army interrogator Tony Lagouranis in Iraq exemplifies how quickly the use of torture can spread; how its use becomes increasingly undisciplined; and how its use encourages incompetence among security personnel. He writes how interrogators first used coercive techniques on two confirmed insurgents who refused to talk following noncoercive interrogations; the interrogators used coercive techniques they had heard were employed by Navy SEALs on high-value targets. Within weeks, interrogators were using these techniques on *all* detainees (most of whom turned out to be innocent) as a matter of course. More experienced interrogators, including Lagouranis himself, initially anguished over whether to use the new techniques. When a new interrogator arrived at the start of the use of the "special treatment," he understood it to be a settled practice, and seeing it as an opportunity for a good night's sleep, ordered all his interrogatees to be kept awake, kneeling in freezing mud the night prior to interrogation.[73]

Lagouranis's story is also valuable in that it shows how many of the elements characterizing programs developed under central government control appear in an ad hoc interrogation program as well. Torture has its own inexorable logic, which undercuts the blithe assumption made in the ticking bomb argument that torture can be limited to only the most desperate situations. The interrogator who tortures the known terrorist to extract information about a rumored nuclear bomb, perhaps thinking it will be a one time occurrence, will do so again in the future, with a lower-ranking terrorist, and then later, with someone only suspected of being a terrorist. At that point, it will be automatic for him, his victims dehumanized, their cries insensible. (Lagouranis writes how he quickly became numb to tormenting detainees, and sometimes abused obviously innocent people simply out of pique.)[74] But that second time, with the lower-ranking terrorist, it will still take some pressure by others to get the interrogator to torture. His reputation will proceed him; his colleagues will regard him with a mixture of awe and fear, and they will demand that he be brought in to interrogate a recalcitrant suspect.[75] Once alone with the suspect, he will feel tremendous pressure to make the man confess—any statements will suffice as a "confession" in the near term—and the interrogator will likely give up on noncoercive methods far earlier than he did the first time. Even if disgusted by what he has done, he will know that he has been given tacit permission to torture: he was brought in to do what few others have the strength to do.

The victims of torture often become willing recruits for terrorists or other criminals,[76] while others remain shattered, withdrawn, unable to participate in social and familial life.[77] While advocates of coercive interrogation will probably acknowledge these effects on detainees, I have not read a pro-torture argument that takes into account the effects of torture on the torturers themselves. They are often blighted, treated as pariahs by the regular security branches—either deviant from the start, or more often not, but brutalized and morally corrupted in the intelligence academies and in the course of their work.[78] A CIA officer said of a colleague, who waterboarded Khalid Sheikh Muhammed, "[He] has horrible nightmares. When you cross over that line of darkness, it's hard to come back. You lose your soul. You can do your best to justify it, but it's well outside the norm. You can't go to that dark place without it changing you."[79] Since torture isn't directly connected to the revelation of truth, and human beings' pain thresholds and psychological makeups vary, torture cannot be measured out with clinical precision; since mentally normal people seem to have a natural aversion to imposing suffering on others, the suggestion that torture can be employed with clinical dispassion seems equally wrong.

The torturers are unstable forces in the government, as their ranks constitute a lawless cell within the legal framework of the state.[80] Institutionalizing torture also tends to actually hinder government counterinsurgency or counterterror operations because security officers tend to forgo the investigative methods that are most efficacious in such operations when given the option of simply torturing suspects.[81] Rejali tells an illustrative anecdote of

French paratroopers torturing a suspected Algerian militant for three days before realizing he had bomb blueprints in his trouser pockets. Rejali also points out, contrary to the circumstances envisioned in the ticking bomb thought experiment, that the torturer is not going to be the same person evaluating the veracity of the confession, much less the person searching out the hidden bombs or weapons caches.[82] The interrogator fills out interrogation reports; success, for him, is having something to put in the report. By the standards used in his professional performance reviews, all statements procured by torture therefore are "confessions."

The necessary secrecy that accompanies intelligence operations creates massive opportunities for criminal corruption.[83] Further, since the acts of the security forces are often extralegal, the routinization of torture requires the corroding of the professional standards and behavior of other branches of society. Police are needed to help in the secret arrests; doctors, to falsify medical reports or keep detainees alive (in violation of their Hippocratic oaths); judges and journalists are pressured to look the other way; and lawyers are pressured to submit to deformed legal procedures designed to allow coerced statements.[84] Governments are rocked when reports of torture become public, and then torturers who had been acting under orders are scapegoated as "bad apples." Recent news reports have said that CIA officers involved in the interrogation of high-value detainees have been contacting lawyers and taking out professional liability insurance in anticipation of being cashiered and/or prosecuted.[85] President Obama has stated that personnel acting under legal authorization will not be prosecuted, but he is under pressure to reverse this position, and a Spanish judge is currently hearing a criminal complaint against six Bush administration officials and lawyers for drafting torture authorizations. In sum, it is has been argued by many that torture is fundamentally at odds with the principles of a democratic society, and this incongruity is reflected in the character of the institutions necessary for the perpetuation of torture. In resorting to its use in times of crisis, a democratic nation subverts the very culture it means to protect.[86]

Weighing Good and Bad Effects

Since consequentialist arguments appeal to anticipated consequences, the consequentialist proponent of coercive interrogation would have to weigh the anticipated good effect of extracted information against the bad effects associated with a regime of coercive interrogation. By "regime," I mean the whole panoply of actions historically accompanying state-instituted systems of coercive interrogation, including the training of interrogators in coercive techniques; the enlistment of doctors to assist the interrogators; the development of novel legal procedures to accommodate coerced testimony; and the establishment of special detention protocols to hold detainees outside the normal penal system, etc.

Before we apply it to the subject of interrogation, consider the following example to get a sense of how a consequentialist might weigh good and bad effects. Greeting a squad of seriously injured soldiers in triage, a military surgeon (with limited supplies) decides to first operate on the patients without head injuries since this plan would likely mean saving seven out of ten patients, whereas operating on patients with head injuries first would likely mean saving only two of ten patients. In this situation, the balance of good versus bad effects anticipated in the first prioritization is clearly more favorable than its alternative.

The consequentialist argument in favor of coercive interrogation cannot succeed, because unlike the data in the triage example, the data on which the consequentialist argument depends is chronically ambiguous. Neither the "weight" of the good or bad effects of a regime of coercive interrogation is measurable. This is the case even when a particular standard of comparison is stipulated, such as the number of lives saved versus the number of casualties caused by a terrorist attack, or the financial cost of a terrorist attack versus the costs associated with the lawsuits, corruption, reciprocal terrorism, and performance degradation brought on by a regime of coercive interrogation. For example, it is impossible to know the number of lives that are directly threatened by criminal plots harbored in the minds of unprivileged irregulars at large today, May 9, 2009. It is also impossible to know how many of these plots would be revealed under torture prior to their realization if every unprivileged irregular currently under surveillance was arrested and coercively interrogated (leaving an unknown number of as-yet-unidentified irregulars at liberty). It is impossible to tell if torture would be worth it. The very secrecy surrounding irregulars' plots and networks, which motivates interrogators to use torture, also will usually preclude using a consequentialist argument to justify torture. True, one *does* have more evidence when it comes to the negative consequences historically associated with regimes of coercive interrogation. Endorsing a regime of coercive interrogation means accepting that torture will be used on innocent persons; torturers will likely become as blighted as the people they torture, and either scapegoated or bought off with secret privileges and monies; these secret funds will in turn create opportunities for corruption; the governments secretly endorsing torture will risk collapse when the scandalous truth is revealed; investigators will likely grow incompetent; extremists will likely find new recruits; and many of the culpable people tortured will be brutalized for what turns out to be trivial bits of information.

That said, the consequentialist could respond that a *particular* state's institution of a regime of coercive interrogation might incur a relatively low number of negative consequences, and that, anyway, these consequences could be outweighed by the successful interruption of one massive plot.[87] Yet this response undercuts the consequentialist's own case. The chronic ambiguity surrounding anticipated consequences of a regime of coercive interrogation prevent *both* pro- and anti-torture advocates from making their cases on consequentialist grounds. Consequentialist assertions in regards to regimes of coercive interrogation are hollow since they rely on evaluations of consequences for support, but the relevant data regarding consequences is chronically ambiguous. Consequentialist reasoning allows for less than certain forecasting of consequences, but the variables associated with a regime of coercive interrogation are endemically cloudy. Without quantifiable data, neither pro- nor anti-torture consequentialist argument is much better than a guess: torture will *probably* have a good—or bad—net effect. The consequentialist approach is therefore ill suited to address questions regarding coercive interrogation.[88]

Thus far, we have noted that refusing the prohibition of coercive interrogation produced by the restricted deontological argument requires jettisoning deontological limits, which entails grotesque consequences in turn. An approach that seeks to justify a regime of coercive interrogation based purely on its consequences is flawed since the data on which the approach depends is chronically ambiguous. The discussion of the systemic negative effects of a regime of coercive interrogation also suggests that torture could not be restricted to a small class of security threats.

Conclusion

Human beings have an inherent right to privacy, and this right entails a right to silence. All other things being equal, one does not have to respond to personal questions posed by a stranger. In most contexts, demanding personal information from a stranger is disrespectful, an inappropriate attempt to gain power over him or inhibit the pursuit of his own goals. States too, must respect their inhabitants' privacy. A signal characteristic of liberal forms of government is their deference to inhabitants' autonomy. Like all other rights, the rights to privacy and silence presuppose their responsible exercise—exercise compatible with all other persons' enjoyment of the same rights to the same extent. Criminal plotting is an illegitimate use of one's privacy, wrongly repaying the deference others express with plans for their harm. Harboring criminal plots is impermissible in the same way holding contraband is impermissible.

While proportionate coercive measures are normally permitted to halt rights violations, other people are usually not in a position to know one is criminally plotting, and so cannot intervene with the assurance of a Good Samaritan acting to stop an assault. Again, all other things being equal, strangers should refrain from bothering one another for personal information. So even criminal plotters are wronged by neighbors or police if pestered for personal information in cases where the plotters' criminal plotting is not manifested by public evidence. The authority of police and other state agents to engage in rights-*infringing* behaviors such as questioning, arrest, violence, and interrogation stems from their role in protecting inhabitants' lives and rights. Given cause, police may question people without *violating* their rights—since this rights-infringing behavior is part of an enterprise necessary over time to protect their rights—so long as police actions are commensurate with what the state has cause to know about the questioned parties' status in the criminal justice arena. A person suspected of criminal plotting or criminal behavior should not to be treated simply as an apparently innocent person or as a guilty person, but in a manner sensitive to the possibility that he could be either one. Deference to this hybrid identity means police may accost, question, arrest, and interrogate a suspicious person—according to the level of external evidence indicating his guilt—but must also defer to his rights to silence and counsel and avoid threats, extortion, and violence in interrogation.

Well-trained police may engage in manipulative and deceptive interrogation techniques to cajole or trick the suspect into revealing the truth if they believe he is withholding criminal information. Police are allowed to use reasonable, reviewable, proportionate, and effective crime-detecting techniques in order to meet their protective obligation, and the (admittedly unsatisfactory) empirical evidence about interrogations suggests that deceptive techniques are reasonably reliable, efficacious, and indispensible in certain cases. Interrogations should be videotaped and the confessions of minors and those with mental retardation should be discounted without strong corroborating evidence.

A state's obligation to protect its inhabitants extends to protection from external enemies, and so military and intelligence officers should be permitted to act prudentially toward foreign enemies including interrogating captured combatants. Prisoners of war are subject to deceptive interrogation despite their right to their professional secrets, because of the privilege both belligerent parties have to act prudentially toward their enemies. There are limits to this prudential behavior: since they have been neutralized as an active physical threat by the time they face an interrogator, POWs may not be physically mistreated or harmed during interrogation. They also may not be threatened with penalties for failing to divulge these secrets since they have a right to their professional secrets.

The salient characteristic justifying POWs' moral impunity and legal immunity for ordinary combat violence (and possible refusal to divulge military secrets) is their role as state agents. Therefore irregular combatants such as insurgents who represent a state, recently defeated state, or nascent state deserve POW status, provided they hew to the other standards of soldierly behavior, including wearing identifying uniforms or emblems, carrying their arms in the open, and otherwise obeying the laws of war. Unprivileged irregulars—militants failing to meet these criteria—are effectively criminals and do not enjoy a right to their operational secrets. Yet the detaining power faces epistemic limitations in dealing with some unprivileged irregulars it does not face in dealing with conventional combatants that complicate its potential response.

An occupying army is responsible for basic policing duties in occupied territory since it is standing in for the defeated government. Agents of the occupying power face the same epistemic limitations when arresting suspected unprivileged irregulars ordinary police face when arresting criminal suspects. Therefore, the occupying power owes inhabitants of occupied territory the same baseline deference due to them from local police during peacetime, including the standard interrogation rights. Since these obligations are based on human rights, they are not affected by the differing nationalities of the occupiers and the inhabitants of the occupied territory.

In the case of ongoing hostilities abroad, affording due process protections for suspected- or positively identified unprivileged irregulars is likely impractical. Further, affording these protections serves no moral purpose since neither suspected- nor positively identified unprivileged irregulars have the relationship with the detaining power justifying the various interrogation and trial rights afforded domestic criminal suspects. *Positively identified* unprivileged irregulars may be interrogated as POWs if the occupying power needs to engage irregular groups militarily instead of with law enforcement personnel, though this treatment will also indicate POW-style detention following interrogation. Affording POW status to irregulars who fail to formally qualify for POW status is the cost of interrogating them without the due process protections required for a fair trial. While the detaining power would not be able to criminally prosecute or execute these irregulars, POW-style detention would meet the detaining power's practical requirements of interrogating detainees at length and removing them from the fight until the end of hostilities.

The situation is more complicated with suspected—and so, presumably non self-identifying—unprivileged irregulars. Any person in civilian dress has his political rights violated if he is detained and interrogated by an agent of a foreign state, regardless of how benignly he is treated during interrogation. This follows because direct prudential behavior by state agents can only be justified against civilians if those civilians are inhabitants of the territory the agents are responsible for policing. Despite the rights-violating nature of their behavior, state agents are justified in detaining and interrogating nonuniformed foreigners abroad who are suspected of being unprivileged irregulars if no other method of securing the agents' national security goals is possible. The violated rights of innocent foreigners can be justified according to the doctrine of double effect in the same manner as would the injuries of innocent civilians sustained in the course of legitimate military attacks. However, with the weight of the "collateral damage" analogy in mind, security personnel should take every precaution to minimize civilian suffering and inconvenience.

There is no cause for establishing an alternative system of interrogation and detention for positively identified unprivileged irregulars since the only potentially efficacious interrogation techniques impermissible for domestic criminal suspects and privileged irregulars—threats and blackmail—also carry serious practical drawbacks for the detaining power. Torture is impermissible because physical violence is only justified when it is the sole means of halting a physical attack in the relevant context where a state agent confronts a criminal. While a positively identified unprivileged irregular such as an al-Qaeda operative may have knowledge posing a deadly threat to innocent people, he is not being violent when under the physical control of interrogators; torture is not directly related to revealing the truth in the way shooting a soldier is related to his incapacitation; and there may be numerous other (even less time-consuming) ways of learning the relevant information. Torture's impermissibility is no hindrance to the detaining power because it is not a reliable interrogation tool anyway. If a person doesn't die under torture or go into shock, he will typically say anything to get the torture to stop; even if some true statements are made, the torturer will usually not be in a position to know which statement is true. Torture programs typically claim vast numbers of innocent people whose false confessions hide the inefficacy of the programs. This dynamic works against the government's goals since their false confessions waste operatives' time on errant leads. Torture also tends to gravely corrupt the personnel implementing it as well as the government authorizing it.

While it may be some time before we have a comprehensive picture of America's recent foray into extralegal forms of detention and interrogation, some recent disclosures have conformed to type. It appears that the CIA tortured Abu Zubaydah because they could—they had this new arrow in their quiver—even though the FBI was apparently already enjoying his cooperation won through noncoercive means. A veneer of professionalism—the clinical specificity of the Department of Justice memos, the minute logs kept of the detainees' treatment, the videotapes of the interrogations (now illegally destroyed), the daily measurements of calf swelling for those detainees forced into stress positions—belied the fact that the program's designers, executors, and defenders were novices improvising on faulty assumptions. The program was designed by psychologists without interrogation experience who drew on Soviet and Chinese methods for producing *false* confessions for show trials; it was implemented against the advice of seasoned FBI interrogators and military officers; and it was championed by administration lawyers and officials with neither interrogation nor military experience who seemed to prefer the most brutal and extralegal measures for ideological, if not character-defect reasons. These "official" programs promoted even more undisciplined and unsophisticated imitations downstream in interrogation centers from Babel to Bagram and in countless field interrogations by ordinary infantrymen and especially roving bands of special operators given carte blanche to find high-value targets like Saddam and al-Zarcawi.[1]

Untold numbers of innocent persons were brutalized by American forces. At least eight people, some likely culpable, some not, died under torture.[2] In regards to confirmed al-Qaeda members like Abu Zubaydah, a slackened pace of revelations was interpreted by his interrogators as recalcitrance rather than ignorance of further operations. This resulted in Zubaydah apparently being tortured far past the point where he had any useful information to reveal. It appears that both he and Khalid Sheikh Muhammed were tortured into making false statements, one of which, concerning the murder of Daniel Pearl, former CIA director Michael Hayden cited in his recent public defense of the CIA's interrogation program. The efficacy of the CIA interrogation program, like the efficacy of all torture programs, is self-obscuring. True statements beaten out of Zubaydah, Muhammed, and others are cited by Hayden, Vice President Cheney, and others as evidence of the program's necessity, while others correctly note that there is no telling *now* if the same or better information would have been elicited through noncoercive means.

The revelations of torture have tarnished America's image abroad; demonstrably increased terrorist recruitment; made foreign government cooperation with the United States more difficult; and legally jeopardized the operators who inflicted the abuse as well as the lawyers and bureaucrats who authorized it. Having been tortured, or detained on evidence procured through torture, the "high-value detainees" may now be unprosecutable and unprisonable; they are currently in the limbo of an extraterritorial prison due to close within a year by presidential writ. The Obama administration is apparently now considering highly unusual—and sure to be controversial—protocols for holding them indefinitely under the guise of preventive detention. In short, torture has reaped its perennial harvest.

The War on Terror is not America's first war, nor is it America's first experience using ruthless methods of intelligence gathering and counterinsurgency. One might ask how we wound up in this same shameful spot, not forty years after the relevant lessons were on view in the aftermath of the Vietnam War. One answer of course is that the same sort of people who blindly supported the government through the outrages of the Vietnam War are the same sort who supported the Bush administration's national security efforts. Also, some of the government personnel are the same. Cheney and Rumsfeld, veterans of the Nixon and Ford administrations, evidently drew the opposite lesson from the Church hearings and the public condemnations of the government's domestic surveillance operations, the Phoenix program and the CIA's other schemes to kill foreign leaders, the official lies and hypocrisy, and the piles of civilian dead in southeast Asia. The details of exactly what occurred over the last eight years will continue to be revealed by journalists and historians. Still, there's something more, I think. When one considers how the willingness to torture has been used in recent American discourse as a criterion for soldiers' toughness, citizens' patriotism, and politicians' "conservative" mettle, it seems appropriate to consider the willingness to torture as a kind of character trait rather than a simple opinion regarding public policy. That torture is connected with something in human beings rather than to cultural or political conditions is suggested by its historical tenacity. After all, many of the juridical practices once associated with torture—corporeal punishment, trial by ordeal, religious inquisition, witchcraft trials—are historical relics in the West, yet torture remains.

With this mention of character traits, we can turn to a theme effectively negated by the humanistic thrust of the modern age, which assumes human reason sufficient to address any problem. I think the reluctance to jettison the all-but-useless ticking bomb thought experiment and finally reject the mostly useless techniques of interrogatory torture—this strange refusal to cast away evil things, really—comes from a reluctance to accept that good may not always triumph over evil. Given the threat of terrorism, some will want to keep torture, locked away perhaps, sealed beneath glass and a placard that reads "only open in case of emergency."[3] Violence commends itself to desperate times since it seems like the maximally efficacious option, a way of cutting through all the frustration and incompleteness of imploring, asking, petitioning, and bargaining to achieve one's ends. The willingness to use violence in its most extreme and ruthless forms in a strange way aggrandizes the actor's ego by showing the extent of his self-control, dedication, and selflessness. There is a perverse glamour in volunteering to do the dirty work, those horribly "necessary" actions that are alleged from time to time to be the price of security, to immolate one's soul for others just as the martyr immolates his body. I choose the simile intentionally: torture is employed as a weapon against terror, but torture is a weapon of terror.

We are a nation famous for its confidence in human progress, and we are a nation that has tortured. We may now be forced to admit what used to be said more often, that there is a dark side to confidence in human potential. The willingness to use even evil things to fight evil expresses a human desire for mastery and control so complete it refuses to accept that perhaps not every problem can be solved, nor even every plot foiled. Finally letting go of these ancient forms of cruelty will be difficult then since doing so may paradoxically require rejecting modernity's greatest promise.

NOTES

INTRODUCTION

1. I happen to find convincing many of the arguments Pragmatist philosophers like Pierce, James, and Dewey deploy against Foundationalism (the search for first principles comprehensive of all forms of inquiry), and for a mode of critique that utilizes tools from the criticized party's own system. Yet it also strikes me that an approach that seeks to draw out the implications of existing practices and modes of speech, instead of contriving a metasystem abstracted from existing practice is appropriate given that our subject concerns rights already recognized in contemporary American law. American jurists are not starting with a tabula rasa when discussing the privilege against compelled self-incrimination and the rights to silence and privacy—they are not asking if such rights are implied by some notion of citizenship—but effectively asking Pragmatic questions: would it not be better to jettison a particular right, or *employ a new understanding* of it in order to modify its practical implementation in one direction or other?

CHAPTER ONE

1. Interrogation transcript of Eugene Livingston, Vallejo, CA, Police Dept., Solano County, CA, Prosecutor's Office, and FBI Office in Albany, GA, 58 (December 18, 1993).

2. Fred E. Inbau, John E. Reid, Joseph P. Buckley, and Brian C. Jayne, *Criminal Interrogation and Confessions*, 4th ed. (Gaithersburg, MD: Aspen Press, 2001).

3. I include Aquinas with the usual quartet despite the thinkers' metaphysical and epistemological differences for the following reasons. The five subscribe to almost identical positions on coercion, and Aquinas's can be seen as the ancestor of the four thinkers linking contract theory with just war theory via his position on coercion and his articulation of natural law. The Vatican's twentieth-century endorsement of human rights as consistent with the Thomistic natural law tradition supports a reading that sees the deontological idiom inchoate in Aquinas's discussion of the duties owed all rational beings.

4. Since the expression of my argument is basically Kantian, it has elements of what philosophers term "agent-centered," "patient-centered," and "contractualist" versions of deontology. Were a different thinker's idiom used, some details of my argument would likely change, but I suspect many of this book's basic conclusions would

remain, barring the use of an overly atomistic deontology. More on the difficulties with atomism in the next chapters.

5. The contrary of this sentence implies that there is no other person whose rights could serve as a legitimate impediment to one's own. If we think of rights in their social setting, properly limited by reciprocal recognition and universal possession, there might be some absolute rights (rights that may never be overridden) though this would seem to depend on the narrowness of their definition. For example, one can think of instances in which a right to bodily integrity can be justly overridden (e.g., in self-defense) but could term certain specifications of this right absolute, such as a right not to be raped.

6. It would take longer for me to reach my destination if all my neighbors get on the highway at the same time, but the delay is a contingent function of the width of the highway, not a feature of our having similar intentions.

7. In this context, "prudential" describes actions that are judged according to the quality of the actor's judgment in selecting them, rather than with respect to the actions' effects on others' rights. An action that is prudentially wrong may be wrong for being inefficient, poorly timed, ineffective, but not wrong in the sense of violating someone's rights.

8. Aquinas and Locke, among others, conceive of the miscreant dropping from the sphere of human moral respect to a bestial level because of his crime. He then can be dealt with prudentially, with reference to his utility or disutility to those defending themselves or the wider community. Kant and Rousseau conceive of the coercion of the criminal as treating him as an end insofar as coercion against injustice is consistent with, and necessary for, the freedom of all, including the criminal. I use the formulation of "means" in this general exposition to capture the sense that the criminal is treated as a means in the immediate term; the defender acts as one does when one illicitly treats another as a means, though his action is in this case justified.

9. H. L. A. Hart, "Are There Any Natural Rights?" *Philosophical Review* 64, no. 2 (April 1955): 183.

10. In some cases, this difference may simply be verbal. "Lying" could be substantively defined in English as a violation of a person's right to honest-dealing, or as an abuse of the right to speak freely; both constructions have enough currency in ordinary English usage to identify distinct concepts. By contrast, an English speaker would not likely define rape, theft, or assault with references to the right the actor was abusing, since a definition of any of them as abuses of the actor's bodily autonomy (which in essence they are) would be too vague a definition to be useful; instead the reciprocal rights violation the victim suffers descriptively distinguishes the actions and, also in a sense, distinguishes the degree to which the actor is abusing his right to bodily autonomy. This is all to explain why I will sometimes refer to rights violations of victims and sometimes to an actor's abuse of his rights.

11. Leslie Mulholland, *Kant's System of Rights* (New York: Columbia University Press, 1990), 189.

12. Wasserman correctly argues that a just defense for all rights violations is not necessarily limited to the same moment in which the rights violation occurred or began to occur (e.g. the act of kidnapping extends to the whole period in which the victim is under the kidnapper's control). David Wasserman, "Justifying Self Defense," *Philosophy & Public Affairs* 16, no. 4 (Autumn 1987): 372.

13. See Fletcher for discussion of the Continental legal systems based solely on the victim's rights. George P. Fletcher, *Proportionality and the Psychotic Aggressor: A Vignette*

in Comparative Criminal Theory, 8 Israel Law Review 367, 378–80 (1973). Fletcher suggests Locke as a proponent of this view. This claim is arguable since Locke writes that natural law allows for punishment in the state of nature "to that *degree*, and with so much *Severity* as will suffice to make it an ill bargain to the Offender, give him cause to repent, and terrifie others from doing the like." And elsewhere, punishment is "only to retribute to [the offender], so far as calm reason and conscience dictate, what is proportionate to his transgression, which is so much as may serve for reparation and restraint" (§§12 and 8, respectively, original emphasis). Yet elsewhere, he seems to abandon proportionalism by describing thieves as having voided *all* their rights. "This makes it Lawful for a Man *to kill a Thief*, who has not in the least hurt him, nor declared any design upon his Life, any farther then by the use of Force, so to get him in his Power, as to take away his Money, or what he pleases from him: because using force, where he has no Right, to get me into his Power, let his pretence be what it will, I have no reason to suppose, that he, who would *take away my liberty*, would not when he had me in his Power, take away everything else" (§18, original emphasis). John Locke, *Second Treatise on Government*. For discussion of this view, see Jeff McMahan, "Self Defense and the Problem of the Innocent Attacker," *Ethics* 104 (January 1994): 252–57.

14. McMahan, 277.

15. The German Supreme Court ruled in the orchard keeper's favor in a famous case from 1920. Discussed in Fletcher, 381.

16. See the Locke quotation from §18 in the above note.

17. For discussions of consequentialist approaches, see Wasserman, pp. 357–58; McMahan, pp. 261–63; Laurence A. Alexander, *Justification and Innocent Aggressors*, 33 Wayne Law Review 1177, 1186–88 (1986–87).

18. Robert Nozick, *Anarchy, State, and Utopia* (New York: Basic Books, 1977), 63. Cheyney Ryan, "Self Defense, Pacifism, and the Possibility of Killing," *Ethics* 93 (April 1983): 512.

19. Interestingly, common law allows killing an attacker when the attack occurs in the defender's home even when escape is possible, and many jurisdictions allow killing under the same circumstances in public places as well. Kent Greenawalt, *The Perplexing Borders of Justification and Excuse*, 84 Colorado Law Review 1897, 1905 (December 1984).

20. An exception might be when penurious background conditions are such that property loss will lead to loss of life.

21. Cf. Ryan, pp. 511, 516. Ryan rejects the justification of defensive homicide that asserts that someone unjustly threatening lethal violence has voided his right to life, on account that attempting murder is not the same thing as committing murder. Rather, insofar as rights violations are expressed in actions, they count as rights violations across the spectrum of the relevant action: Y is "stealing X's purse" when he suddenly reaches for it; when he grabs it; when he pulls it away; and when he runs away with it in his hand. So X could react coercively when Y first lunges for it (note, that with the exception of lethal force, all kinds of coercive reactions can be "dialed down" if the defender realizes she was mistaken about Y's intentions).

22. Locke, §16; St. Thomas Aquinas, *Summa Theologica* II–II Q 64.2 (in consideration of murderers and so, presumably, murderous attackers). As noted in n. 13, there is a reasonable alternate reading to Locke on this point. For Otsuka, a bestial nature obviates the need to inquire about permanently psychotic aggressors' rights; Michael Otsuka, "Killing the Innocent in Self-Defense," *Philosophy & Public Affairs* 23, no. 1 (Winter 1994): 92.

23. Aquinas goes on to explain all actions have to be proportionate to their intended goal to be morally permissible, but this concern is related to the defender's soul, not due to concern with the offender; II–II Q 64.7.

24. Fletcher, 374.

25. My advocated view is closer to Kant's. Kant argues that the offender makes himself servile by following nonuniversalizable maxims, probably ones generated by his passions and imposed on his will. Therefore, coercion against him to restrain his unjust actions does not do him moral injury (he has already made himself un-free), but just responses have to precisely match his original rights-violating deeds lest they offend his remaining rights.

26. I do not have the space here for a full discussion of the problem of the "innocent aggressor," who nonculpably threatens an innocent person (an example of an innocent aggressor might be someone who behaves violently as a result of psychosis). Since the innocent aggressor has not chosen to threaten others, he has not ceded his otherwise legitimate expectation against coercion and so would be wronged by defensive coercion. However, the defender would not be wrong in exercising defensive coercion, because unable to choose an action that protects both himself and the nonculpable attacker. This scenario will be further discussed in reference to the doctrine of double effect in chapter 7.

27. Ryan, 512.

28. Locke, §§8, 11.

CHAPTER TWO

1. There may be other ways to link moral duty with political coercion beside the way described in this chapter, as well as ways to defend political coercion without a link to a moral conception of autonomy. What follows is one way of linking political coercion with moral autonomy, which creates a basis for determining the scope of rights to privacy and silence, a privilege against compelled self-incrimination, and the proper limits of police powers. So far as I can see, it survives fatal challenges to other extant understandings of political coercion that have been made within the social contract tradition.

   Police powers would seem to attend any type of liberal state, as a relatively crime-free environment would seem to be a precondition for any conception of autonomy and attendant rights exercise. By contrast, other government programs or institutions (e.g., subsidized school lunches, public art, the electoral college, etc.) would each seem more contestable and more dependent on contingent national needs or on theoretical starting points more specialized than the ones I am using.

2. Moral duties are owed by all persons *to* all persons irrespective of particular relationships or promises. "Obligations" generate special rights for the obligee: a legitimate expectation that the obligor will perform a specific future action the nature of which is described, and right to which is transferred, by a mutually understood sign made by the obligor to the obligee. Drawn from H. L. A. Hart, "Are There Any Natural Rights?" *Philosophical Review* 64, no. 2 (April 1955): 183; A. John Simmons, *Moral Principle and Political Obligation* (Princeton, NJ: Princeton University Press, 1979), 14. Moral duties are what Hart calls "general duties," while obligations are a species of "special rights," on his usage.

3. For purposes of style, I will use the following pairs of terms interchangeably: "idea" and "concept," "freedom" and "liberty," "area" and "arena," and "nation" and "state."

4. There are undoubtedly other preconditions for positive freedom, likely including things like education, familial love, health, etc., but this chapter will only focus on the precondition of negative freedom since it directly relates to police powers. On the relation of police powers to negative liberty, see Seamus Miller, "Moral Rights and the Institution of the Police," in *Human Rights and the Moral Response of the Corporate and Public Sector Organizations*, ed. T. Campbell and S. Miller (Dordrecht: Kluwer, 2004), 177.

5. By "community," I mean a group of persons living in close enough proximity that their actions could directly affect other persons.

6. Immanuel Kant, *The Metaphysical Elements of Justice*, 71–72, 307. Locke makes a similar argument, though focusing on passions and self-regard as the source of potential trouble, *Second Treatise*, §13. The point about well-intentioned error follows depending on the level of abstraction with which the theorist conceives the moral system. Viewing the deontological system as a whole, from the "top down," the theorist's emphasis on the harmony of the system typically abstracts the choosers within the system to their most ideal instantiation, always self-directing in ways that really are consistent with all other actors similarly self-directing. For example, the theorist might describe the system in this manner when defending it against the illiberal critique that freedom is inconsistent with social order (e.g., Kant, "What Is Enlightenment?"). What the theorist is really doing in this instance is arguing that it is theoretically possible for there to be an orderly community of autonomous persons—that there is *at least* one instance in which all can fully exercise their rights and not violate the rights of their fellows. However, when the same system is explored from the perspective of the rational actor—who is still conceived abstractly, but with at least one detail associated with actual decision making, non-omniscience, now brought to the fore—the possibility of well-intentioned error is evident.

7. The relevant time slice would extend backward to include the time required for the development of his abilities to jog and the time required to become comfortable with it, such that he saw jogging in the park as his right and an arena of freedom in which he could conceive of himself operating. The time slice would extend forward to what Livingston considered the "foreseeable future," meaning that temporal horizon conceptualized by Livingston as being relevant to his current plans.

8. It is possible that rights violators could be dissuaded without coercion, say through rational argument, but coercion remains a right of the restrainer. Strictly speaking, the restrainer does not have to refrain from coercive measures to restrain rights violators, because the rights violation is the very thing that gives him leave to use coercion. The deterrence of those who inadvertently infringe on other's rights is not direct since such people are not choosing to bother their neighbors. The state's legal framework and law enforcement powers serve as an indirect deterrent in these cases in the following sense. Just as these mechanisms may give people confidence that they will be safe from rights violations, and so are free to do as they will in the future, they will also have the confidence that inadvertent infringements will be quickly and peaceably resolved through legal mechanisms.

9. This condition could obtain with *most* persons behaving morally, because a few rights violations may be trivial in nature and so have no effect on the overall system, or because they might remain undiscovered and unfelt by everyone, thereby having no effect on people's positive freedom. For example, if one tomato is stolen from my garden, unnoticed by me, I would not alter my behavior or hesitate to plant tomatoes

in the future. For the sake of simplicity at this point, I will discuss perfect states of moral compliance and rights exercise.

10. Thomas Hobbes, *Leviathan*, chap. 13.

11. Here I mean *conceptually actual* rather than *empirically actual*, where the latter term means "existing in the real world." For example, in the imagined universe of the novel *The Brothers Karamazov*, the character Alyosha Karamazov is conceptually actual—he is a human being who exists *in the novel*. We also know his father actually exists or existed in the world of the novel: *his* actual (conceptual) existence is implied by the actual existence of someone, Alyosha, who could possibly not exist.

12. Suppression could be prospective in the sense of deterrence. Potential violators are deterred from attempts due to the presence of some impressive coercive power. Assuming all persons in the community are choosing morally (with the possibility of error), the prospective force of the coercive power is to give persons the confidence that neighbors will be restrained from inadvertently committing rights violations.

13. The possibility that the human species evolved from a nonhuman species was not one they entertained.

14. Since Hegel, many have made the point against Kant—if for different reasons—that autonomous persons cannot be coherently conceived without certain background conditions. My argument is not meant to be a critique of Kant, but a critique of atomistic views of autonomy that conceive of autonomy wholly apart from a social-political background. Such views see political coercion as inherently in tension with persons' moral rights.

15. While the above argument may strike some as surprising, I think it simply exposes the connection between the enabling conditions for action, on one hand, and rights to those actions, on the other—inchoate in the ideal grounds of deontological moral theory. Typically, the theoretical grounds for moral judgments are presented as ideal states of affair, with actors' deliberate departures from ideal behavior being characterized as instances of immoral behavior. For example, Kantian systems assume networks of autonomous beings who are due, and reciprocally bound to show, equal levels of deference to one another's autonomy. The system "works" in its ideal instantiation because all actors are conceived as freely willing to act or being able to freely will actions consistent with all others making and acting on the same sort of choices. Moral choices are rational choices since judgments in favor of immoral actions lead to practical self-contradictions when made on a system-wide level. Immoral judgments and behavior then are "noise" that cannot be accommodated in the system if others are to fully enjoy their rights. Although the legitimacy of coercion is inherent in the idea of a right, the coercive restraint necessary for persons' rights enjoyment in a moment when rights violations threaten will often appear *added* to the original, ideal instantiation of the system, a special case. Coercion functions as a fail safe for the system. It takes a little bit of explaining for the theorist to account for why coercion is now acceptable when it was neither present nor acceptable in the first instantiation of the moral system. Yet all the theorist has done is articulate an inherent element of the system that was not articulated in the first expression of the theoretical grounds of the system, because the impetus for it (a rights violation) was not expressed in that instantiation.

While it is true that one actor's successful, freely chosen act presupposes an immediate environment free of rights violations affecting him, it would seem odd to say so when the actor is conceived in a solitary manner, as is often the case when considering questions in ethics. Absent an explicitly thematized social framework, the statement seems only trivially true. However, when speaking of a community of persons exercising their rights, the potential for rights violations becomes clearer, as does the salience of mentioning a background free of rights violations. What, for the individual, is a right retained in reserve to act in case of threatened rights violations must be an extant (i.e., actualized) coercive power that either coerces rights violators or threatens/promises to do so in the case of a community of autonomous persons actually enjoying full rights exercise in all instances. When the community of autonomous persons as a whole is viewed, the presence of a commonly recognized coercive power then appears as a precondition rather than a fail safe for the ideal system. See Kant, *The Metaphysical Elements of Justice*, 37–38, 233.

16. Smaller groups of persons might not require the formal institutions we normally associate with government. However, we are accustomed to seeing the basic functions of government present even in small voluntary associations (e.g., sports teams, housing co-ops, charitable organizations, etc.), including rules, leadership, and discipline and arbitration procedures. I see no reason to not take these occurrences as manifestations of the relations I have argued are implied by the idea of autonomy. That these features are even implicitly at work in the smallest ad hoc groups, like a group of friends taking a road trip, is evident when some disagreement thematizes divergent interpretations of these implicit rules. (E.g., "We listened to your music for the last hour; now we should listen to mine.")

17. The conceptual argument circumvents the contention that fear of widespread disorder will not often motivate citizens' preference for government coercion, because as a matter of fact, few people directly experience such social breakdowns. C. W. Cassinelli, "The 'Consent' of the Governed," *Western Political Quarterly* 12, no. 2 (June 1959): 403. (Looking for such empirical motivations signals a voluntarist standard for political obligation at odds with the rationalist model I'm advancing.) I'm also not sure about Cassinelli's point as a matter of fact; there are presently several "failed states" in the world where disorder and danger are the rule, and even more young nations with a collective memory of recent chaos. On why it is rational to prefer a single governing authority in a given territory, see Robert Nozick, *Anarchy, State, and Utopia* (New York: Basic Books, 1977), 12–17; Jeremy Waldron, "Special Ties and Natural Duties," *Philosophy & Public Affairs* 22, no. 1 (Winter 1993): 23.

    My exploration of autonomy's conceptual entailments, rather than of rational egoists' probable choices signals a departure from Nozick's state of nature thought experiment as well. The relevance of this difference will be clearer as we proceed. See Nozick, chap. 2.

18. Egon Bittner, *The Function of the Police in Modern Society* (New York: J. Aronson, 1975), 39.

19. I will use "criminal" to refer only to legal offenses that are also violations of moral rights or secondarily related to rights violations in order to maintain the linkage between the subpolitical (i.e., interpersonal) and political realms and avoid the complexities associated with claims about the social construction of criminality. This restriction should limit postmodern critiques to the possible social construction of autonomy and rights. (Even if autonomy is merely historical, its invocation still has certain logical implications this book means to develop with respect to interrogation.)

    In order to maintain the link between political coercion and just coercion on the subpolitical level, "crimes" will refer to external actions (i.e., in principle observable by another person) that violate another person's moral rights, such as murder, rape, assault, kidnapping, etc. Not all moral rights violations are necessarily illegal;

crimes are those moral rights violations that are salient to the state's police powers. "Crimes" will also refer to those actions concerning general social order and the maintenance of a state that are secondarily associated with core rights and likely salient only within an empirical state. Laws concerning general social order like those concerning contracts, torts, traffic rules, etc., prescribe moral behaviors insofar as these laws are applications of major moral duties in a particular social-political setting. Insofar as law-guided government coercion is implied by autonomy, the duty to obey laws concerning the state's maintenance, like taxation, is a moral one as well.

I will beg the question of whether acts with more controversial moral status, outlawed in some states, like abortion, polygamy, consensual sodomy, flag-burning, etc., are immoral and will not use the term "crime" with such acts in mind. Nor will I use "criminal" to refer to deontologically permissible (coherent if universalized) practices that certain governments have outlawed at various points in their history, like free religious worship, interracial marriage, reading *Ulysses*, etc. On my usage, "a criminal" could refer to either a core rights violator or a violator of the two types of law secondarily associated with core human rights (likely only salient in a state), though I will most often use the term only to mean the former. So, in sum, when I write that people do not have a right to plot, commit, or conceal crimes, I am not talking about African Americans sitting at "whites only" lunch counters, colonial Bostonians' refusal to pay the tea tax, Nazi generals plotting to kill Hitler, etc.

20. Continued autonomous existence and rights exercise may well presuppose many other state actions, such as providing education, heath care, equal suffrage, etc. but we are only here concerned with those steps necessary to directly protect negative freedom.

21. See Kant, *The Metaphysical Elements of Justice*, 64–65; 256; Waldron, "Special Ties," 15.

22. Howard Cohen and Michael Feldberg, *Power and Restraint* (New York: Praeger, 1991), 35.

23. It is necessary to specify a specific state for one's life and rights exercise because it is not contradictory to assert "I want to enjoy my rights" and to reject the legitimacy of the police powers of a particular state (which may not be respectful of its inhabitants' rights). It is contradictory to both assert that one desires to exercise one's rights and to generally reject the notion of government coercion. A solitary person could exist without a state (e.g., the proverbial castaway on a deserted island), free in both senses, though talk of rights is not apposite as the concept presupposes a social context.

24. Sentences describing his current situation ("He is living his life and enjoying his rights.") and the state of affairs he demands ("The state has no police powers in support of a legal-political regime.") are also *conceptually* opposed. I am not asserting that the dissenter is necessarily in *performative* self-contradiction: that his very act of dissenting contradicts the content of his assertion, which is to say that his dissenting would not be possible without a relatively crime-free environment. Dissenting to any state of affairs for a long period of time might presuppose a relatively crime-free environment in that continued life, bodily integrity, and probably some education are necessary prerequisites, though it seems to stretch the argument to say a given instance of communication presupposes a general material state of affairs like a relatively crime-free environment in the way that Apel and Habermas argue an instance of communication presupposes an ideal communication community. While making a basically Kantian argument, I am refraining from the transcendental-semiotic

approach and maieutic maneuver favored by Apel and Habermas, because so far as I can see, an argument for the transcendental salience of the maneuver is viciously circular. Michael Skerker, "Pragmatism, Pluralism, The Salience of Doubt" (Ph.D. diss., University of Chicago Divinity School, 2004), 76–202. In fairness to them, my project is less ambitious than theirs, starting with givens about autonomy and rights rather than seeking a nonfalsifiable starting point for philosophy. Instead, I am focusing on practical opposition accruing between the desired end states of a speaker's actions, expressed in the content of a speaker's assertion, and the actual end states that would be brought about by the same actions. The practical contradiction accrues, strictly speaking, between the speaker's assertion ("In doing X, I want to achieve Y") and his implied assertion ("In doing X, I want to achieve the opposite of Y").

25. The state's efforts to protect negative liberty may well go beyond traditional policing and include all manner of legal compliance review (e.g., with respect to occupational safety, food and drug purity, honesty in advertising, transportation safety, environmental stewardship, etc.). I will focus on traditional policing duties and refer to them alone for ease of exposition. See Cohen and Feldberg for a similar social contract-based list of police standards, 39.

26. See John Rawls, *A Theory of Justice* (Cambridge, MA: Belknap, 1971), 343, 353.

27. The recognition of authority is meant in a relative sense. One recognizes the authority of government if one recognizes it as the official promulgator and enforcer of law, rather than some other body or person. The sense of recognition I mean does not necessarily mean recognizing some quality on the part of government that confers authority, in the sense that recognizing a person's experience or intelligence might confer on her the right to issue orders. With his rigorous and somewhat idiosyncratic definition of "political obligation," Simmons seems to have in mind this kind of deep bond consequent to a quasi-existential recognition of a particular government's authority, like a feudal peasant's quasi-religious identification of his lord's authority over him. Simmons, 11–16, 29–30, 192–96.

28. Locke, Rawls, and Kant make similar points, John Locke, *A Letter Concerning Toleration* (Indianapolis: Hackett, 1983), 48; Rawls, §53; Kant, "What Is Enlightenment?" 59, and "On the Common Saying . . . ," 84, in *Kant's Political Writings*, ed. Hans Reiss, trans. H. B. Nisbet (Cambridge: Cambridge University Press, 1970).

29. William Galston, *Liberal Purposes* (Cambridge: Cambridge University Press, 1991), 220.

30. Miller, 181.

31. The foregoing argument may appear counterintuitive if the reader is thinking of dissent and obedience as antonyms. It should be emphasized that I am speaking of *reasons* to obey and mean "dissent" in the sense of "criticize" rather than "disobey." Dissent is *inconsistent* with obedience on a purely *volitional* model of autonomy, which would hold that one is not obliged to follow laws to which one does not consent. (E.g., Nozick, 95; Simmons, 139, 149; Cynthia A. Stark, "Hypothetical Consent and Justification," *Journal of Philosophy* 97, no. 6 [June 2000]). Such a view is wedded to an incoherently *atomistic* view of autonomy in which human beings are viewed as completely self-sufficient and without precontractual obligations to others. This view ignores the conditions for autonomy, reciprocal respect paid to others, discussed in chapter 1, and the preconditions for autonomy discussed above. (For the rational/volitional distinction, see Waldron, "Theoretical Foundations of Liberalism," *Philosophical Quarterly* 37, no. 147 [April, 1987]: 144.)

32. Cohen and Feldberg make a similar argument, 39.

33. Violations of even seemingly unimportant laws (e.g., curbing one's dog) can be expected to encourage more widespread legal disobedience since citizens would not have a prelegal moral hesitance to break such laws as they would with laws duplicative of moral duties. While a single minor legal violation may not be of great consequence, the widespread disobedience of even "minor" laws, such as those concerning pet waste would obviously lead to very unpleasant conditions. Also, the willingness to disobey laws one finds inconvenient displays a kind of arrogance—an unwillingness to submit oneself to laws applying to everyone—that might manifest in less trivial offenses when more important laws also become "inconvenient." Cf. M. B. E. Smith, *Is There a Prima Facie Obligation to Obey the Law?* 82 Yale Law Journal 950–76 (1972–73).

34. I would include a law that individually is not so onerous but part of a broader set that collectively deny persons their rights, like a law racially segregating lunch counters or drinking fountains.

35. Rawls, §53.

36. See Kant, "On the Common Saying . . . ," 74. The conception of autonomy I am using sees autonomy as a nested concept, necessarily implying moral duties, the possibility of just coercion, negative and positive freedom, and an overarching, law-guided coercive power. While the rights associated with this conception of autonomy are "natural" in the sense that they do not exist merely by being legally conferred by a polity (i.e., "positive rights"), they are not natural in the "strong," atomistic sense employed by Hobbes, Locke, and Nozick. On this formulation, autonomy is abstracted from its nested concepts and so can be thought of fully actualized in a state of nature, even for a solitary human forever apart from a community. So far as I can see, the concept of autonomy is incoherent without its companions, and so errors attend contrary juxtapositions of self-preservation and moral duty (Hobbes, xiv, para. 29–30) or freedom and subscription to a rule-guided protection service (Nozick, chaps. 2–5). In both cases, the privileges of autonomy are asserted in a state of nature as potential checks against state power or social coercion, even though the concept of autonomy assumes both an overarching, law-guided coercive power and the possibility of just coercion.

37. Waldron, "Special Ties," 28.

38. (By implication) Kant, *Metaphysical Elements*, §§44, 77, 312; Waldron, 21.

39. Waldron, 26; Walzer, *Just and Unjust Wars* (New York: Basic Books, 1977), chap. 11, especially, 195–96.

40. Waldron, 8; Walzer, *Obligations* (Cambridge, MA: Harvard University Press, 1970), 103–5. By just laws, I mean those overlapping with morality (defined, for our purposes, deontologically) or pertaining to the general structure of society. Here the nature of the regime is immaterial, murder or rape being as wrong in a liberal society as in an illiberal one, and in a democracy as much as a dictatorship. Unjust laws are those that are deontologically invalid (say, prescribing lesser rights to certain ethnic groups), and could exist in just or unjust regimes. There may be ambiguous cases, like laws pertaining to general social order supporting an illiberal regime; in such cases, tax monies are perhaps being utilized for both bad and good purposes, for paying the secret police who torture dissidents and the regular police who pursue muggers. Disobeying such "dual-use" policies or laws may negatively affect inhabitants in the sense that a refusal to pay taxes starves both the secret police and the regular police of funds, perhaps weakening the unjust government, but also exposing

inhabitants to the depredations of common criminals. I cannot address these issues in detail here, beyond pointing out that it is rationally inconsistent for a dissident who is motivated by concern for inhabitants' lives and rights to attack inhabitants (unaffiliated with the government) for the purposes of sowing fear and destabilizing the government (i.e., terrorism).

41. Waldron, 10; Rawls, 343.

42. I phrase the matter in this way rather than designate the police the agents of inhabitants, empowered by their consent, because inhabitants do not directly choose their police in the way they do accountants or attorneys. It is irrational to dissent to law-guided political governance as a whole, and police power is part of this governance. Therefore, it is more fitting to speak of police officers' direct relation to the state rather than to the state's inhabitants whom they potentially protect. In principle, private citizens could take on policing duties of their own accord, patrolling dangerous areas, prepared to intervene on behalf of innocent crime victims. Were they to accost a rights violator, a moral evaluation of their action would proceed in the same way as would the behavior of a police officer. Crimes are ones perpetrated against other inhabitants of the state, not against the state.

CHAPTER THREE

1. www.bbc.co.uk, November 7, 2006.

2. By "personal information," I mean any information regarding one's life that strangers would not normally know as a result of casual contact, including passing thoughts, beliefs, opinions, and facts about one's private relations.

3. Mark Alfino and G. Randolph Mayer, "Reconstructing the Right to Privacy," *Social Theory and Practice* 29 (January 2003): 10; H. J. McCloskey, "Privacy and the Right to Privacy," *Philosophy* 55 (January 1980): 21; Jean L. Cohen, "Equality, Difference, Public Representation," in *Democracy and Difference*, ed. S. Benhabib (Princeton, NJ: University Press, 1996), 192; Thomas Nagel, *Equality and Partiality* (New York: Oxford University Press, 1991), 142–43; Stanley Benn, "Privacy, Freedom, and Respect for Persons," in *Nomos* XIII, ed. J. R. Pennock and J. W. Chapman, (New York: Atherton Press, 1971), 3; Ernest Van Den Haag, "Definition: The Nature of Privacy," in *Nomos* XIII, 151. Alan F. Westin distinguishes four functions of privacy, one of which, "reserve," "protects the personality" by creating invisible walls between the person and the rest of the world. *Privacy and Freedom* (New York: Atheneum, 1967), 32.

4. Alfino and Mayer, 10.

5. Sissela Bok, *Secrets* (New York: Vintage, 1989), 21–23. See also Westin, 34; Benn, 24–26; Arnold Simmel, "Privacy Is Not an Isolated Freedom," in *Nomos* XIII, 73.

6. Van Den Haag, 151, and Benn, 10, make similar points.

7. Jean L. Cohen, *Redescribing Privacy: Identity, Difference, and the Abortion Controversy*, 3 Columbia Journal of Gender and Law 43, text accompanying no. 58 (1992).

8. The right to privacy is broader than the right to silence in that it also includes at least the right to control physical access to personal information such as a diary or entry into one's home and can also regard how and where one may be physically viewed by others.

9. The questioner might have an extraordinary claim to the requested information in certain emergencies. In emergencies that affect both questioning and questioned parties (e.g., a gas leak in the area, a fugitive on the loose, etc.), there is also an argument to be made that the questioned party would want to volunteer the relevant information for her own safety, and so she is not wronged by being questioned.

There is probably an attendant duty in this case for the questioner to give the reason for his questions, signaling to the questioned party that the questioner does have a right to the information (because he is endangered by its nondisclosure), or that the information is of the sort that the questioner would want to be disclosed. The duty to disclose information about other person's criminality stems from the prohibition on abetting criminals, explained below.

10. Greenawalt terms this a right to silence in a "very weak sense." Kent Greenawalt, *Silence as a Moral and Constitutional Right*, 23 William and Mary Law Review 15, 25 (1981–82). See text accompanying notes 11–13, for reasons why the right to silence is nontrivial.

11. Fields of information that are not unique to any particular person are not necessarily privileged by privacy rights (e.g., the current time, the location of a given store, etc.), and so it is not disrespectful to ask a stranger questions relating to this type of information. The questioned party is not wronged by the questioner, though the questioned party need not respond.

12. This is certainly the case for strangers, though one could argue that the intimacy of certain relationships creates a sort of "relationship right" to know what the other person is thinking. Yet this special right is probably a matter of degree, entitling one spouse to inquire what is on his or her spouse's mind, and expect a response, but both spouses are still autonomous beings, needing some privacy to form their own thoughts and identities, and so cannot be forced to answer questions. If parents are entitled to know what their children are thinking, it is because children are not fully morally autonomous and so are not due the deference due another adult.

13. I will use "demand" to mean "explicitly request the provision of something to which the demander has a right to own, use, possess, hold, exploit, sell, know, etc., and to which the holder does not have a right to own, use, possess, hold, exploit, sell, know, etc."

14. I am using the term "crime" instead of "rights violation" because the former is more of an everyman's term and so seems more appropriate for a context in which private citizens might justifiably find a neighbor's behavior alarming. It is likely that only rights violations that are of so public and serious a nature as to be made illegal would consistently be of the sort to motivate a person to confront and question a neighbor.

15. Greenawalt, *Silence*, makes the point with respect to friends, 20.

16. By "weak grounds of suspicion," I mean grounds that are less compelling than those a reasonable person would could consider obvious cause for suspicion, (e.g., holding a bloody knife next to a blood-splattered corpse).

17. This critic will have to be hypothetical because I have not found any extended treatment of this issue in the literature.

18. Kant writes that wishing to deprive another of his rights is "unethical" (displaying bad character) rather than "unjust": this follows, because on his usage, "strict justice" is only concerned with external actions. The implication is that criminal plotting is not something that can be made the object of political coercion. Kant, *The Metaphysical Elements of Justice*, §C, 35, 231.

19. I am not asserting that this is an analytic identity, nor that the definition is incontestable, but simply describing how I will be using the term.

20. I make the distinction because it seems that while people can be generally angry with someone for a sustained period of time, they usually do not nurse a desire to do a particular form of harm to someone (like punching him in the nose) for more than

a moment. The latter often occurs to someone as an imagined scene ("I saw myself punching him in the nose"), imagined in a "flash."

21. Guy Martin, "Al Qaeda's New York," nymag.com, May 2, 2005.

22. Manifesting the plot in some external way gives an observer potential grounds for saying it is a plot, but does not definitively determine for an observer that it is a real criminal plot.

23. Some crimes require little planning—or are at least carried off without much planning—and some fictional schemes are complicated and well researched. A shopper's idle thought "I sure would like that expensive shirt" could lead, in sort of a dreamy way to "How *do* shoplifters operate? Could I just stick it under my coat and walk out? Does it have one of those little security devices on it?" At this stage, only the shopper knows if he "means it"—if, at any point, his daydream becomes a plot.

24. The rational and practical elements of a plot further distinguish it from a fantasy in that the plot can be communicated *as a plot* to another person. Another person who shares the original plotter's motivation can choose to make the communicated plot his own like he can choose to use a tool another person gives or sells to him. By contrast, fantasies have unique emotional connections to fantasizers—it is not a fantasy, properly speaking, unless it "emerges" from the fantasizer. One can hear of another's fantasy but cannot *choose* to make it one's own: it either turns him on or it doesn't.

25. Say I regularly fantasize about assaulting my cruel, belittling boss, such that I imagine myself doing it every time he yells at me. If one day I snap and do assault him, I have acted on my fantasy rather than acted on a plot. My imagined assaults were emotional reactions; the image of striking him pops into my head in reaction to his harangues rather than being summoned up by my own rational deliberation. Assaulting my boss was a result of my failure to rationally restrain my fantasy instead of a deliberate, proactive marshalling of my will. Afterward, I am shocked by what I have done, where I would not have been shocked had it been the result of a plot. Granted, these are all subjective, psychological distinctions—and not everyone would necessarily experience such distinct mental modes—but these terms do indicate different moral casts to the action to the extent that the agent can describe his mental phenomena with distinct terms. (There is a point where the attempt to label subtle gradations in mental phenomena runs up against the limits of a given language's descriptive vocabulary for mental events—potentially muddying the distinction between plots and fantasies.)

26. The caveat is necessary because the right to privacy also is usually thought to cover physical privacy in one's domicile. Things a person does in the privacy of his apartment could violate the rights of other tenants in the building, (e.g., mixing volatile chemicals to make explosives, breeding goats, etc.)

27. For the constitutional analogue of this argument, see Jessica Pae, *The Emasculation of Compelled Testimony*, 70 Southern California Law Review 473, 501 (1997). It is arguable whether universal criminal plotting is coherent. Universal mendacity is incoherent because lies depend on an expectation of honest-dealing for efficacy. Many criminal plots depend on a general expectation of moral behavior, but since criminals can plot against one another (plots per se are not parasitic on particular forms of moral conduct in the manner of lies), it seems that one cannot draw a necessary connection between expectation and violation as one can with honesty and lying. One might be able to carry off the argument that universal criminal plotting is incoherent—even allowing that all plots do not lead to crimes—because universal

plotting implies continual attempts at criminal behavior, and criminal behavior is definitionally parasitic on moral or lawful behavior. However, this argument would require the caveat that either plotters do nothing but plot and commit crimes (never behaving morally) or that the occasional moral behavior all plotters exhibit is not consistently sufficient to form a background against which crimes can parasitically function.

28. "Used as a plot" as opposed to being referenced, say, in a lecture about presidential assassins.

29. John Locke, *A Letter Concerning Toleration*, 27; Martin Luther, "Secular Authority," in *Martin Luther: Selections from His Writings*, ed. John Dillenberger (New York: Anchor Books, 1962), 384.

30. Rights to privacy and silence do not protect things that are goods unto themselves (i.e., there is nothing humanly significant about silence or the act of withholding information per se) but function as prophylactics to the right to think freely as well as prophylactics and applications of autonomy more broadly. On the practical level then, there is a sequential layering of the *actions* expressing the prophylactic and the protected rights: a person's *remaining silent* in the face of questioning protects her *free thinking*, or *conscience* (which is in service of autonomy). Criminal plotting utilizes the same thought processes used by all other forms of deliberation, equally protected in a practical sense by the rights to privacy and silence. By contrast, the actions that express the rights to free speech, bodily autonomy, and property are not protected by actions expressive of prophylactic rights separating what is public from what is private. Whereas an outsider would have to infringe on one set of rights (privacy and silence) in order to see if the right to think freely is being misused, a misuse of speech, bodily autonomy, or property is more or less obvious, there being no prophylactic right separating the offending agent from others.

31. Rawls's "political conception of a person" is a famous example of a practical model. *Political Liberalism* (New York: Columbia University Press, 1993), 29–35.

32. I do not mean to say that the moral conception of autonomy is without a political analogue, nor the political conception, a moral one. I also do not mean to say the moral conception of autonomy is moral theory's characteristic view of autonomy and the political conception of autonomy, political theory's characteristic of autonomy. Each conception is an expression of a moral theory in that it is a normative account of an aspect of human experience; some thinkers use the political conception to discuss interpersonal responsibilities, and some use the moral conception to judge the appropriate limits of state behavior. I use the tags "moral conception" and "political conception" in part descriptively, because the two accounts are most often used by thinkers in moral (i.e., subpolitical or interpersonal), and political arenas, respectively. I also use the terms in part prescriptively; for the purposes of this book, I will suggest the moral conception is an appropriate candidate for abstractly considering questions of interpersonal responsibilities, because a conception of a community of equal rights-bearers who do not have reciprocal duties runs into the problem of parasitism. The political conception is apposite for considering questions regarding the liberal state's interactions with its inhabitants, at least in the criminal justice arena.

33. These are the conceptions of autonomy associated with Isaiah Berlin's positive and negative versions of liberty, respectively. Berlin discusses the conceptions as distinct ones affiliated with different thinkers. "Two Concepts of Liberty," in *Four Essays on Liberty* (Oxford: University Press, 1969), §§ I and II. The moral and political concep-

tions also track with Kant's positive and negative freedoms, respectively. The distinction is between a view of freedom as inherently, constitutively entwined with regard for others—so that it is incoherent to oppose an agent's freedom with the other persons' legitimate moral expectations—and a conception of freedom as presocial, and so not constitutively related to obligations to others. Rousseau and Kant offer examples of the former view; Locke and Hobbes, the latter. For Rousseau, man is only free when moral, that is, making rational decisions with the rights of others in mind. This only occurs in a society in which one alienates his natural rights to the state in exchange for other citizens' reciprocal alienation. Criminals can be "forced to be free," that is, forced to meet the social obligations they implicitly endorsed, which also provide the context for their true freedom. Kant offers a more detailed version of Rousseau's conception of freedom only being possible when a rational being legislates maxims for himself that are logically coherent (i.e., universalizable). A state is not in principle necessary to make rational beings morally free, as is the case for Rousseau, but is necessary to ground property rights given the factual finitude of land on which humans are set. Once a state exists, Kant includes an atomistic element to his theory, allowing that the state only enforces citizens' outward perfect (juridical) duties to others, without concern for their ethical character. Coercion against unjust behavior is consistent with the freedom of all.

A rigid, atomistic conception of autonomy is shared by Hobbes and Locke, though they disagree as to whether social obligation is conventional (Hobbes) or natural (Locke). Hobbes believes that natural man makes compromises in his natural liberty in society as a means to survival. Thus while bound to respect the conventional rights of his fellow citizens in society, he maintains an inchoate atomistic and adversarial instinct that is to be privileged over social obligation when his survival is at stake. Locke's natural man does not need (at least) other adult men for survival or moral formation but is not naturally ill disposed to their company either. Each man is competent to judge when a miscreant has violated natural law, so the state and the formal alienation of natural rights do not serve any moral purpose, as they do for Rousseau. Rather, for both Locke and Hobbes, civilization is to be prudentially preferred—it does not make people free—because it relieves *already* free men from the "inconveniences" (Locke) or "brutishness" (Hobbes) of nature.

34. In the case of observation, the criminality is apparent. On a liberal state's disinterest in its citizens' moral character, see e.g., Rawls, *Theory*, 311–12 and Kant, "On the Common Saying . . . ," 37.

35. For example, Rousseau proposes a moral conception of autonomy, to be employed as an authentic understanding of the person. On his view, truly free (moral) acts are only possible in a political society in which one has the opportunity to control one's impulses in deference to a rational assessment of those impulses' effects on others. Apart from civic education, the state enforces morality by preventing immoral *actions*. However, the state is not able to detect mere immoral judgments where citizens put self-interest ahead of deference to others.

36. Historical experience indicates that certain models of citizenship tend to have a practical effect when grounding government policy many in the West (at least) would argue are undesirable, such as a conception of the citizen, and of the citizen-state relationship, justifying government compulsion in regards to consensual adult sexual behavior.

37. Nagel, 142. I take it that fears of government abuse, coupled with an increasing appreciation of moral and cultural pluralism, drives the political and

legal trend toward proceduralism in the West lamented by communitarians. Proceduralism does presuppose a degree of atomism and anomie that is probably false anthropologically—it is incoherent morally—but historical events recommend employing an atomistic practical model to prevent overreaching by the state. American examples of overreach might include the McCarthy-era hounding of suspected communists, the seizure of children of polygamists in 1950s Utah, the proscription of married couple's use of contraceptives (*Griswold v. CT*), and consensual sodomy between adults (*Lawrence v. TX*), etc.

38. Hobbes, Locke, and perhaps Nozick seem to treat the political conception of autonomy as an authentic account of persons, adequate for answering normative questions in both subpolitical (i.e., interpersonal) and political arenas. I argued in Chapter 1 that this atomistic view of autonomy cannot serve as a basis for a coherent system of moral rights if all people have equal rights. It *is* possible for a theorist to simultaneously employ both conceptions of autonomy if they are employed in different ways. This is possible, for example, if the theorist conceives of the political conception as a practical model for use in determining appropriate state action, and the moral conception as an authentic understanding of the person, to determine what persons are owed on an interpersonal level. For example, one might judge a teleological anthropology (e.g., a Thomistic one) to be authentic, and so hold that there are specific choices humans *should* make, but then also allow that a rights-based idiom is a good lingua franca to use with people loyal to other teleological or nonteleological views. The teleologist may reject the deontologist's claim that all universalizable decisions freely made by an adult are morally licit but concede that acting as if this were the case in the public square has the double benefit of allowing the teleologist to pursue her own vision of the good life, and of precluding the greater evil (e.g., coercion) that might accompany demands that all persons choose the actions favored by the teleologist.

39. For example, Dworkin argues that a serious respect for rights requires government to err on the side of inflating rights rather than infringing on rights. Ronald Dworkin, *Taking Rights Seriously*, (Cambridge, MA: Harvard University Press, [1978] 2001), 199.

40. Westin, 23. On the subject of privacy and totalitarianism, see Benn, 21–24. The practical impediments to judging moral or political desert are not problems for the illiberal state, because it does not normally restrict its behavior based on qualities associated with individual citizens like guilt or innocence.

41. Cohen argues that the legal meaning of constitutionally protected privacy rights with respect to personal matters is that such rights *confer* decisional autonomy, rather than *recognize* a preexisting feature in citizens. In other words, the rights enumerated in the Constitution are indexed to a certain *model* of a citizen, rather than formulated in deference to the empirical qualities of a particular group of citizens. Cohen, "Equality," n. 46.

42. Thomas S. Schrock, Robert C. Welsh, Ronald Collins, *Interrogational Rights: Reflections on Miranda v. Arizona*, 52 Southern California Law Review 1, n. 185 (1978). On the portability and possible plurality of one person's moral and legal "personas," see Cohen, "Equality," 198; Cohen, "Redescribing," 35; Charles Larmore, *Patterns of Moral Complexity* (Cambridge: Cambridge University Press, 1987), 40–91. This plurality of views should not strike us as novel from a policy point of view. The current statutory regime of the United States has elements from different schools of theology, political philosophy, and political economy, instituted at different times and by different parties.

43. See Richard Schmidt, *Beyond Separateness* (Boulder, CO: Westview, 1995); Michael Sandel, *Democracy's Discontent* (Cambridge, MA: Belknap, 1996), chap. 4, and *Liberalism and the Limits of Justice* (Cambridge: Cambridge University Press, 1998); Charles Taylor, *Philosophy and the Human Sciences* (Cambridge: Cambridge University Press, 1985), chaps. 7 and 8; Mary Ann Glendon, *Abortion and Divorce in Western Law* (Cambridge, MA: Harvard University Press, 1987), 33–39; Will Kymlicka, *Contemporary Political Philosophy*, 2nd ed. (Oxford: University Press, 2002), 212–28.

44. I am here interested more in communitarians' and feminists' charge of atomism and illusory self-sufficiency than the specific reasons they proffer for why human nature is not atomistic. The moral conception of autonomy I am using would still be substantively criticized by them for atomism in that it assumes a decontextualized moral self without concrete material, familial, or communal attachments. Again, I am not asserting that this conception is authentic, but developing it in an effort to show how it is assumed in various discussions related to interrogation.

45. Cohen makes a similar point regarding a right to privacy's role in protecting moral autonomy. Her definition of privacy includes a right to refrain from justifying one's existential views to others that my argument does not require and which I would hesitate to endorse. "Redescribing," 203.

46. Of course, this preference is based on contingent liberal preferences. Competency in pursuing one's interests is assumed provided the autonomy constituted by moral responsibility.

47. Michael Walzer makes an interesting, related point about the benefit of the atomistic model of citizenship in the modern state. *Obligations*, 113.

48. "Flagrant" means: first, the actor is behaving in a publicly visible way that appears to an observer as criminal. Second, given the nature of the action and the context, it is *highly likely* that the action is criminal. Third, since the trigger for observers' interference with the actor is a visible action, the categorization of the action as criminal is prima facie. It is possible that there is an innocent explanation for the actor's behavior. Given epistemic limitations and the opacity of other minds, actors can rarely act with the assurance that their actions are done in response to how things really are, as opposed to how they appear from the actor's perspective. Regarding state agents' special privileges, see Kent Greenawalt, *The Perplexing Borders of Justification and Excuse*, 84 Colorado Law Review 1897, 1922 (December 1984).

49. Bittner argues that police must initially act on less information than is necessary for conviction; Egon Bittner, *The Function of the Police in Modern Society* (New York: J. Aronson, 1975), 33.

50. Any type of action prompted by a stranger's behavior is subject to the actor's epistemic limitations. In this case, strange behavior that is potentially suspicious does not look any more criminal if seen through a video camera than with the naked eye. Similarly, the number of informants who have actually witnessed criminal behavior will still pale next to the number of people reporting mere suspicious behavior, no matter the total number of police informants.

51. Jerome Skolnick, *Justice without Trial* (New York: Wiley, 1966), 8–10.

52. By protective obligation, I mean the obligation to protect all inhabitants' lives and rights equally.

53. Howard Cohen and Michael Feldberg, *Power and Restraint* (New York: Praeger, 1991), 51.

54. There are certain actions that most if not all observers would consider suspicious, (e.g., holding a smoking gun in the immediate vicinity of a corpse, running wild-eyed

down the street in an orange prisoner's jumpsuit, etc.). Yet since "appearing suspicious" is a subjective designation, and since these actions could have innocent explanations, we cannot say such actions are *inherently* suspicious. In most contexts, such actions would entail a level of privacy forfeiture, such that a person could not complain if he was questioned, but he would still have the right to remain silent.

55. From the perspective of the person whose privacy is being respected, the moral and political rights to privacy function in the same way when respected by neighbors and by state agents, respectively. A person is more obliged to respond to state agents' questions than a neighbor's because of the assumption (in a basically just state, at least) that the state's protective interest is operative when a state agent is asking questions. So the distinction between moral and political rights does not make much of a difference in this section.

56. Greenawalt, "Silence," 36.

57. David O'Brien, *The Fifth Amendment: Fox Hunters, Old Women, Hermits, and the Burger Court*, 54 Notre Dame Law Review 26, 52 (1978–79).

58. A person does not have a standing right to know the thoughts of another such that he can legitimately expect a stranger to divulge her thoughts on demand. One is entitled to demand that a criminal divulge his plot, because one may demand that people refrain from criminal behavior and plotting is sometimes integral to criminal behavior. Yet all other things beings equal, it is disrespectful to assume a stranger is a criminal; barring public evidence of criminality, one should not demand that a random stranger reveal possible criminal intentions. Police ought not to ask persons pointed questions without some public safety purpose either. However, since public safety is their standing concern, they may be more proactive in questioning, and in circumstances less obviously to do with public hazards than a private citizen. For example, an officer would probably be justified in questioning Smith even if he has no particular reason to suspect Smith of a specific crime, but simply because Smith's being in an area at a time when pedestrians are not usually present is strange. Or an officer walking a beat might politely engage people to get acquainted with them and get a lay of the land. By contrast, a uniformed officer acts inappropriately if he accosts and questions a woman about her plans that evening by way of asking her out on a date. The authority police have to be more proactive than private citizens in accosting and questioning people stems from police officers' protective obligation. They are therefore operating out of the bounds of their authority if using their power for reasons unrelated to public safety.

59. Bok, 121. Also, see John Henry Wigmore, *Evidence* §2286 (1961).

60. Some of these rights and privileges are no longer all operative in the United Kingdom. Following the passage of the Criminal Justice Act of 1987, suspects in the United Kingdom do not have a per se right to silence, and according to the Criminal Justice and Public Order Act of 1994, a suspect's pretrial silence *can* be held against him during trial. Australia's laws on the matter largely reflect the status quo ante.

61. See Dorsey D. Ellis, Jr., *A Comment on the Testimonial Privilege of the Fifth Amendment*, 55 Iowa Law Review 829 (1970); Eben Moglen, *Taking the Fifth: Reconsidering the Origins of the Constitutional Privilege against Self-Incrimination*, 92 Michigan Law Review 1086 (1994); Alan Dershowitz, *Is There a Right to Remain Silent?* (Oxford: Oxford University Press, 2008), chap. 5. The privilege largely gained currency in the early seventeenth century in England as a reaction against religious persecution by the Stuarts and, later, Cromwell. The accused (often dissenters to official Anglicanism and, later, Calvinism) were required to make oaths ex officio prior to learning of

the charges brought against them, the identity of their accusers, or the nature of the evidence against them. The magistrate's interrogation then proceeded (there was no defense counsel) without the accused even being told of the crime the prosecutor was pressuring him to admit. As several authors point out, these practices purportedly justifying the privilege are historical relics.

62. David Dolinko, *Is There a Rationale for the Privilege against Self-Incrimination?* 33 UCLA Law Review 1063, 1065 (1985–86).

63. *Chambers v. Florida*, 309 US 227, 235–38 (1940).

64. Robert S. Gerstein, *The Demise of Boyd: Self-Incrimination and Private Papers in the Burger Court*, 27 UCLA Law Review 343, 350 (1979–80).

65. *Murphy v. Waterfront Commission*, 378 US 52, 55 (1964).

CHAPTER FOUR

1. David Dolinko, *Is There a Rationale for the Privilege against Self-Incrimination?* 33 UCLA Law Review 1063, 1065 (1985–86) (emphasis added).

2. Robert S. Gerstein, "Privacy and Self-Incrimination," *Ethics* 180 (1970): 90.

3. Dolinko, 1074; Joseph D. Grano, *Voluntariness, Free Will, and the Law of Confessions*, 65 Virginia Law Review 859, 937 (1979); Donald A. Dripps, *Against Police Interrogation— and the Privilege against Self-Incrimination*, 78 Journal of Criminal Law & Criminology 699, 731 (1987–88).

4. Fred E. Inbau, *Police Interrogation—a Practical Necessity*, 89 Journal of Criminal Law & Criminology 1403, 1404, 1408 (1998–99). Many of these questions apply if the privilege is seen as grounding the right to silence in the trial phase as well. The strengths of my recommended construal mostly apply in the trial phase as well; space restrictions have forced me to omit an extended discussion of the trial phase.

5. Most of my interlocutors in this section are interpreting the Constitution and/or justices' interpretations of the Constitution. Their discussions pick up moral and political content as the justices and scholars interpret the Constitution's meaning in light of the Framers' intent to enshrine and protect political and moral values. In writing these chapters, I am trying to provide the moral grist some jurists have requested for their jurisprudential mills.

6. Hobbes, *Leviathan*, I, xiv, 3.

7. Ibid., I, xiv, para. 29–30.

8. Kent Greenawalt, *Silence as a Moral and Constitutional Right*, 23 William and Mary Law Review 15, 36 (1981–82).

9. Ibid., 39.

10. Ibid., 50. Historically, it seems early commentators were moved to compassion based on the intractability of the perjury horn of the "cruel trilemma" of contempt, perjury, or self-incrimination faced by the accused. To a religious mind, perjury entailed damnation inasmuch as the oath to tell the truth was an oath to God. See John Lilburne, in *The Levellers Tracts, 1647–1653*, ed. William Haller and Godfrey Davis (New York: Columbia University Press, 1944) quoted in *Miranda v. Arizona*, 384 US 436; S Ct 1602, 459; Sir Thomas Tresham, quoted in Leonard Levy, *The Origins of the Fifth Amendment* (Chicago: Dee Publishing, 1968), 103, 134.

11. Gerstein, "Privacy," 93; Donald A. Dripps, *Self-Incrimination and Self-Preservation: A Skeptical View*, University of Illinois Law Review 329, 331 (1991).

12. Dripps, *Self-Incrimination*, 344. Certainly Hobbes, and perhaps Greenawalt as well, commits a naturalistic fallacy by conflating what a class of people often do with what they should do.

13. I will use "citizen" rather than "inhabitant" if the author under discussion uses that term. I will refer to "inhabitants" when developing my own position.
14. Greenawalt, 36.
15. Gerstein, *The Demise of Boyd*, 27 UCLA Law Review 343, 348 (1979–80).
16. Gerstein, *Privacy*, 91, 93.
17. Gerstein, *Boyd*, 349.
18. Though Dolinko is right to wonder what it does to one's moral development to go unpunished for a crime, 1125.
19. Ibid., 1129.
20. Gerstein, *Boyd*, 349.
21. Ibid., 353–54.
22. Grano, 901.
23. Ibid., 933; Dolinko, 1074, 1081; Dripps, *Self-Incrimination*, 331, 346.
24. Thomas S. Schrock, Robert C. Welsh, Ronald Collins, *Interrogational Rights: Reflections on Miranda v. Arizona*, 52 Southern California Law Review 1, n. 185 (1978).
25. Grano, 887; Dripps, *Against Police Interrogation*, 700; Yale Kamisar, *What Is an Involuntary Confession?* 17 Rutgers Law Review 728, 747 (1962–63); George C. Thomas and Marshall D. Bilder, *Aristotle's Paradox and the Self-Incrimination Puzzle*, 82 Journal of Criminal Law & Criminology 243, 273 (1991–92).
26. Dripps, *Against Police Interrogation*, 700; Grano, 944. On the *Miranda* procedure as a compromise, see *Columbe v. Connecticut*, 367 US 568, 578–81 (Frankfurter, plurality opinion); *Miranda v. Arizona*, 481.
27. Grano, 905.
28. Thomas and Bilder, 271.
29. Dripps, *Self-Incrimination*, 350.
30. Dripps, *Against Police Interrogation*, 701.
31. Welsh S. White, *Police Trickery in Inducing Confessions*, 127 University of Pennsylvania Law Review 581, 585 (1979); *Miranda's Failure to Restrain Pernicious Interrogation Practices*, 99 Michigan Law Review, 1211, 1236 (2000–2001); James G. Thomas, *Police Use of Trickery as an Interrogation Technique*, 32 Vanderbilt Law Review, 1167, 1190 (1979); David W. Sasaki, *Guarding the Guardians: Police Trickery and Confessions*, 40 Stanford Law Review, 1593, 1609 (1987–88).
32. Kamisar, 759.
33. Dripps, *Self-Incrimination*, 350.
34. Ibid., 350; Albert Alschuler, *Constraint and Confession*, 74 Denver University Law Review, 957, 957 (1996–97).
35. Even if he is caught red-handed, the state does not enjoy the equivalent of certainty of a person's criminal status until there is a legal verdict of guilt. There may be a legitimate reason for his apparent criminal behavior. State agents may begin to deal prudentially with him though in the moment of interdiction.
36. John Henry Wigmore, *Evidence* §224 (1961).
37. Grano, 934; Dripps, *Against Police Interrogation*, n. 78.
38. I mean here to bracket the question of whether political rights may be curtailed in public emergencies like natural disasters or military attack.
39. Cf. Dripps, *Against Police Interrogation*, 700.
40. Justice Holtzoff, Hearings on S 300, S 553, et. al., Before the Subcommittee on Criminal Laws and Procedures of the Senate Committee on the Judiciary, 90th Cong., 1st Sess. 925 (1967), at 263–64.

41. Grano, 914.

42. By contrast, Hobbes and Greenawalt argue that those actually guilty do not have to cooperate in their demise, just because of their guilt, and the therefore certain nature of their punishment if they cooperate. See n. 35 above on the question of being caught "red-handed."

43. I'm speaking in reference to the criminal justice arena, rather than those arenas in which justification may be given for the state's collection of taxes, institution of a draft, or seizure of property as eminent domain, etc., all of which ought to follow the provision and review of reasons.

44. It would be irrational to dissent to privacy violations necessary to preserve public safety. These rational grounds would also apply to questioning for the sake of public safety implying that the questioned party is the one threatening public safety; silence in the face of accusations is tantamount to a rejection of the state's grounds for considering one suspicious.

45. The two attitudes demand practically incommensurable behavior in a given moment: on one hand, complete deference and, on the other hand, prudential treatment. Yet the attitudes are consistent on a macro view in the sense that suspicious people must be questioned in order for innocent people to enjoy their rights. Practically, the behavior demanded is consistent in series, as are Aristotle's demands that a citizen learn how to give and to take orders: a given person can be treated as an object of suspicion in one moment, and then go back to being an apparently innocent citizen whose rights are secured by the questioning of suspicious people.

46. This is why I think it wrong to claim police exist primarily to protect victims, rather than criminals' rights. At first blush, the police are not necessarily in the epistemic position to distinguish criminals from innocent people. Cf. Seamus Miller, "Moral Rights and the Institution of the Police," in *Human Rights and the Moral Response of the Corporate and Public Sector Organizations*, ed. T. Campbell and S. Miller (Dordrecht: Kluwer, 2004), 185.

47. Another way of protecting this status is the right to counsel. While having counsel present during interrogation is a practically more efficacious way of preserving apparently innocent status and political autonomy than silence, silence has more of an ultimate status insofar as it is the suspect's direct control.

48. Dripps rejects the assertion that the privilege protects citizens from harassing "fishing expeditions" by the government by pointing out the Fourth Amendment already protects citizens from criminal prosecution without reasonable grounds for suspicion, *Against Police Interrogation*, 714. Dripps's argument begs the question, because it is still the government's determination whether or not reasonable grounds for suspicion exist, and suspicion is inherently subjective and contextual. From the government's point of view, its grounds for indicting a citizen may be reasonable, but from the point of view of the wrongly suspected citizen, an indictment passed down by an upright, well-meaning government may appear just as arbitrary as that passed by a tyrannical one. This notion is implicitly endorsed by Dolinko, who rejects a rationale for the privilege as a prophylactic against government harassment, because the government could still harass a person by compelling damaging, but noncriminal testimony (at least during the grand jury stage), 1081.

49. Kamisar, 759; Dripps, *Self-Incrimination*, 330; Wigmore, §2251. See David O'Brien, *The Fifth Amendment: Fox Hunters, Old Women, Hermits, and the Burger Court*, 54 Notre Dame Law Review 26, 42–43 (1978–79).

50. David Simon, *Homicide* (New York: Ballantine Books, 1991), chap. 2.
51. Grano, 907.
52. Reck v. Pate, 367 US 433 (1961); Blackburn v. Alabama, 361 US 199 (1960); Fikes v. Alabama, 352 US 191 (1957).
53. Colorado v. Connelly, 107 S Ct 515 (1986).
54. Brown v. Mississippi, 297 US 278 (1936).
55. Ashcraft v. Tennessee, 322 US 143 (1944).
56. Stroble v. California, 343 US 181 (1952); Lisenba v. California, 314 US 219 (1941). The mere age of a fifteen-year-old defendant in Haley v. Ohio, 332 US 596 (1948), was judged to render his confession involuntary. Schrock et. al. suggest that American justices' reluctance to speculate about suspects' mental states during interrogation has led to a complacency regarding police interrogation methods. For example, the traditional "totality of circumstances" test has been judged a sufficient measure of voluntariness even when police failed to explicitly warn the suspect that he had the right to remain silent. This complacency follows a reduction of *Miranda*'s concern for "free and rational choice as a constitutional good independent of the trial" (via its novel application of the Fifth Amendment to pretrial interrogation), to the pre-*Miranda* due process standard that ensured the "protection of the accused's *trial rights* from pretrial subversion by unfair methods" 37. (Second quotation from *Developments in the Law—Confessions*, 79 Harvard Law Review 938, 973–74 [1966]; emphasis added.) The authors argue that this reductive reading of *Miranda* loses the Court's interest in ensuring that the suspect's waiver was rational (i.e., with full knowledge and understanding of his or her rights) in addition to freely volunteered.
57. Alan Dershowitz, *Is There a Right to Remain Silent?* (Oxford: Oxford University Press, 2008), 22–24.
58. Cf. Grano, 905.
59. David W. Sasaki, *Guarding the Guardians: Police Trickery and Confessions*, 40 Stanford Law Review, 1593, 1595 (1987–88).
60. Cf. Schrock et. al., 49.
61. While the shocking to the conscience and totality of circumstances tests might also be pegged to a "reasonable man" standard, they are not easily modeled by that standard, because they depend on the judge's own intuition in judging what she feels is shocking to the (read: her) conscience or what she would consider "overbearing" if in the suspect's position. By contrast, my proposed standard relates to the professionalism of police officers, which is partly assessable based on objective factors like the evidence they had in their purview and currently accepted best practices in policing.
62. Greenawalt, 51.
63. The former removes all justification for law enforcement and the criminal courts' interaction with inhabitants, and the latter voids the role of the courts and turns the police into a mere retrieval service for suspicious, and therefore "guilty," persons.
64. E.g., Ziang Sung Wan v. United States, 266 US 1, 10–12 (1924).
65. E.g., Greenwald v. Wisconsin, 390 US 519 (1968).
66. E.g., Brooks v. Florida, 389 US 413 (1967).
67. E.g., Rogers v. Richmond, 365 US 534 (1961).
68. Cf. Griswold, 223.
69. Wigmore, 8 §2251, 296, n. 1.
70. Richard Leo, *Inside the Interrogation Room*, 86 Journal of Criminal Law and Criminology, 266, 281 (1995–96).

71. See Edwin Driver, *Confessions and the Social Psychology of Coercion*, 82 Harvard Law Review, 42 (1968).

CHAPTER FIVE

1. Fred E. Inbau, John E. Reid, Joseph P. Buckley, and Brian C. Jayne, *Criminal Interrogation and Confessions*, 4th ed. (Gaithersburg, MD: Aspen Press, 2001), 360. The manual was originally printed in 1947 and is now in its fourth edition.
2. Allison D. Redlich, "Law & Psychiatry: Mental Illness, Police Interrogations, and the Potential for False Confession," *Psychiatric Services* 55 (January 2004): 19–21, http:/ psychservices.psychiatryonline.org/cgi/content/full/55/1/19 (accessed May 5, 2007).
3. Ariel Neuman, "Custodial Interrogations . . . ," in *Educing Information* (Washington, DC: NDIC Press, 2006), 215.
4. Inbau et. al., 6.
5. Ibid., 8.
6. Ibid., 93.
7. I will use the male pronoun to refer to interrogator and suspect since the overwhelming majority of American police detectives and criminal suspects are male.
8. Inbau et. al., 104.
9. Ibid., 108.
10. Ibid.
11. Ibid., 125.
12. Ibid., 111.
13. Aldert Vrij cites extensive agreement between independent researchers. See his bibliography in "Detecting Deceit via Analysis of Verbal and Nonverbal Behavior," *Journal of Nonverbal Behavior* 24, no. 4 (Winter 2000). Vrij's research also suggests an important qualification: while there are strategies that can yield around 80 percent success in detecting lies, not all police officers are good at detecting lies, and many overestimate their skill at lie detection, 240.
14. Inbau, et al., 155–72.
15. Ibid., 190–93.
16. Ibid., 212.
17. Neuman, 215.
18. Inbau, et al., 210.
19. Ibid., 223.
20. Interrogation transcript of Alan Adams, Sonoma County, CA, Sheriff's Office 7 (July 4, 1991) (Case No. 910605-16).
21. Inbau, et al., 219–23. Vrij notes that behavioral tics *alone* are not a reliable indicator of deception. "Credibility Judgment of Detectives: The Impact of NonVerbal Behavior, Social Skills, and Physical Characteristics on Impression Formation," *Journal of Social Psychology* 133, no. 59 (1993): 610.
22. David Simon, *Homicide* (New York: Ballantine Books, 1991), 519.
23. Inbau et al., 235–80.
24. Ibid., 233.
25. Interrogation transcript of Michelle Duke, Kern County, CA, Sheriff's Office 27 (August 27, 1995) (Case No. 95-95-33322).
26. Inbau et al., 281.
27. Ibid., 304.

28. Ibid., 313.

29. Ibid., 337–45.

30. Ibid., 353.

31. Ibid., 364.

32. To be clear about the distinction between the last two clauses, the interrogator might deceive the suspect without uttering a lie, for example, by affecting through tone and expression sympathy when he feels none.

33. Since all interrogations, definitionally, begin with an accusation, nondeceptive interrogations would be ones where the opening accusation is coincident with the interrogator's *knowledge* of the suspect's guilt and no other deceptive tactics are used. Even these interrogations are manipulative, and so potentially in tension with or in violation of inhabitants' rights. I will focus on deceptive interrogations below for offering more robust objects of study. Many of the concerns that could be associated with manipulation consequent to knowledge of a suspect's guilt will be addressed in the discussion of deceptive interrogations.

34. See n. 25 in chapter 4.

35. Richard Leo's 1994 study is the only empirical study of American police practices since 1971. Leo viewed 182 police interrogations conducted by seventy-one different detectives over a nine-month period in three urban American police departments. According to Leo, only two empirical studies preceded his own—Neal Miller, "Supreme Court Effectiveness and the Police Organization," 36 Law and Contemporary Problems 467 (1971); Michael Wald et al., "Interrogation in New Haven: The Impact of Miranda," 76 Yale Law Journal 1519 (1967)—and neither were conducted in large urban departments. Leo, 281. Gudjonsson cites these earlier studies reporting lower rates of confessions in critique of Inbau's optimistic promise of an 80 percent confession rate (Inbau, et al., 364). Gisli Gudjonsson, *The Psychology of Interrogations and Confessions* (London: Wiley, 2003), 136. Leo urges caution in comparing studies on account of researchers' differing definitions of what constitutes a confession, 281. Seventy-eight percent of suspects waived their right to silence after hearing the *Miranda* warning, 286.

36. Leo found that 70 percent of interrogations were concluded in under one hour and only 2 percent of the interrogations involved coercion, liberally defined in the study as omitting the *Miranda* warning, using threats, and engaging in hostile questioning. Leo, 279.

37. Leo observed both nondeceptive and deceptive tactics. Among the former tactics, interrogators made truthful assertions (e.g., telling the suspect about actual evidence implicating him, used 88 percent of the time), identified inconsistencies in the suspect's story (used 42 percent of the time), or appealed to his conscience (used 23 percent of the time). Leo also frequently observed deceptive tactics (used no more than 43 percent of the time), including deception achieved through the interrogator's affect and through lies. Interestingly, the tactics laypeople probably most associate with police interrogations due to their prominence in television police dramas—yelling at the suspect and employing the good cop/bad cop routine—were almost never used (3 percent and 1 percent of the time, respectively), 278. The only variables Leo found related to the likelihood of a successful interrogation were the length of the interrogation and the number of tactics used, 292.

   With respect to efficacy at inducing a confession, the two most successful techniques did *not* employ deception: appealing to the suspect's conscience (97 percent success rate; used 23 percent of the time) and identifying contradictions in the suspect's story (91 percent success rate; used 42 percent of the time). The next two most effective techniques could be categorized as deceptive in that the interrogator presumably did not believe the suspect worthy of praise for his crime (91 percent success rate; used in 30 percent of the interrogations), nor did the interrogator necessarily believe the psychological or moral excuses he suggested on the suspect's behalf (90 percent success rate; used 34 percent of the time). Other deceptive techniques included confronting suspects with false evidence of guilt (83 percent success rate; used 30 percent of the time), minimizing the moral seriousness of the offense (81 percent success rate; used 22 percent of the time), and praising or flattering the suspect (91 percent success rate; used 30 percent of the time), 294.

38. Hugo Bedau and Michael Redalet, *Miscarriages of Justice in Potentially Capital Cases*, 40 Stanford Law Review 20 (1987).

39. Richard Leo and Richard Ofshe, *The Consequences of False Confessions: Deprivations of Liberty and Miscarriages of Justice in the Age of Psychological Interrogation*, 88 Journal of Criminal Law and Criminology 429 (1997–98).

40. Gary Hamblet, *Deceptive Interrogation Techniques and the Relinquishment of Constitutional Rights*, 10 Rutgers Law Journal 109, 125 (1978–79); Welch S. White, *Miranda's Failure to Restrain Pernicious Interrogation Practices*, 99 Michigan Law Review, 1211, 1230 (2000–2001).

41. Leo and Ofshe, 434.

42. These facts suggest normative comment. It is incumbent on states to track the relevant data so state agents and policymakers can judge whether they are diligently executing their protective function, and also so inhabitants can assess whether their government is exceeding the scope of its power. A significant percentage of confirmed false confessions to true confessions would constitute legitimate grounds for inhabitants to dissent to police interrogations in general. Clear evidence of this nature might render moot the following *theoretical* discussion of the political legitimacy of deceptive interrogation. Further, all interrogations should be videotaped: this will help protect suspects from abusive police practices and will protect police from false charges of abuse. (Leo and Ofshe, 494; Albert Alschuler, *Constraint and Confession*, 74 Denver University Law Review, 957, 976 [1996–97]; Paul Cassell, *Guilty and Innocent: An Examination of Alleged Cases of Wrongful Convictions from False Confessions*, 22 Harvard Journal of Law and Public Policy, 526, 533 [1998–99].) Recording the interrogations should also work to promote police professionalism and serve as a reviewable record for attorneys, judges, and juries to consider the reliability of confessions.

43. Fifty-six of the 350 wrongful convictions in the Bedau and Redalet study involved errors by eyewitnesses. One hundred seventeen convictions were the result of witness perjury. Bedau and Redalet, 57.

44. Cassell, 584.

45. White, 1235.

46. Lynumn v. Illinois, 372 US 528 (1963).

47. Laura Hoffman Roppe, *True Blue . . .* , 31 San Diego Law Review 754, 770 (1994).

48. Leyra v. Denno, 347 US 556 (1954).

49. Leo and Ofshe, 495.

50. Ibid., xii–xiv.

51. It is worth considering that contrary to public perception, crime scenes yielding usable DNA evidence are fairly rare, and trace analysis (e.g., of hair, chemicals, fibers) can often only provide vague information like the race of the hair's owner. Jeffrey Toobin, "The CSI Effect," *New Yorker*, May 7, 2007, www.newyorker.com.

52. Cassell, 526.

53. James G. Thomas, *Police Use of Trickery as an Interrogation Technique*, 32 Vanderbilt Law Review, 1167, 1190 (1979); White, 1223; Hamblet, 142; David W. Sasaki, *Guarding the Guardians: Police Trickery and Confessions*, 40 Stanford Law Review, 1593, 1609 (1987–88); Alschuler, 974; Roppe, 758; Margaret Paris, *Lying to Ourselves*, 76 Oregon Law Review 817, 819 (1997).

54. Simon, 35–36, 34.

55. While the following discussion will assume the context of an interrogation, the known liar's rights are the same if a private citizen rather than a police officer is the one who knows he is lying.

56. Cf. David Hume, *Enquiry concerning the Principles of Morals*, § 3, pt. 1, ed. Henry Aiken, (New York: Hafner Press, 1948), 188–89; Jan Narveson, "Terrorism and Morality," in *Violence, Terrorism, and Morality*, ed. R. G. Frey and Christopher Morris (Cambridge: Cambridge University Press, 1991), 161.

57. See Hugo Grotius, *On the Law of War and Peace*, bk. 3, chap. 1 (Indianapolis: Bobbs-Merrill, 1925); Benjamin Constant, "De Reactionspolitiques," *France* 6, no. 1, (1797): 124. I hope to publish separately an omitted response to thinkers who make arguments against lying in all cases.

58. Roppe, 769.

59. The discussion of the latter consequence can also apply to interrogators in military and intelligence settings.

60. Hamblet, 145, n. 209; Paris, 38; Roppe, 764; Jerome H. Skolnick and Richard Leo, *The Ethics of Deceptive Interrogation*, 2 Criminal Justice Ethics 9 (1992); Christopher Slobogin, *Deceit, Pretext, and Trickery* . . . , 76 Oregon Law Review 775, 798 (1997); Deborah Young, *Unnecessary Evil: Police Lying in Interrogation*, 28 Connecticut Law Review 425, 461 (1995–96).

61. Paris, 25, 44; Young, 457; Sasaki, 1610.

62. Paris, 38; Young, 456.

63. Paris, 31.

64. Police act on behalf of all inhabitants, even criminals. For example, they investigate crimes committed against criminals, like murders of drug dealers. I couch the sentence in the text this way, because innocent people presumably think of the police as being in the business of protecting them from criminals.

65. See Skolnick, 216, and Lawrence Sherman, "Becoming Bent," in *Human Rights and the Moral Response of the Corporate and Public Sector Organizations*, ed. T. Campbell and S. Miller (Dordrecht: Kluwer, 2004), 291, for discussions of how the pressures of police work tend to alienate police from the public.

66. Young, 463; Hamblet, 142; Roppe, 764; Slobogin, 783, 800; Skolnick and Leo, 9; Skolnick, "Deception By Police," 1 Criminal Justice Ethics 40, 43 (1982).

67. Skolnick, 52.

68. Sherman, 294.

69. There is an awareness in the American military and intelligence communities that a person's initial emotional and moral profile may make him or her less able to play certain professional roles. I've been told by CIA officers that the Agency's division between operations and intelligence (i.e., analysis) directorates corresponds to a basic division in the personality types of those working in the directorates, and that the operations directorate, where officers are often called on to lie, blackmail, and manipulate, is not for everyone. A retired Navy SEAL told me that his organization

has found the best special operators are those who are not very emotionally sensitive, and an Army interrogator told me that the Army has found that the best interrogators are those who score relatively low on a personal ethics test.

CHAPTER SIX

1. Cicero, "De Officiis" 1, in *War and Christian Ethics*, trans. W. Miller and ed. Arthur F. Holmes (New York: Brown Pub Group, 1975), 29.
2. For analysis of the disparate strands of the Western just war tradition, see James T. Johnson, "Historical Roots and Sources of the Just War Tradition in Western Culture," in *Just War and Jihad.*, ed. J. Kelsay and James Turner Johnson (New York: Greenwood, 1991). See my "Jesus and Mars," in *Enemy Combatants, Terrorism, and Armed Conflict Law*, ed. David Linnan (Westport, CT: Praeger, 2008), for a brief history of the Christian just war tradition.
3. Cf. Paul W. Kahn, "The Paradox of Riskless War," in *War after September 11*, ed. Verna Gehring (Lanham, MD: Rowman, 2003), 39. Also, if it were the mere threat of force that made one vulnerable to being harmed or killed—suggested by some to justify combat violence—criminals would be justified in harming or killing police officers who attempted to apprehend them at gunpoint.
4. Walzer, *Just and Unjust Wars* (New York: Basic Books, 1977), 39.
5. Even in a circumstance where soldiers' superiors order them to commit war crimes, individual soldiers are responsible for knowing that these sorts of things could not be legitimate aims of the state, because they are not the sort of things that directly and efficiently contribute to military victory.
6. Text accompanying photographs, Chris Hondros, Getty Images, August 29, 2007, http://bop.nppa.org/2006/still_photography/winners/INS/63710/124342.html.
7. W. Winthrop, *Military Law and Precedents* (Washington, DC: Government Printing Office, 1920), 788.
8. From the late seventeenth century through WWI, captured officers were sometimes even paroled home or to a neutral country, having given their word as gentlemen not to return to the fight. Since the fight was between governments, it was thought that there was no point in further inconveniencing officers who had been removed from the martial equation. A. J. Barker, *Behind Barbed Wire* (London: B. T. Batsford, 1974), 9–10.
9. Geneva Convention Relative to the Treatment of Prisoners of War, August 12, 1949.
10. As will be made clear, they do not need to actually be members of a conventional military. The 1977 First Protocol of the Convention states that POW rights can apply to certain irregular groups.
11. By implication, Walzer, 36.
12. Nicholas Fotion and G. Elfstrom, *Military Ethics* (Boston: Routledge, 1986), 224.
13. Walzer, 182; Michael Ignatieff, "Lesser Evils," *New York Times Magazine*, May 2, 2004, 86; Sidney Axinn, *A Moral Military* (Philadelphia: Temple University Press, 1989), 48, 76, 78; Andrew C. McCarthy, "Torture: Thinking the Unthinkable," in *The Torture Debate in America*, ed. Karen Greenberg (Cambridge: Cambridge University Press, 2006), 99.
14. Derek Jinks, *The Declining Significance of POW Status*, 45 Harvard International Law Journal 367, 441 (2004); Heather MacDonald, "How to Interrogate Terrorists," in ed. Greenberg, 87.

15. Fotion and Elfstrom, 213.
16. Axinn, 104.
17. Douglas P. Lackey, *The Ethics of War and Peace* (Englewood Cliffs, NJ: Prentice Hall, 1989), 66.
18. Axinn also makes the point that some cultures tend to look at POWs with disdain, on the assumption that the prisoners abandoned their military duty and surrendered, 94.
19. Walzer, 180. Also see my "The New Face of War," *Journal of Military Ethics* 3, no. 1 (2004).
20. See Shlomy Zachary, *Between the Geneva Conventions: Where Does the Unlawful Combatant Belong?* 38 Israel law Review 378, 382 (2005).
21. E.g., Steven R. Ratner, "Revising the Geneva Conventions to Regulate Force By and Against Terrorists: Four Fallacies," 1 *IDF Law Review* 7, 13 (2003); MacDonald, 87.
22. Jinks, 438.
23. "Suicide Bomber Suspected in Mess Hall Attack," www.cnn.com/2004/WORLD/meast/12/22/iraq.main/index.html (accessed August 10, 2007).
24. Barker, 20; Jinks, 441.
25. The prudential reason related to the safety of civilians is indirectly a moral reason. First, scrupulous government soldiers are endangered when they hesitate to shoot someone who might be a civilian, but might be a disguised irregular combatant. Second, the scrupulous soldier wishes to exercise discrimination and does not want to have the killing of an innocent on his conscience for the rest of his life. (On this point, it is worth mentioning that the shooting in Tal Afar was the First Battalion's only engagement during its entire tour.) The government acting on his behalf is in effect offering a material incentive to the irregular to behave in such a way as to allow the government soldier to act morally and avoid this psychological trauma.
26. Jon Lee Anderson, "The Taliban's Opium War," *New Yorker*, July 9, 2007.
27. T. E. Lawrence, *Seven Pillars of Wisdom*, quoted in R. Ernest Dupuy, "The Nature of Guerilla Warfare," *Pacific Affairs* 12, no. 2 (1939): 142.
28. Dupuy, 143.
29. Col. Thomas Hammes, *The Sling and the Stone* (St. Paul, MN: Zenith Press, 2004), 2.
30. Recategorization would be indicated, for example, depending on the temporal scope for what is considered a new form of government. For example, despite the IRA's self-described rebellion against foreign occupation, I nonetheless place the group in the category involving a settled form of government because Northern Ireland has been occupied by British forces in one form or other for seven hundred years.
31. For a discussion of the anomalous nature of levee en masse in international law, see Richard Baxter, *So-called "Unprivileged Belligerents": Spies, Guerillas, and Saboteurs,* 28 British Yearbook International Law, 323, 335, 343 (1951).
32. Richard Shultz, "The Limits of Terrorism in Insurgency Warfare," *Polity* 11, no. 1 (1978): 75.
33. Walzer makes a similar argument, though he looks to civilians' active support of irregulars to determine if the irregulars qualify for POW status, 185.
34. There are also more complicated arguments appealing to property rights and/or patriotism to justify resistance.
35. Shultz, 75, 80.
36. Richard Weitz, "Insurgency and Counter-Insurgency in Latin America, 1960–1980," *Political Science Quarterly* 101, no. 3 (1986): 410.

37. Ian F. W. Beckett, *Modern Insurgencies and Counter-Insurgencies* (London: Routledge, 2001), 154, 170, 174.

38. Ibid., 170.

39. Oliver O'Donovan, *The Just War Revisited* (Cambridge: Cambridge University Press, 2003), 64. See Skerker, "The New Face of War."

40. O'Donovan, 65.

41. The POW status of conventional troops is independent of the justice or wisdom of the campaign in which they are engaged because of the idea of invincible ignorance. By contrast, it is an open question whether a given irregular combatant represents a politically legitimate entity. In order to answer this question, we need to ask whether the tactics and mission of his group are ones to which inhabitants of the relevant territory could rationally dissent. Also, there is plausibly more culpability for involvement in the insurgency for individual insurgents in groups with flat hierarchies than there is for conventional troops in wars undertaken by a state.

42. Regis Debray, *Revolution in the Revolution?* (New York: Grove Press, 1967), 42.

43. Walzer, 182.

44. Fotion and Elfstrom, 213.

45. Anonymous, *Imperial Hubris* (Washington, DC: Brassey's Inc., 2004), 217.

46. Cf. David Meltzer, "Al Qa'ida: Terrorists or Irregulars?" in *Law after Ground Zero*, ed. John Starwson (Portland: The Glass House Press, 2002), 82.

47. Ratner makes a similar point, 16.

CHAPTER SEVEN

1. John Wahlquist, "Educing Information: Interrogation—Science and Art," in *Educing Information: Interrogations: Science and Art* (Washington, DC: NDIC Press, 2006), xxiv.

2. Randy Borum, "Approaching Truth," in *Educing Information*, 18.

3. *Human Intelligence Collector Operations*, FM 2-22.3 (Washington, DC: Department of the Army, 2006), 8–20.

4. Ibid., 8-6.

5. See *Miranda v. Arizona* 384 US 436; 86 S Ct 1602, HN 8A.

6. Bok and Fried draw the analogy between lying and self-defense, with Bok doing so in the context of a state's protective function, though neither mentions interrogations. The authors who argue that the rights violator loses the right to truth can be presumed to allow for lying to protect oneself or others from unjust attack. Sissela Bok, *Secrets* (New York: Vintage, 1989), 144; Charles Fried, *Right and Wrong* (Cambridge, MA: Harvard University Press, 1978), 74. Cf. Rev. Francis J. Connell, *Morals in Politics and Professions* (Westminster, MD: Newman Bookshop, 1946), 54; Maureen Ramsey, "Justifications for Lying in Politics," *The Politics of Lying* (New York: St. Martin's Press, 2000), 25. Space limitations forced the omission of a section considering of interrogators' virtue I hope to publish separately.

7. More extensive prudential behavior than deemed necessary in retrospect could be justified based on what the interrogator had reason to suspect; see Chapter 1.

8. The relationship between an enemy soldier and the detaining power is different than between a criminal suspect and his own government. The detaining power does not have a policing responsibility toward enemy soldiers, and so war crime prosecutions consequent to illegal attacks on the detaining powers' troops would not suggest the same rationale for interrogation rights used in domestic situations. However, if the

war crime prosecutions are for crimes against the civilian population (e.g., rape, pillage, murder) during a period of time when the detaining power was not occupying the territory in question, then the detaining power would be prosecuting crimes against humanity and therefore occupying a quasi-policing role. Given this duality, it seems conceptually neater to justify interrogation rights based on the need to garner trustworthy evidence for a fair trial. See further discussion below.

9. Ronald J. Sievert, *War on Terrorism or Global Law Enforcement Operation?* 78 Notre Dame Law Review 307, 320–29 (2002–3).

10. The mobster, for example, does not wish to bring down the state but instead to corrupt its institutions (e.g., winning rigged municipal contracts, infesting unions, etc.). Kidnappers depend on people having regular sorts of jobs to pay ransom. Also, while the demands of justice, particularly with respect to the victim, demand that a thief or murderer be caught, the police department's failure in this regard will not cause society to crumble.

11. The POW can, for example, demand to use the bathroom or be allowed to sleep, but neither necessarily brings an immediate halt to the interrogation in the way that a domestic suspect's request for a lawyer must. Rather, the POW's demand for sleep informs the interrogator that he is in danger of violating the POW's rights if he refuses.

12. This notion unto itself suggests treating unprivileged irregulars as POWs rather than criminal suspects if useful intelligence rather than indictable evidence is indeed sought from their interrogations.

13. Were the attack in Uruzgan the first of its kind, detainees should initially be treated as criminal suspects; in the context of Afghanistan's current Taliban-led insurgency, it seems reasonable to treat the detainees as suspected insurgents.

14. If the detainees are determined to be illegal aliens, they can be deported without further interrogation or prosecution if the detaining power wishes.

15. This is insofar as they are suspects, rather than self-declared enemies of the state.

16. U.N. Commission on Human Rights, E/CN.4/Sub.2.2002/4, July 9, 2002, 12–13.

17. Sievert, 328–29.

18. Ibid.

19. Statement of Pierre-Richard Prosper, "Preserving Freedoms while Defending against Terrorism: Hearings before the S. Comm. on the Judiciary," 107th Cong. (2001).

20. Sievert, 325.

21. While the U.S. Supreme Court has ruled that "truly voluntary" statements given prior to *Miranda* warnings are admissible, and that information a state agent learned from asking questions meant to avert an immediate danger (and so, in the absence of a warning) are admissible as well, it seems that the inherent coerciveness of the military interrogation environment ought to trump the rationales behind these rulings. U.S. v. Lonetree, 31 M.J. 849, 868 (N-M Ct. Crim. App. 1990); New York v. Quarles, 467 US 649 (1984).

22. E.g., Brian W. Earley, *The War on Terror and the Enemy Within: Using Military Commissions,* 30 New England Journal on Criminal and Civilian Confinement 75, 102 (2004).

23. Statement of George Terwilliger III, "Preserving Freedoms."

24. Statement of John Ashcroft, "Preserving Freedoms."

25. For legal critiques of Bush's military order, see Neal Katyal and Laurence Tribe, *Waging War, Deciding Guilt: Trying the Military Tribunals,* 111 Yale Law Journal, 1259 (2001–2); Manooher Mofidi and Amy Eckert, *"Unlawful Combatants" or "Prisoners of*

War": The Law and Politics of Labels, 36 Cornell International Law Journal, 85 (2003); Silvia Borelli, "The Treatment of Terrorist Suspects Captured Abroad: Human Rights and Humanitarian Law," in *Enforcing International Law Against Terrorism,* ed. Andrea Bianchi (Oxford: Oxford University Press, 2004), 39.

26. David Meltzer advocates classifying al-Qaeda members as POWs in part because it eliminates the need to collect evidence and go to trial. "Al Qa'ida: Terrorists or Irregulars?" in *Law after Ground Zero,* ed. John Strawson (Portland, OR: The Glass House Press, 2002), 83.

27. Louis Fisher, *Military Tribunals and Presidential Power* (Lawrence: University of Kansas Press, 2005), 125.

28. I will not make a detailed argument for this position as I have not addressed justifications for punishments in this work. I will note that if basically humane treatment is judged acceptable for serial killers or child molesters, it does not immediately seem "too good" for terrorists or guerillas.

29. That censorship might need to be heavy with high-ranking irregulars, given the risk of letters containing coded messages.

30. Tony Lagouranis, *Fear Up Harsh* (New York: Caliber, 2007), chap. 8.

31. Ibid., 197.

32. Specifically, the civilians suffer *harms* (e.g., death, property damage), and their political rights are violated since a foreign power is acting coercively against them. Their moral rights are not violated though, because it would be irrational for them to dissent to their own country's military defending their country, and it would be incoherent to assert that foreigners' militaries cannot perform the same function. The same applies for the political rights of covert unprivileged irregulars. They do not suffer harms since they do not have a right to their professional secrets and ought not to be storing military materiel in civilian dwellings.

33. See e.g., Erik Saar and Viveca Novak, *Inside the Wire* (New York: Penguin Press, 2005), 153, 173; Lagouranis, 63, 103.

34. Lagouranis, 38.

35. E.g., Heather MacDonald, "How to Interrogate Terrorists," in ed. Greenberg, 85.

36. Lagouranis, 53; Chris Mackey and Greg Miller, *The Interrogators* (New York: Little, Brown, and Co., 2004), 115.

37. Mackey and Miller, 215, 461.

CHAPTER EIGHT

1. For an especially good discussion of the thought experiment, see David Luban, "Liberalism, Torture, and the Ticking Bomb," in *The Torture Debate in America,* ed. Karen Greenberg (Cambridge: Cambridge University Press, 2006), 44–51.

2. It is telling that the bulk of normative articles written on the subject written prior to 2001 were written in the early 1980s and refer to the U.S. marine barracks bombing in Lebanon and contemporary airplane hijackings.

3. I took a more detailed approach in an earlier piece, "Interrogation Ethics in the Context of Intelligence Collection," in *Ethics of Spying,* ed. Jan Goldman (Lanham, MD: Scarecrow Press, 2006). My conclusions in this book are somewhat different than in that article. I argued a weak justification of coercive interrogation of positively identified terrorists was possible *if* reliable coercive techniques existed; information that has subsequently come to light about even those coercive techniques designed to avoid the unreliability of more traditional forms of torture suggest that there are no reliable coercive techniques.

4. The 1983 CIA "Human Resource Exploitation Training Manual"(HRETM) largely repeats the KUBARK manual's section on coercion verbatim, though with inserted emendations (presumably added prior to its public release under force of a FOIA lawsuit), crossing out the most controversial sections and including provisos couching in the passive voice what had originally been in the imperative. HRETM includes manipulation of time, meal times, sleep schedules, and interrogation schedules as noncoercive while the KUBARK manual includes those methods in the chapter on coercive techniques, HRETM, 9.

5. Edward Peters, *Torture* (Philadelphia: Blackwell, 1985), 13.

6. Ibid., 42.

7. Ibid., 43.

8. Ibid., 41.

9. Alfred McCoy, *A Question of Torture* (New York: Metropolitan, 2006), 21–60.

10. Jane Mayer, "The Experiment," July 11, 2005, newyorker.com; Katherine Eban, "Rorschach and Awe," July 17, 2007, Vanityfair.com.

11. KUBARK, 90–91.

12. KUBARK, 82; HRETM, 2.

13. KUBARK, 82. The bracketed text replaces "these functions" and is taken from the preceding sentence.

14. KUBARK, 40; HRETM, 2.

15. KUBARK, 40.

16. E.g., Rick Francona's testimony in Eric Weiner, "Are Tough Interrogations Necessary?" March 19, 2008, NPR.org, available at E:\Interrogation Ethics book\Are Tough Interrogations Necessary NPR.mht. Also note Assistant Attorney General Jay Bybee's focus on data about the health effects of SERE training in his memo authorizing coercive techniques, Memorandum from Assistant Attorney General Jay to John Rizzo, "Interrogation of al Qaeda Operative," August 1, 2002, 5–6.

17. Tom Malinowski, "The Logic of Torture," *Washington Post,* June 27, 2004, B7.

18. It also seems there would be more obvious and direct means than those described if the tormentor was motivated by sadism or a desire to punish.

19. Cf. Heather MacDonald, "How to Interrogate Terrorists," in ed. Greenberg; Mark Bowden, "The Dark Art of Interrogation," Atlantic.com, October 2003.

20. Plotting also involves the abuse of mental freedom, or the right to think freely. Torture can interfere with or destroy a person's ability to think freely, so one might think that torture is a proportionate defensive measure against a known plotter. Yet describing plotting chiefly as a matter of the plotter abusing his mental freedom is as unhelpfully vague as calling rape a matter of the rapist abusing his right to bodily autonomy. Mental freedom and bodily autonomy are abused in nearly every type of rights violation. Thus, if abusing one's mental freedom was justification for torture, torture could be prescribed universally to interfere with anyone planning or concealing plans for rights violations, including petty thieves, adulterers (who are violating wedding vows), deceitful business partners, corrupt bureaucrats, sorority girls intent on cruel pranks, etc.

21. See Matthew Cole, "Blowback," GQ, March 2007, 229–36.

22. See Randy Borum, "Approaching Truth," in *Educing Information: Interrogations: Science and Art* (Washington, DC: NDIC Press, 2006), 17–38.

23. Joseph Lelyveld, "Interrogating Ourselves," June 12, 2005, nytimes.com.

24. John Schmertz and Mike Meier, "Citing International Human Rights Conventions,

Supreme Court of Israel . . . ," *Human Rights* 6, no. 3 (March 2000): 2 of electronic version.

25. Lelyveld.

26. *Ireland v. UK*, para. 98.

27. John Conroy, *Unspeakable Acts, Ordinary People* (Berkeley: University of California Press, 2000), 46.

28. Ibid., 4.

29. David Luban, "The War on Terrorism and the End of Human Rights," in *War after September 11*, ed. Verna Gehring (Lanham: Rowman & Littlefield, 2003), 58.

30. Lelyveld.

31. Don Van Natta, Jr., "Interrogation Methods in Iraq Aren't All Found in Manual," May 7, 2004, nytimes.com.

32. Eban; Ali Soufan, "My Tortured Decision," April 22, 2009, nytimes.com,.

33. Soufan; Michael Hayden and Michael Mukasey, "The President Ties His Own Hands on Terror," April 17, 2009, online/wsj.com; David Johnston, "At a Secret Interrogation Site, Disputes Flared over Tactics," September 10, 2006, nytimes.com; Scott Shane, "Interrogation Effectiveness May Prove Elusive," April 22, 2009, nytimes.com. See Mark Danner, "US Torture: Voices from the Black Sites," *New York Review of Books*, vol. 56, no. 6, sec. 7, April 9, 2009.

34. Ron Suskind, "The Unofficial Story of the al-Qaeda 14," *Time*, September 10, 2006; Peter Finn and Joby Warrick, "Detainee's Harsh Treatment Foiled no Plots," *Washington Post*, March 29, 2009, A1.

35. James Risen et. al., "Harsh C.I.A. Methods Cited in Top Qaeda Interrogations," *New York Times*, May 13, 2004, A1.

36. Suskind.

37. Jane Mayer, "The Black Sites," *New Yorker*, August 13, 2007, 56.

38. Ulpian, *Digest*, 48.18.1.23.

39. See Eben Moglen, *Taking the Fifth: Reconsidering the Origins of the Constitutional Privilege against Self-Incrimination*, 92 Michigan Law Review 1086, 1101–2 (1994); Peters, 81.

40. William R. Johnson, "Tricks of the Trade: Counterintelligence Interrogation," *International Journal of Intelligence and Counterintelligence* 1, no. 2 (1986): 103; Michael Ignatieff, "Lesser Evils," *New York Times Magazine*, May 2, 2004, 93; Jean Maria Arrigo, "A Utilitarian Argument against Torture Interrogation of Terrorists," *Science and Engineering Ethics* 10, no. 3 (July 2004): 16; Chris Mackey and Greg Miller, *The Interrogators* (New York: Back Bay Books, 2004), 32. For additional classical authors' views, see Stephen Holmes, "Is Defiance of Law a Proof of Success?" in ed. Greenberg, 120–23.

41. Aleksandr Solzhenitsyn, *The Gulag Archipelago* (New York: Harper Row, 1973), 146–47.

42. Mayer, "The Black Sites," 46. Muhammed told the ICRC, "I gave a lot of false information in order to satisfy what I believed the interrogators wished to hear in order to make the ill-treatment stop. . . . I'm sure that the false information I was forced to invent . . . wasted a lot of their time and led to several false red-alerts being placed in the US." Quoted in Danner, sec. 7.

43. Stephen Grey, "CIA Rendition: The Smoking Gun Cable," http://blogs.abcnews.com/theblotter/2007/11/cia-rendition-t.html, accessed August 18, 2008.

44. Darius Rejali, "Five Myths about Torture and Truth," *Washington Post*, December 16, 2007, B3; Cole, 229–36.

45. Matthew Cole, personal correspondence, January 27, 2007.

46. Mayer, "The Black Sites," 57.

47. KUBARK, 93. Darius Rejali, "Five Myths about Torture." In cases of widespread inter-rogatory torture, intelligence agencies can be overwhelmed by the sure volume of false information proffered by suspects desperate to placate the interrogators. Alistair Horne, *A Savage War of Peace: Algeria 1954–1962* (London: Macmillan, 1977), 204.

48. Luban, "War," 45; Rejali, "Torture's Dark Allure," salon.com, June 18, 2004; Merle Pribbenow, "The Man in the Snow White Cell," *Studies in Intelligence* 48, no. 1, 64, https://www.cia.gov/library/center-for-the-study-of-intelligence/kent-csi/pdf/v48i1a06p.pdf.

49. Rejali, "Does Torture Work?" salon.com, June 21, 2004.

50. E.g., Alan Dershowitz, "Want to Torture? Get a Warrant," *San Francisco Chronicle,* January 22, 2002, A19.

51. Henry Shue, "Torture," *Philosophy and Public Affairs* 7, no. 2 (1978): 135. The KUBARK manual warns against using coercion to the point that the subject is delusional, at which points his statements are unreliable; rather, interrogators are to relent (at least temporarily) once the subject has made an initial confession (e.g., to membership in a terrorist organization), 83.

52. Rejali, "Five Myths."

53. "Military Studies in Jihad against the Tyrants," chap. 17, 14, UK/BM-172 translation, available at www.thesmokinggun.com.

54. Arrigo, 7; Christopher Tindale, "The Logic of Torture," *Social Theory and Practice* 22, no. 3 (Fall 1996): 369; KUBARK, 93.

55. Arrigo, 7–8.

56. Tony Lagouranis, *Fear Up Harsh* (New York: Caliber, 2007), 98, 129; Memorandum from Assistant Attorney General Jay Bybee to John Rizzo, 2.

57. Arrigo, 5; HRETM, 3; KUBARK, 83; Darius Rejali, "Does Torture Work?" The CIA manuals stress that the stage of disorientation desired by the interrogation is not so great as to render the suspect unsure of basic facts about himself, such as whether or not he is a spy. It grants that the suspect is no longer reliable once he has been driven to the point where he is delusional.

58. Cf. Andrew C. McCarthy, "Torture: Thinking about the Unthinkable," in ed. Greenberg, 107.

59. See n. 39 above; Ronald Kessler, *The CIA at War* (New York: St. Martin's Press, 2003), 277; Mackey, 477.

60. Steven Kleinman, "KUBARK CounterIntelligence Interrogation Review," in *Educing Intelligence,* 103.

61. Michael Bond, "The Enforcer," newscientist.com, November 20, 2004; Lelyveld; Eban; Erik Saar and Viveca Novak, *Inside the Wire* (New York: Penguin Press, 2005), 151, 170; Kleinman, 107.

62. Lagouranis, 63, 103, 119, 129; Saar and Novak, 153, 173.

63. McCarthy would seem to endorse this view, 107–8.

64. Ibid., 109.

65. Cf. ibid.

66. As discussed in chapter 1, Locke could be fairly read as endorsing proportionate limits on just coercion, and also be read as not recognizing any limits. The strain in Continental law that exonerates the killing of apple thieves is consistent with the latter interpretation.

67. Dershowitz, A19; Andrew C. McCarthy, "Abu Ghraib and Enemy Combatants," NationalReview.com, May 11, 2004.
68. Tindale, 350.
69. The Israeli High Court of Justice outlawed the relevant techniques in 1999.
70. Memorandum from Assistant Attorney General Jay Bybee to Alberto Gonzales, "Standards of Conduct for Interrogation under 18 U.S.C. §§2340–2340A," August 1, 2002.
71. Shue, 138, 141, 143; Douglas Lackey, *The Ethics of War and Peace* (Englewood Cliffs, NJ: Prentice Hall, 1989), 80; Nigel S. Rodley, *The Treatment of Prisoners Under International Law* (Paris: UNESCO, 1987), 76.
72. Ronald Crelinsten, "In Their Own Words: The World of the Torturer," in *Violence, Terrorism, and Morality*, ed. R. G. Frey and Christopher Morris (Cambridge: Cambridge University Press, 1991), 53. See Saar and Novak, 154.
73. Lagouranis, 92–93.
74. Ibid., 134.
75. Idid., 65.
76. Ariel Neuman and Daniel Salinas-Serrano, "Custodial Interrogations," in *Educing Information*, 222; Conroy, 46. The al-Qaeda manual mentioned in n. 53 **above** uses truly heinous instances of Arab security officials' abuse of terrorists' relatives to raise readers' fervor, 12.
77. Ignatieff, 93, *Miranda v. Arizona*, 384 U.S. 436; S. Ct. 1602, 447.
78. Lackey, 80; Crelinsten, 59; *Miranda*, 447; Arrigo, 11; HRETM, 2; Mayer, 56; Conroy, 106, 119.
79. Mayer, "Black Sites," 56.
80. Arrigo, 17.
81. See n. 69 in chap. 4; Lagouranis, 92–93.
82. Rejali, "Does Torture Work?"
83. See Solzhenitsyn, 144–59.
84. Arrigo, 5, 14–16.
85. Mayer, "Black Sites," 50; Scott Shane, "CIA Agents Sense Shifting Support for Methods," nytimes.com, December 13, 2007.
86. Ignatieff, 93, 86; Bowden, 38, *Miranda*, 447; *Public Committee against Torture in Israel v. State of Israel*, H.C. 5100/94 et al. (Sup. Ct. Israel, September 9, 1999), para. 39. In an anecdote that seems to undercut and support this point at the same time, Mackey relates how one relatively high-value detainee "broke" after twenty-nine straight hours of questioning (the interrogator was awake for the same duration). When asked why he finally capitulated, the detainee said he realized that he was fighting for the wrong side if this was the worst that America would do to him. Mackey, 426.
87. Gen. Jacque Massu's argument that torture could be a legitimate, efficacious tool of the state and torturers, responsible servants of the state, led to the labeling of this term *Massuisme*. Peters, 177.
88. At best, one can speculate about the likely conclusion a consequentialist argument would reach if there *was* unambiguous data. Perhaps *in retrospect,* all of these costs *would* be worth the lives and monies (measured in lives and monies) saved by forestalling a massive attack through the desperate, last ditch use of coercive techniques. However, a realistic, prospective weighing of potential consequences would likely have to conclude that the host of negative effects would *not* be worth the possible

failure to reveal any plots or the revelation of some insignificant, poorly planned attacks.

CONCLUSION

1. Seymour Hersh, "Moving Targets," newyorker.com, December 15, 2003.
2. "Command Responsibility: Detainee Deaths in U.S. Custody in Iraq and Afghanistan," http://www.humanrightsfirst.org/us_law/etn/dic/exec-sum.asp.
3. Joseph Lelyveld, "Interrogating Ourselves," June 12, 2005, nytimes.com. See Walzer, *Just and Unjust Wars* (New York: Basic Books, 1977), chap. 16 on "Supreme Emergency."

INDEX

Abu Ghraib, 1, 186
Abu Omar, 191
Abu Sayyaf, 133
Abu Zubaydah, 193, 210–11
accusation, 94, 97
al-Masri, Khalid, 174–75, 177–78
al-Qaeda, 117, 133, 143, 161, 170, 181, 191, 194–95
al-Shibh, Ramzi bin, 193
alternative question, 96
anarchism, 32
ANC, 133, 141
apparently innocent, 55, 75, 78, 80–81
Aquinas. *See* Thomas Aquinas, Saint
arrest, 97
article 31B rights, 167
assault, 16
atomism: appropriate for consideration of negative duties, 55; attendant governmental attitude, 53; critique of, 216n4, 220n14, 230n37; defined, 52; model of citizenship, 231n47; relevance to self-incrimination, 67
Augustine, Saint, 119
Augustus, Caesar, 193
Auld, Jim, 193
autonomy: as affected by police investigations, 57; atomistic view, 223n31, 229n33, 230n38, 231n44, 231n45; background conditions for, 220n14; bodily, 216n10; communal context of, 28; critiques as atomism, 55; definition, 11; entailments of, 30; grounds of curtailment, 56; Lockean view of, 198–99; moral

conception of, 11, 52, 71, 83, 218n1, 228n32; necessity of responsibility, 37; political conception of, 52–53, 67, 69, 71–72, 75, 79, 83, 228n32, 230n38; preservation of, 19; relation to political coercion, 25, 35, 38, 221n16; relation to political legitimacy, 137; rights as expression of, 27; two conceptions of, 51

Barot, Dhiren, 41, 50, 144
basically just, 35–36
Batista, Fulgencio, 137
Bin Laden, Osama, 117, 142
Boers, 132
Bok, Sissela, 42, 60
brainwashing, 186
Bush, George W., 161, 169, 211, 244n25

Castro, Fidel, 137
Chambers v. Florida, 60
Cheney, Richard, 211–12
Chindits, 133
chivalry, 119–20, 126
Chu Teh, 130
CIA, 133, 191, 212
Cicero, Marcus Tullius, 119
citizenship, relation to legal protection, 38
coercion, definition of, 13, 56, 219n8
colonialism, as justification of insurgency, 138
communitarianism, 230n37, 231n44
confession: false, 87, 99–102, 239n42; general, 44, 68, 96, 170; grounds for compulsion, 71; police-procured, 71